IMAGES
of Rail

RAILROAD DEPOTS OF WEST CENTRAL OHIO

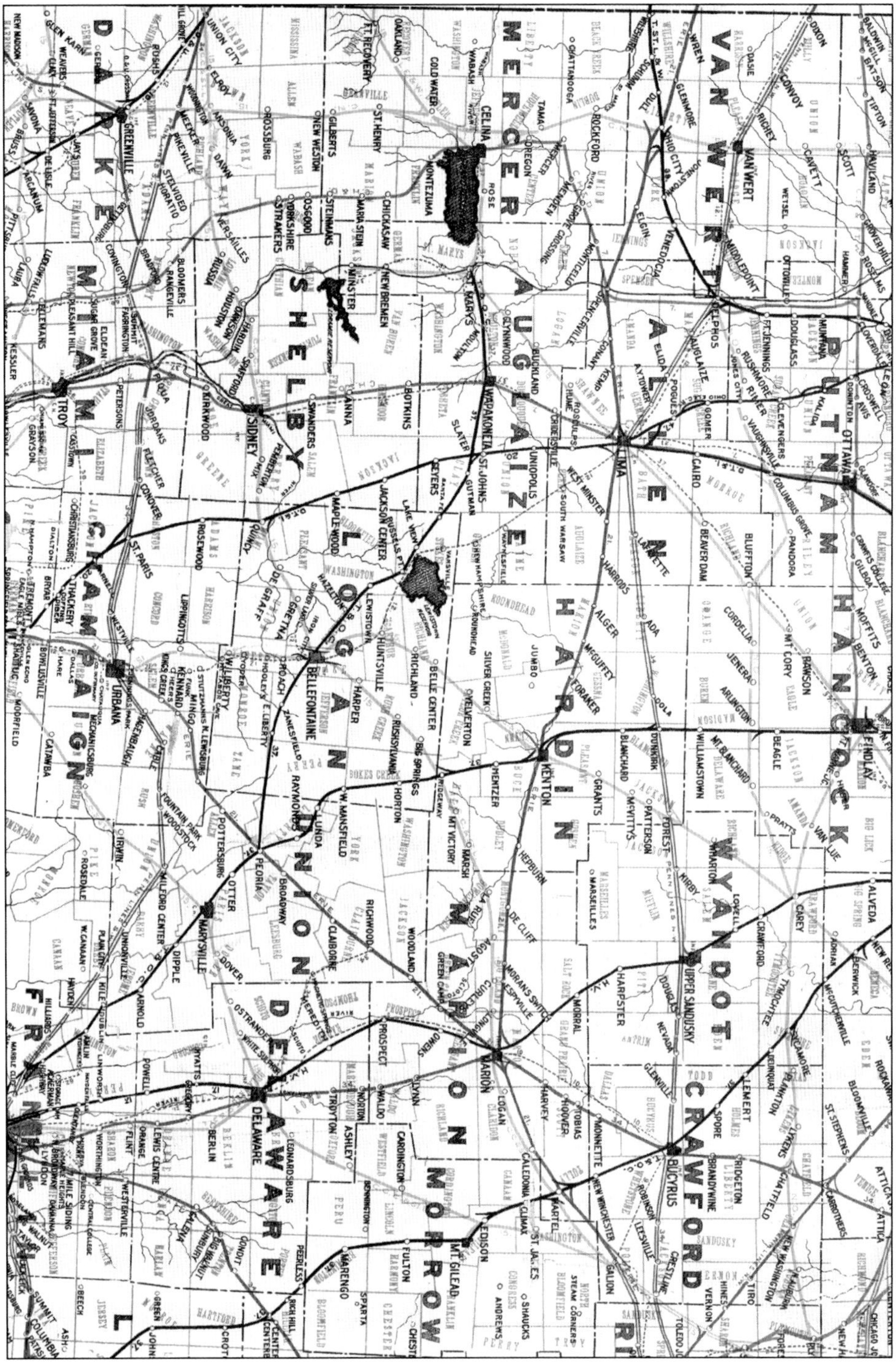

Railroads served many communities of west central Ohio in 1909. (Railroad Commission of Ohio state map.)

On the cover: Mark J. Camp collection.

IMAGES
of Rail

RAILROAD DEPOTS OF WEST CENTRAL OHIO

Mark J. Camp

ARCADIA
PUBLISHING

ISBN 978-0-7385-4009-2

Published by Arcadia Publishing
Charleston, South Carolina

Printed in the United States of America

Library of Congress Catalog Card Number: 2005935867

For all general information contact Arcadia Publishing at:
Telephone 843-853-2070
Fax 843-853-0044
E-mail sales@arcadiapublishing.com
For customer service and orders:
Toll-Free 1-888-313-2665

Visit us on the Internet at www.arcadiapublishing.com

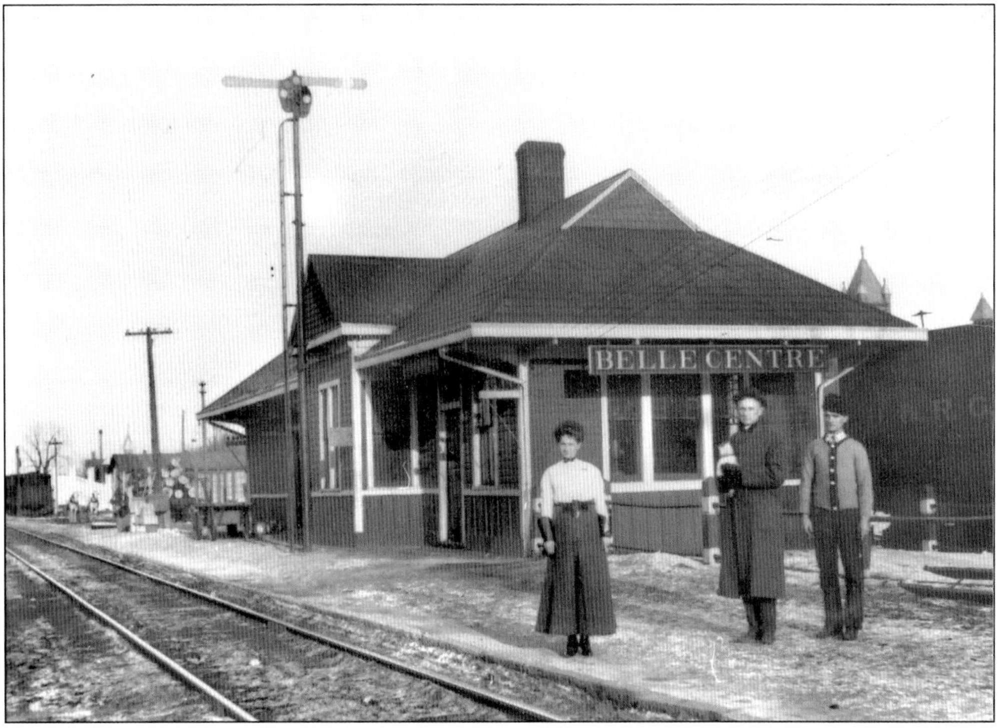

The Big Four depot at Belle Center is a typical example of a small-town combination depot with facilities for handling both passengers and freight. Seen in 1911 are Elizabeth Roll, the first trick telegraph operator and John Mains, second trick operator, flanking Ross "Nick" Carter. The depot still stands along the abandoned right-of-way. (Logan County Historical Society collection.)

Contents

ACKNOWLEDGMENTS

Since my photographing did not begin until the 1960s, I am indebted to numerous individuals, many unknown to me, that had the fortitude to take photographs of their surroundings through the years. Some did it for a living—postcard and newspaper photographers—others were rail fans or historians, and still others were just taking family pictures. Although this work is far from a complete record of railroad structures, the following individuals added to its historical content: Charles Bates, Terrell Berryman, the late Charles Garvin, the late Clyde Helms, the late Si Herring, the late John Keller, Bob Lorenz, K. Todd McCormick, the late Eldon Neff, and David P. Oroszi. Also of particular help were the Allen County Historical Society, Logan County Historical Society, Mary Lou Johnson Hardin County District Library, Oberlin College Library, Railroad Station Historical Society, Spencerville Historical Society, Toledo-Lucas County Public Library, University of Toledo Carlson Library, and all the other libraries and societies of west central Ohio that maintain historical materials. Thanks also to Kevin Capurso of the University of Toledo for technical assistance.

Historical information came from *Reports of the Ohio Railway Commission*; *Annual Reports of the Public Utilities Commission of Ohio*; *Poors Manuals*; *Railroad Gazette*, *Railway Age*, and other trade journals; various newspapers of west central Ohio; numerous centennial, sesquicentennial, and bicentennial compilations and histories of west central Ohio communities; and firsthand interviews conducted over the last 40 years.

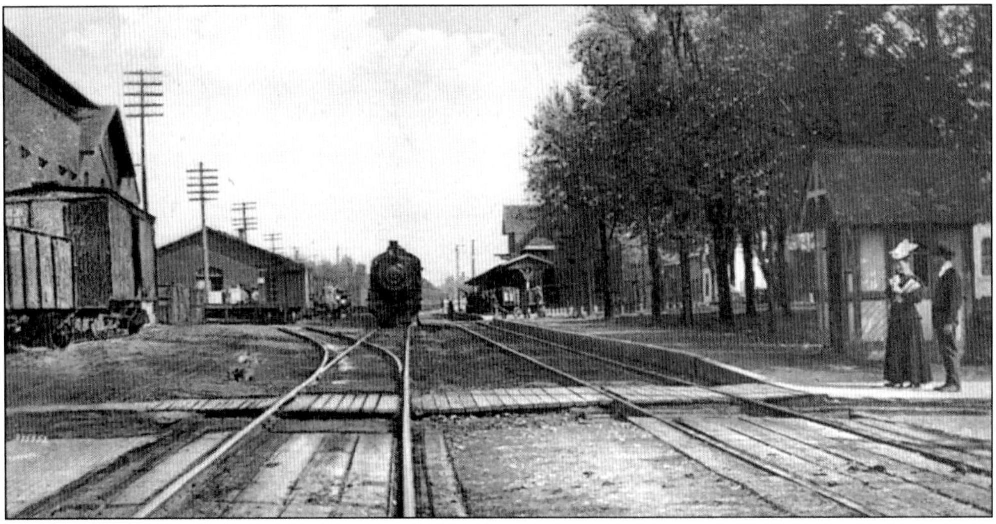

Larger communities had separate passenger and freight depots. This c. 1907 scene on the Pennsylvania Railroad at Bucyrus shows a brick freight house on the left and a passenger depot on the right, both dating to the 1870s. At the road crossing in the foreground is a shanty for the crossing watchman. (Mark J. Camp collection.)

INTRODUCTION

Railroad fever reached western Ohio in the 1830s when the Mad River and Lake Erie surveyed its route from Lake Erie to Dayton by way of Tiffin, Carey, Kenton, Bellefontaine, Urbana, and Springfield. The line opened to Springfield in 1848, the first railroad in west central Ohio. Most lines came after the Civil War. Eventually the Akron, Canton and Youngstown; Cincinnati, Hamilton and Dayton; Cincinnati Northern; Cleveland, Cincinnati, Chicago and St. Louis; Detroit, Toledo and Ironton; Erie; Lake Erie and Western; Pennsylvania; Toledo and Ohio Central; and Toledo, St. Louis and Western crisscrossed the region.

The first rail lines used strap iron rails, strips of thin metal fastened to wood rails, mounted on ties that rested on lengths of timbers (or stone), called sleepers, imbedded in the earth. Later they were replaced with more durable T-rail. Until the standard rail width of four feet eight and a half inches was adopted, rails varied from broad gauge, with widths up to six feet, to narrow gauge, with widths as little as three feet. As rail lines spread across Ohio, stations were necessary to accommodate the railroads and the people they served. Stations were designated points along the railroad, often where it passed through a community, crossed a major river, joined or crossed another line, or just a stop necessitated by the fuel and water needs of the locomotives. Often stations became the seed from which a village or town grew. The railroad depot was a building built at a station to shelter passengers, railroad employees, and freight and baggage. This book aims to present a little of their history and importance to the development of west central Ohio.

Depots ranged from a simple umbrella shelter on an open platform, to a fully enclosed building, to a multi-floor building occupying the better part of a city block. Those in smaller communities generally handled both passengers and freight, so-called combination depots. Cities, county seats, and important junction and transfer points often had separate passenger and freight depots. Where two railroads crossed or joined, a depot might be shared, or each line would maintain separate facilities. Depots varied in design, but most combination depots had a passenger waiting room separated from a freight room by a central agent's office. The agent's office housed the agent and helpers, who sold tickets, maintained records, handled the mail, observed passing trains for physical problems that could lead to accidents, and communicated with other depots on the line, first by telegraph, later by telephone. The depot became the connection between communities and the world. The agent's office often projected from the trackside of the depot in a bay window, awarding the operator an unobstructed view up and down the track. A signal, or order board, was often located outside the bay window. Controls for the order board in the bay window allowed the agent to notify passing trainmen to slow down or stop at the depot. A special metal stand allowed the operator to post "orders" on paper that would be hooked or grabbed by trainmen as the train slowed passing the depot. Each line had its own style of order boards.

Depot designs evolved through time. Engineering departments of the various railroad companies often designed their depots, having several styles and sizes depending on the size and importance of a community or station. Although similarities made the depot a recognizable structure, each line had distinct depot features. This is perhaps most noticeable along the Columbus and Hocking Valley, Erie, Ohio Southern, and Pennsylvania railroads. Lines that absorbed other lines may have several styles dating to the original lines; the Detroit, Toledo and Ironton is a good example. Junction depots, like Ansonia, were often L-shaped, extending along each line. Some depots had a second story, serving as additional office space or living space for the agent and family. Live-in arrangements were not common in Ohio since many communities predated the railroad and had available housing. Freight depots consisted of large windowless rooms for storage with large doors for easy loading and unloading, usually with an elevated platform on trackside for transfer of items between railroad cars and depot. Street side doors allowed transfer to wagons and, later, trucks. Smaller freight depots may have had an office area for the freight agent at one end. Larger ones often had a two-story headhouse attached to a long freight shed. These buildings could be easily extended or shortened to accommodate changing business needs.

Stations also had other structures like interlocking or signal towers, watchtowers, telegraph offices, division office buildings, water tanks, coaling stations, engine houses, roundhouses, and maintenance shops. Interlocking or signal towers were two- or one-story manned buildings located along lines and at all major junctions or railroad crossings (diamonds) to control traffic flow, like traffic lights. Few remain today due to radio and computers. Smaller elevated towers sat at road crossings and points of limited visibility to control crossing gates; many were equipped with bells rung by the operator. These also disappeared as automatic gates replaced the manual ones. Some towers lacked signal control and only served as checkpoints for train travel. The Pennsylvania Railroad, for example, commonly had towers spaced every two to three miles along the line. Steam locomotives required an assortment of buildings to handle servicing. Coal, sand, and water needed to be replenished at certain stations, and some stations like Bellefontaine, Bradford, Bucyrus, Crestline, Galion, Lima, Marion, and Van Wert were terminals where locomotives could be stored and/or serviced. Some had complete car and locomotive repair and construction facilities. The roundhouse was a series of locomotive stalls surrounding a central turntable—a garage for steam locomotives. Some doubled as repair shops. As diesels appeared in the 1950s, these facilities became unneeded, and today few remain.

This book picks up where *Railroad Depots of Northwest Ohio* left off. It includes illustrations of selected passenger and combination depots from some 18 counties south of a line east and west from Findlay and southern Seneca County to the Indiana line, to a line from Union City to Troy and Urbana. The compilation is far from complete for this part of Ohio since through the years it has been served by some 300 depots. Readers willing to share photographs and information are urged to contact the author through the Railroad Station Historical Society Web site (www.rrshs.org) or the University of Toledo Web site (www.eeescience.utoledo.edu/Faculty/Camp/Default.htm).

One

Baltimore and Ohio Lines

The Dayton and Michigan Railroad connected Dayton and Toledo in 1859 by way of Sidney, Wapakoneta, and Lima. Construction began in Dayton in 1853; the line was in operation to Sidney in 1856 and Lima in 1858. The Cincinnati, Hamilton and Dayton Railroad (CH&D) had a vested interest in this line since it had recently ended its agreements with the Mad River and Lake Erie Railroad (MR&LE) for access to a Lake Erie port by way of MR&LE tracks from Dayton to Sandusky. In 1863, the line came under the control of the CH&D, and the CH&D had a port of its own at the growing city of Toledo. In 1887, a line began west from Findlay, eventually reaching Fort Wayne in 1895. The original name, New York, Mahoning and Western, hinted at great aspirations; it became the American Midland and, eventually, the Findlay, Fort Wayne and Western (FFW&W), often called the Tangent line because of its relatively straight course. It connected with the Toledo and Ohio Central (T&OC) in South Findlay and the Pennsylvania Railroad (PRR) and Wabash on the east side of Fort Wayne. After the CH&D gained control in 1902 and reorganized it as the Cincinnati, Findlay and Fort Wayne (CF&FW), it connected the new acquisition to its Delphos-Dayton branch by laying track from a new wye junction called East Mandale south to Delphos in 1904. The Delphos-Dayton branch, chartered as the narrow-gauge Toledo, Delphos and Burlington Railroad in 1879, began service in 1883 as the Toledo, Cincinnati and St. Louis Railroad. It was taken over by the CH&D and converted to standard gauge. The main business along the line was lumber, and when the forests disappeared, so did the future of the line; traffic did not develop as projected. The CH&D encountered financial difficulties around 1905, receiverships followed, and the 1913 Flood wreaked havoc along the road. The Baltimore and Ohio (B&O) bought the CH&D minus its line from Hamilton to Indianapolis and Springfield, Illinois, and the Pere Marquette system in Michigan, which it had controlled, in 1916. The Delphos-Mandale stretch was removed in 1918. The CF&FW was scrapped in 1919 with the exception of a stretch from Grover Hill to the Cincinnati Northern connection at Haviland, which reportedly operated until June 1920. The Delphos-Dayton line came up in 1923.

The Dayton and Greenville Railroad opened between Greenville and Union, west of Dayton, in June 1852. After extending the line to Union City, it became the Dayton and Union Railroad. A two-story frame office building and depot was built on Martin Street in Greenville. After several corporate changes the Greenville-Union portion was taken over by the B&O. The Greenville depot was demolished around 1951; a metal prefab building served the line in later years.

The CH&D, and later B&O, erected significant brick passenger depots at Lima, Sidney, and Wapakoneta and a larger frame structure at Columbus Grove. Other depots were small combination depots built to a number of standard plans. Depots along the Delphos-Dayton branch and FFW&W were particularly spartan, and since the lines were abandoned by the early 1920s, few survived. Apparently only Wapakoneta and the relocated and modified Anna, East Mandale, and Versailles depots survive in this part of the state.

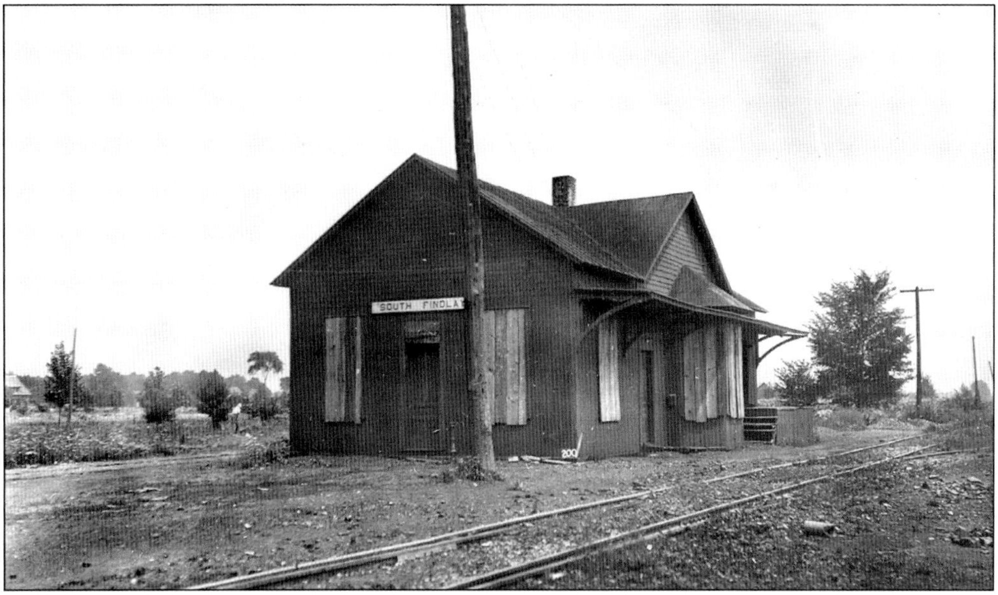

The New York, Mahoning and Western used Findlay's Lake Erie and Western (LE&W) depot initially. Later the FFW&W connected with the T&OC at this depot on the south edge of Findlay. The depot was used for less than 30 years. In this 1918 evaluation photograph, the depot is boarded and grass grows between the rails. (T&OC photograph; Allen County [Ohio] Historical Society collection.)

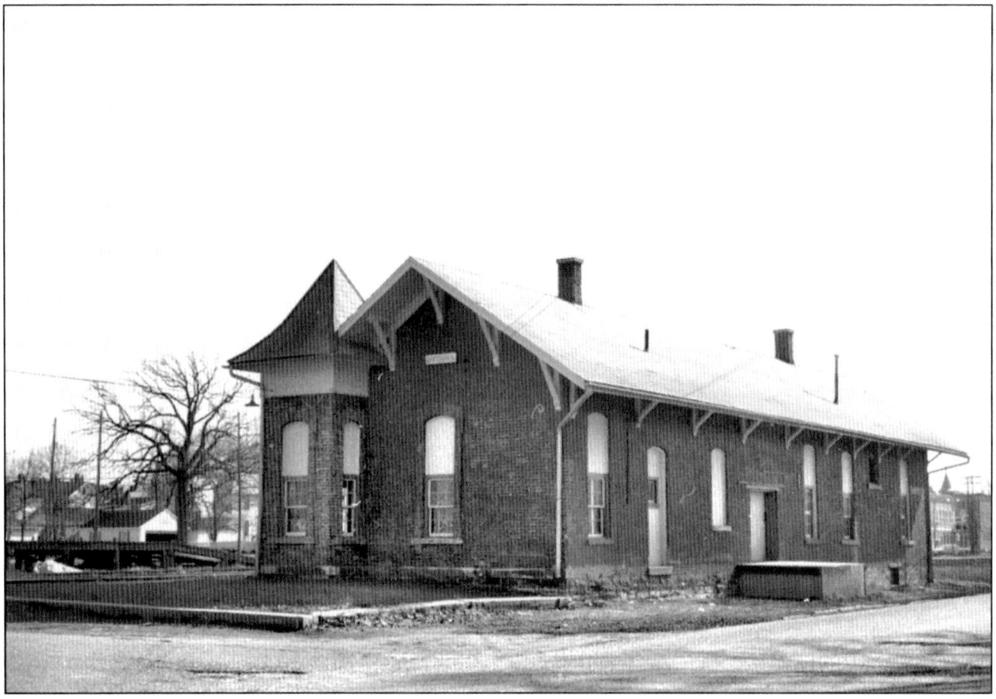

This depot replaced an earlier passenger depot located at the crossing of the FFW&W and CH&D on the north edge of downtown Ottawa. The tracks of the FFW&W have been gone for many years, but the corner bay window calls attention to its former existence.

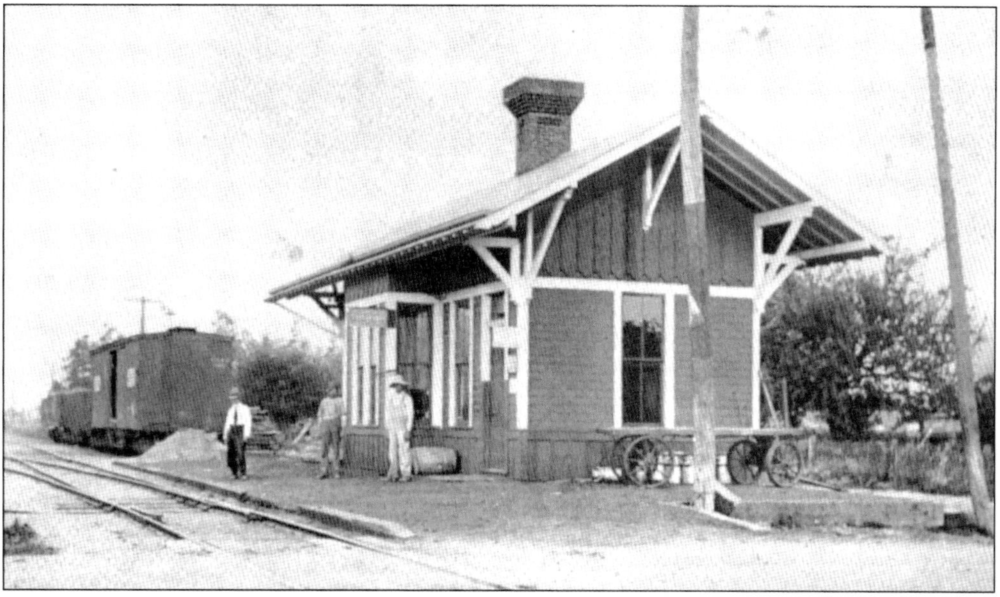

With the exception of Findlay, Ottawa, and Fort Wayne, the communities served by the FFW&W were small farming communities and adequately served by standard plan combination depots like this 1894 structure at Glandorf. The paint scheme dates to the time of CH&D control. After abandonment of the line, the depot was moved off-site to become a garage. It has since been demolished. (Mark J. Camp collection.)

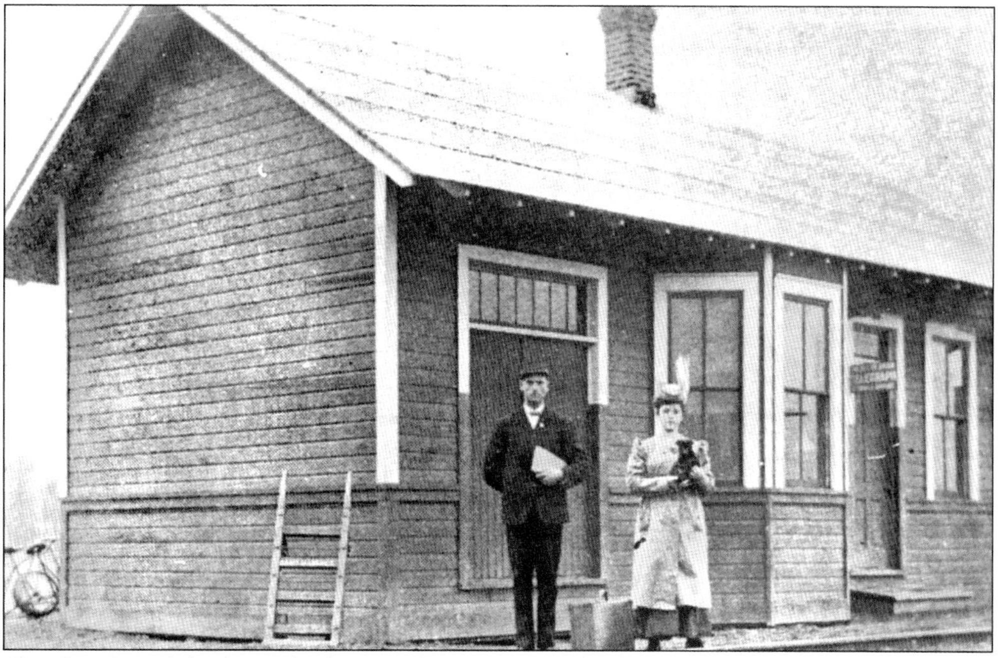

The East Mandale depot, built around 1904, was indeed spartan, but sat at the important junction of the FFW&W and the CH&D branch to Delphos and Dayton. The depot agent, William Dray, and his wife, Flossie, pose on the platform. After abandonment around 1919, it was relocated to a nearby farm. (Mark J. Camp collection.)

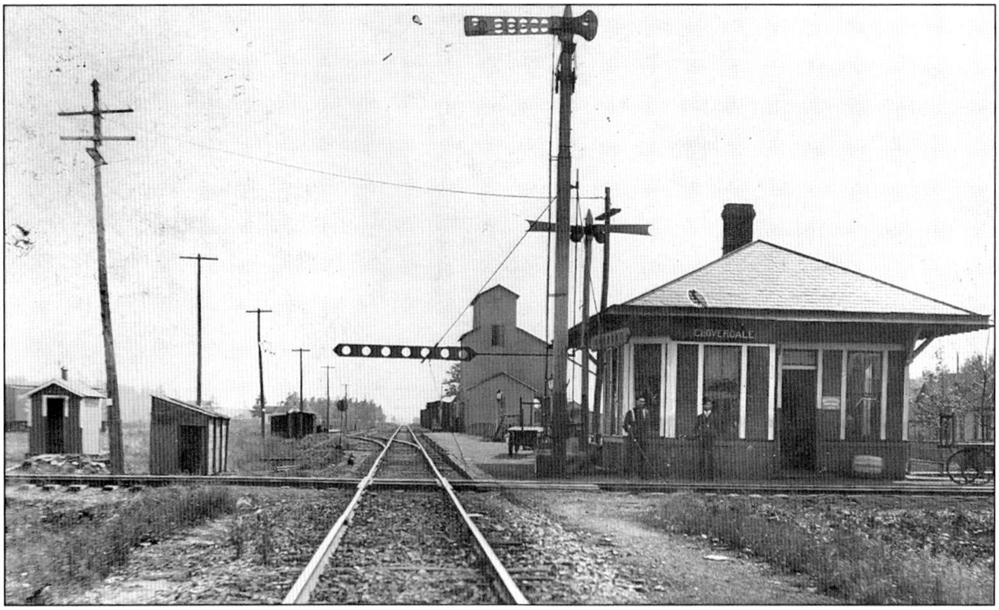

Cloverdale's depot sat at the diamond with the Toledo St. Louis and Western (Clover Leaf). This view looks down the FFW&W. Smash boards are across both tracks, and baggage carts await the stop of local passenger trains. Down the track is a grain elevator. In the days before indoor plumbing, the little vented house across the track was a necessity. Just out of view is the local railroad hotel. (Mark J. Camp collection.)

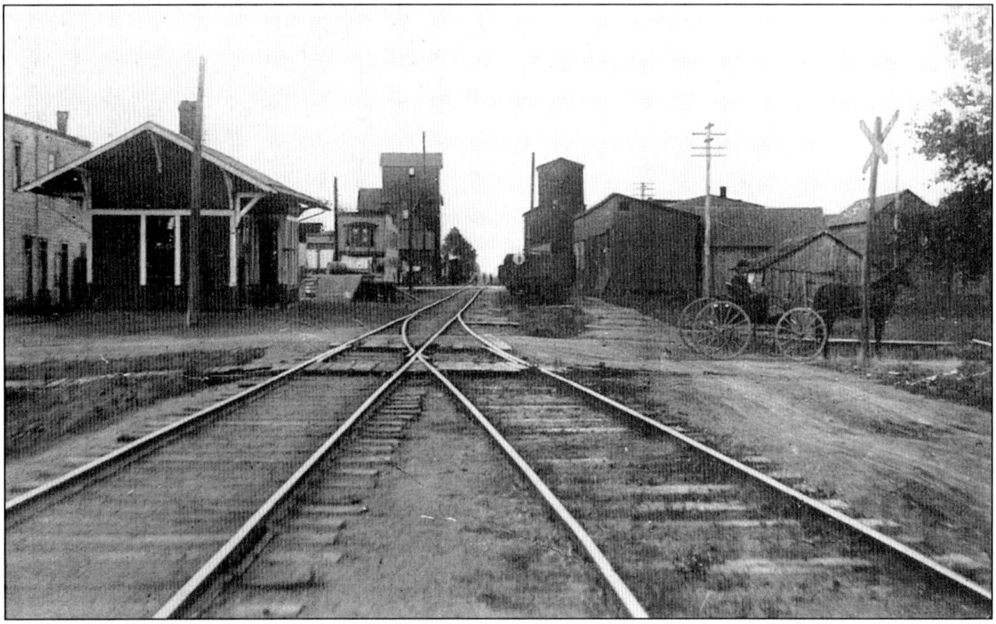

Looking east at Grover Hill are the depot, freight platform, grain elevators, and, to the left, a restaurant. The combination depot is built to the same plan as Glandorf and probably dates to the same time. The siding veering off to the right leads to stockyards and straw sheds. The depot remained on-site for about 10 years after abandonment in 1920. Since then, it was moved twice and later torn down. (C. U. Williams photograph; Mark J. Camp collection.)

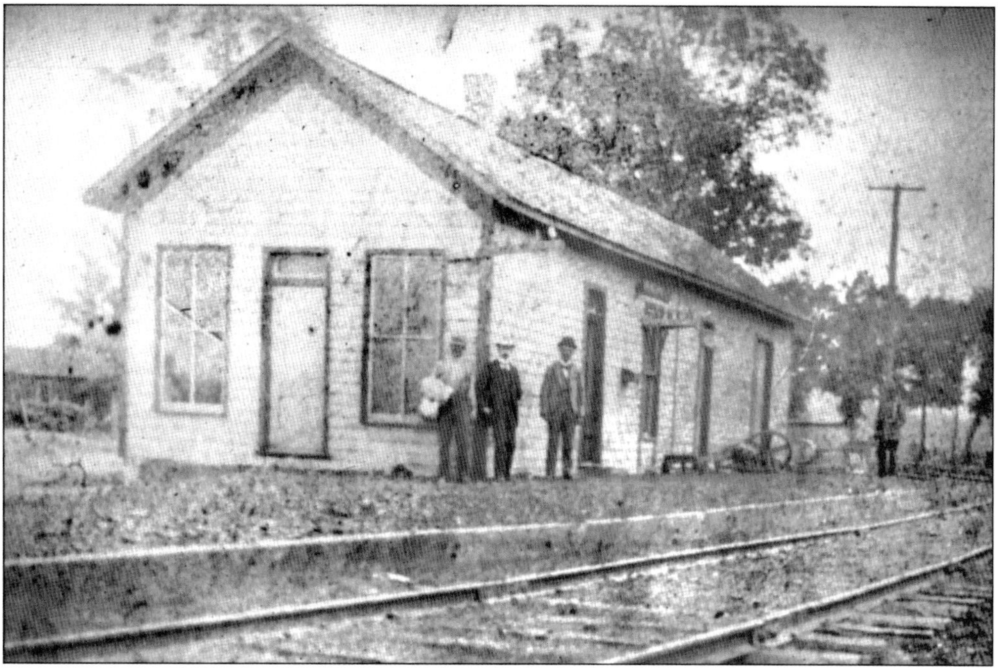

This is the "old Narrow Gauge," later CH&D, depot in Spencerville in the early 1900s. The structure reportedly dates to around 1879 and served the community until 1923. Even the right-of-way is hard to find today. (Spencerville Historical Society collection.)

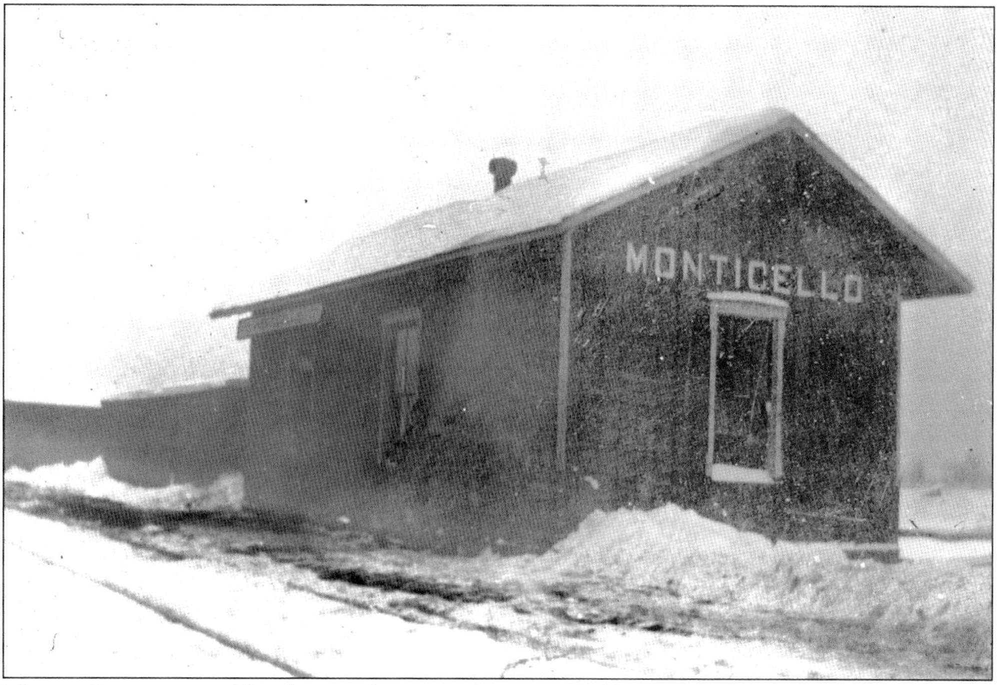

Monticello was served by this combination depot, probably erected around 1880. It is spartan but contained a small waiting room and agent's office complete with a potbelly stove. The depot and track are long gone. (Spencerville Historical Society collection.)

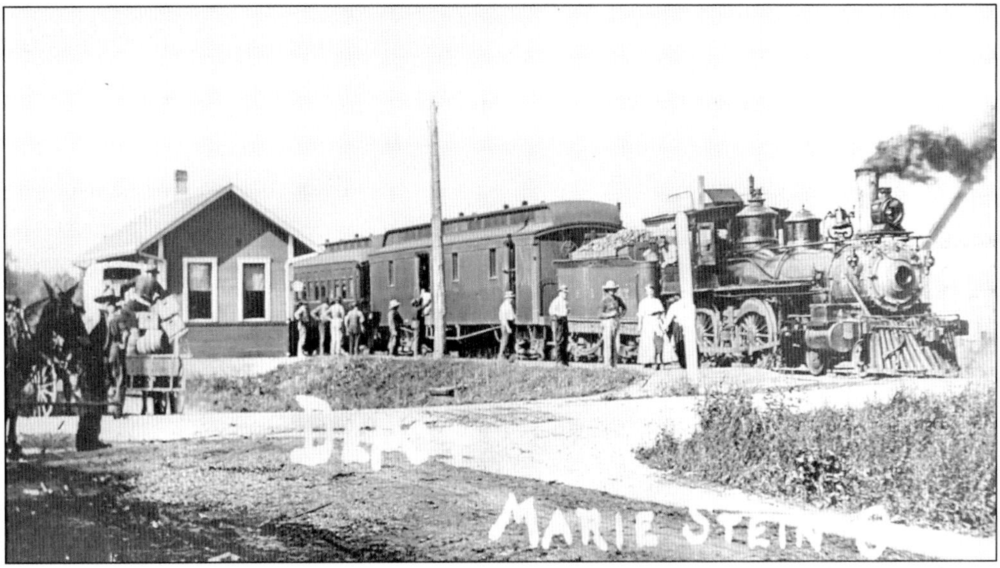

It is train time at Maria Stein! The CH&D accommodation has just arrived at the *c.* 1883 depot, and while workers load express and others wait to board, others pose for the photographer. Such was the daily activity at many towns along the old Narrow Gauge. Unfortunately, only these pictorial memories survive. (Mark J. Camp collection.)

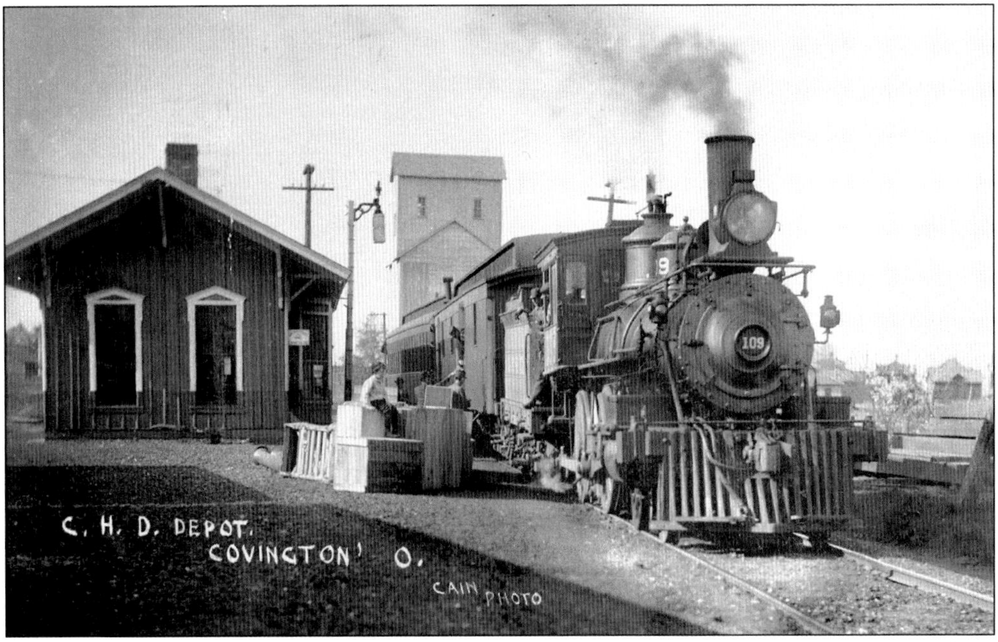

Farther south near the crossing with the Pittsburgh, Cincinnati, Chicago and St. Louis Railway (Pennsylvania Railroad) at Covington, the scene is repeated. Note the early-style order board. The depot no longer exists. A depot still exists in Versailles, but it was relocated in 1923 and converted to an automobile repair shop. (Cain photograph; Mark J. Camp collection.)

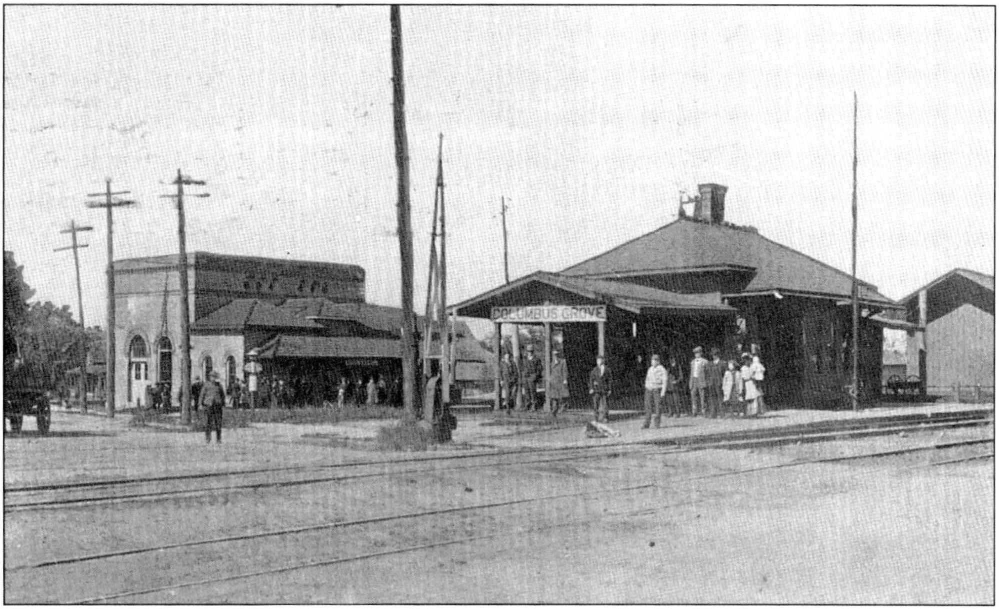

Columbus Grove, on the main line of the CH&D, had separate frame passenger and freight depots. To accommodate the increased passenger business at this transfer location, three other depots were within walking distance the CH&D maintained a covered outside waiting area. Note the adjacent Ohio Electric depot/substation. By 1960, the shelter and freight house (former combination depot) were gone; the depot disappeared by the early 1970s. (Mark J. Camp collection.)

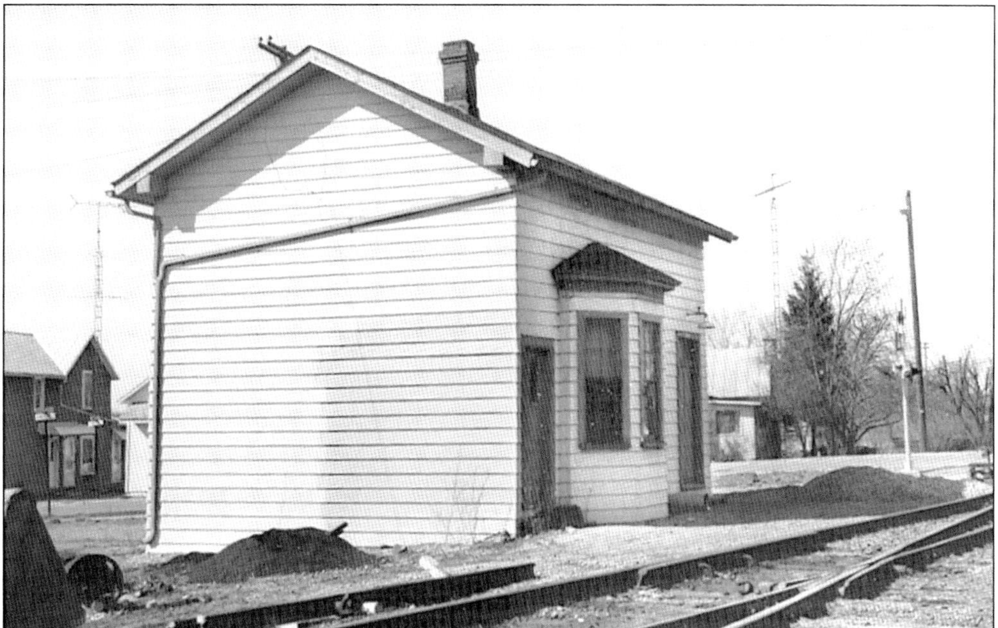

The Cairo depot had been shortened and significantly modified by the time of this 1975 photograph. It is now gone. The B&O, in later years, covered many of its depots with aluminum siding and eliminated any unnecessary architectural details, including some windows and doors.

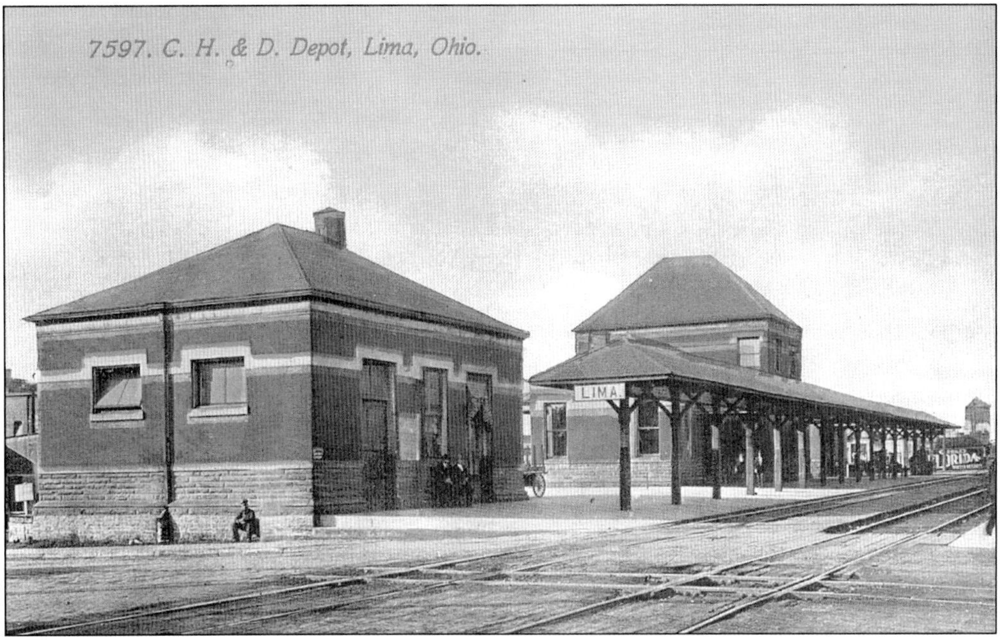

The track first reached the city of Lima in 1858. This CH&D passenger depot opened in December 1891. Nearby was the old stone downtown depot of the Detroit, Toledo and Ironton (DT&I) and brick Pennsylvania Railroad passenger depot. Across and down the tracks were a number of large railroad hotels and CH&D and LE&W freight houses. In the foreground is the baggage/express building, which at one time was used by the LE&W for passengers. In the foreground of the 1971 view below is the Pennsylvania Railroad crossing. This was a very busy junction until the early 1970s. The B&O also had an engine terminal on the north side of town. Unfortunately, all buildings in these views are now gone.

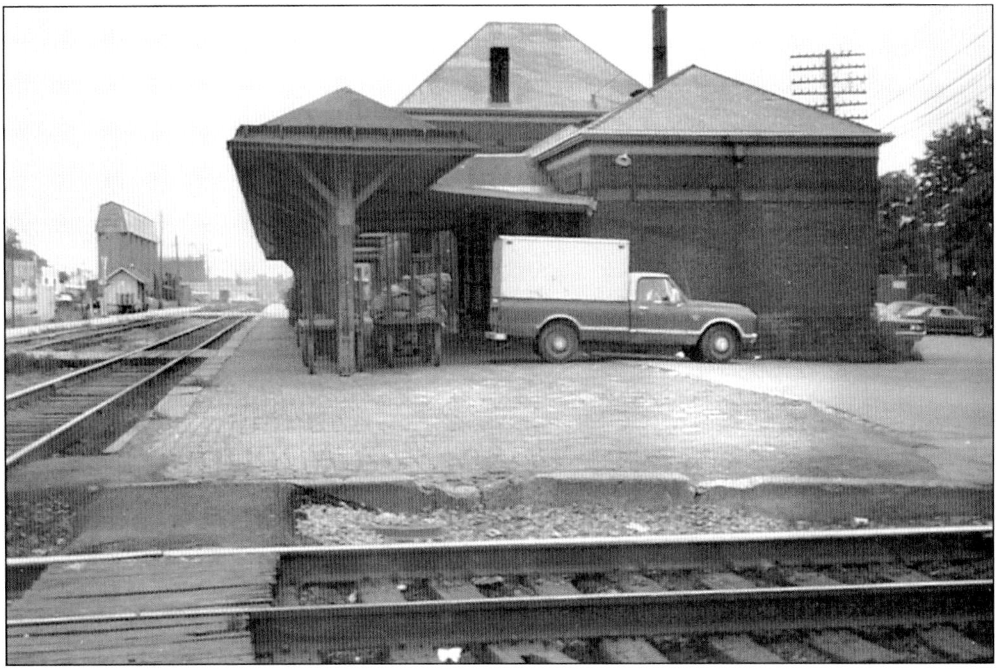

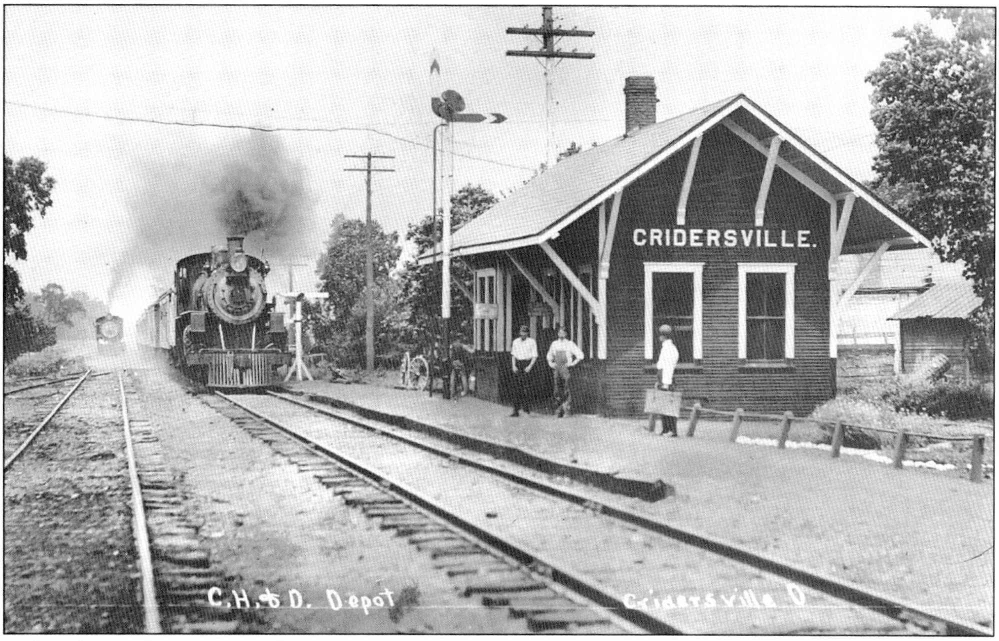

A local switcher sits on the siding as a passenger train pulls into Cridersville depot around 1910. A hack waits to transport passengers to the local hotel while a traveling salesman awaits boarding. Note the wooden mail crane adjacent to the locomotive and the lowered blade of the order board, signifying that there is business to be done at this station. The depot is long gone. (Mark J. Camp collection.)

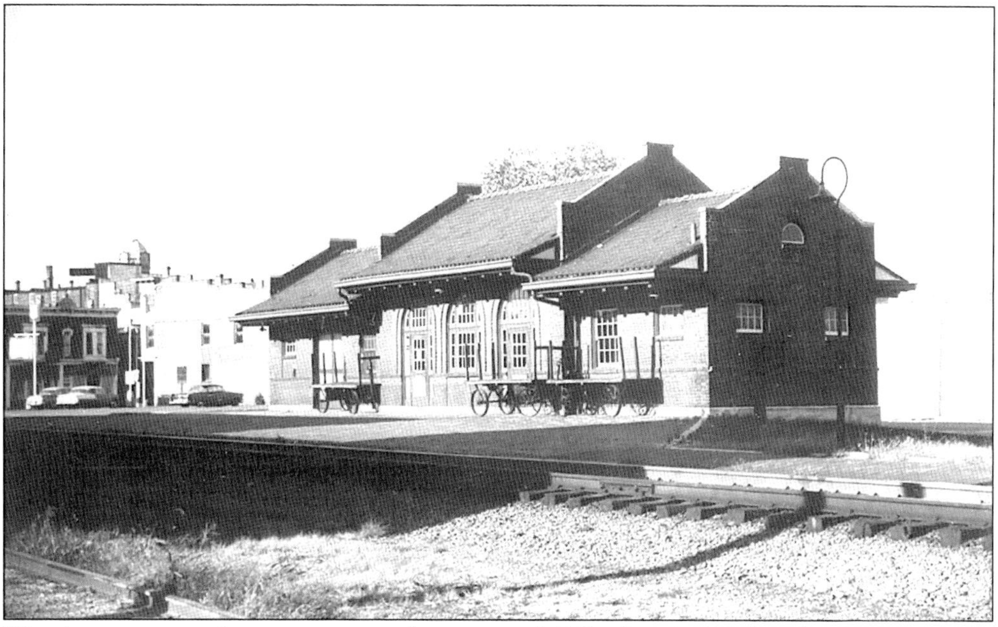

Wapakoneta received a new passenger depot around 1917 when the B&O took over the CH&D. The waiting rooms were flanked by a baggage room and ticket/agent's office. Note the baggage wagons and characteristic gooseneck platform light. Across the tracks was a frame freight house, now gone. CSX still uses the building. (Charles Garvin photograph; Mark J. Camp collection.)

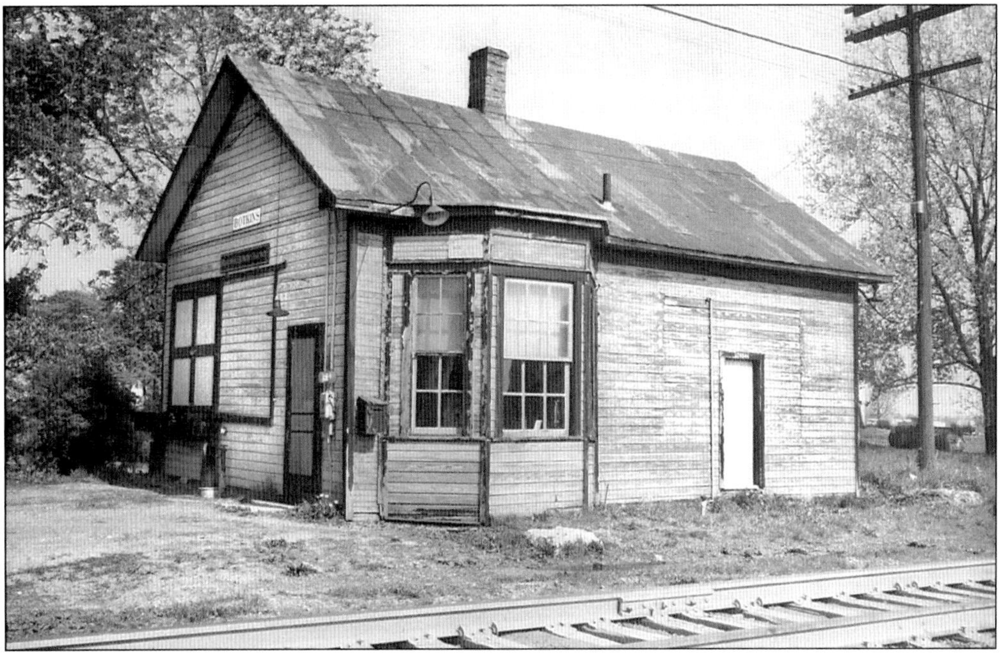

The B&O made many changes to the Botkins depot over the years. By this 1969 view, the depot had long since seen its last passenger; it has since been removed. (Charles Garvin photograph; Mark J. Camp collection.)

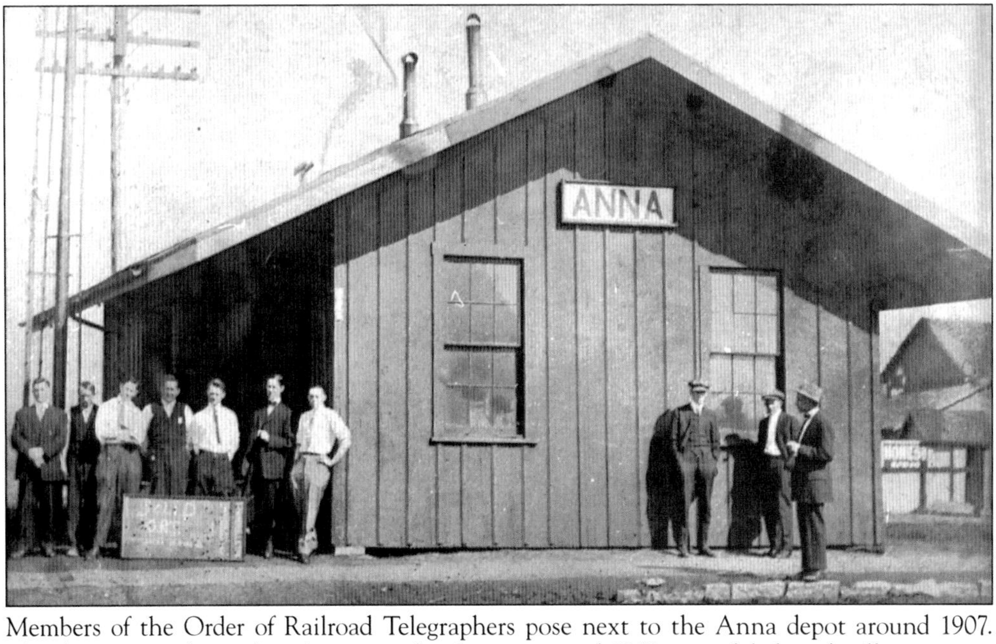

Members of the Order of Railroad Telegraphers pose next to the Anna depot around 1907. The depot was relocated to the west side of town around 1950, remodeled, and still exists as a residence. (Mark J. Camp collection.)

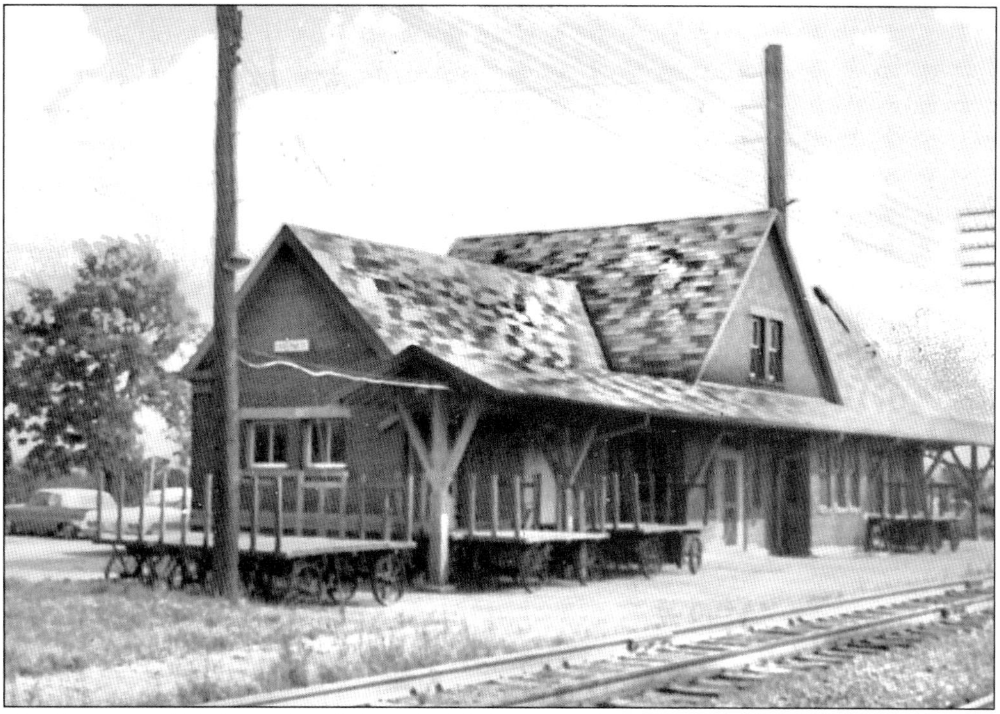

The Dayton and Michigan (D&M) reached Sidney in 1856. The CH&D built this depot around 1900 during a track elevation project. The last passenger service was in 1971; the depot has been reportedly gone since the 1980s.

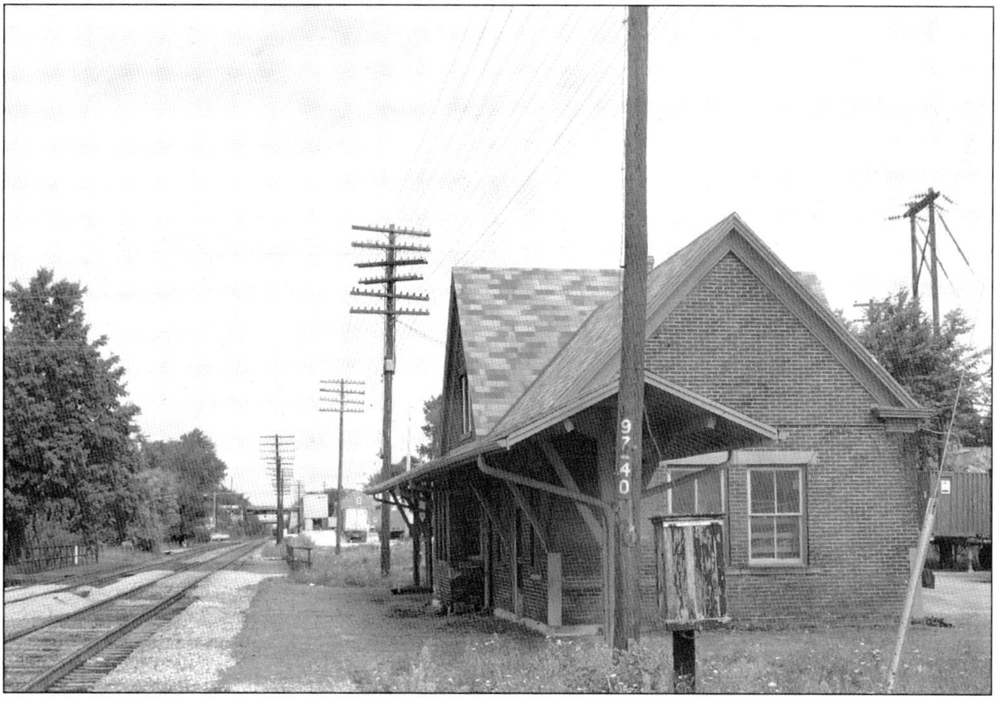

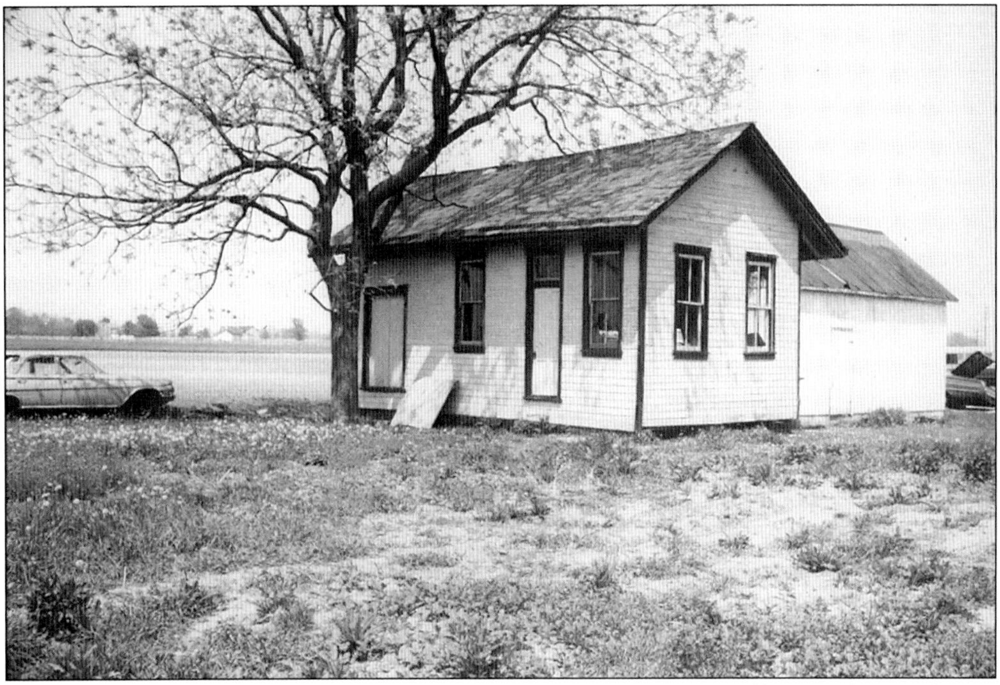

The small combination depot that once served Kirkwood was reportedly moved around 1954 to property of a former agent after it was declared surplus by the B&O. In later years, it served as a storage building on this farm. Falling into disrepair, it was removed around 1993. (Charles Garvin photograph; Mark J. Camp collection.)

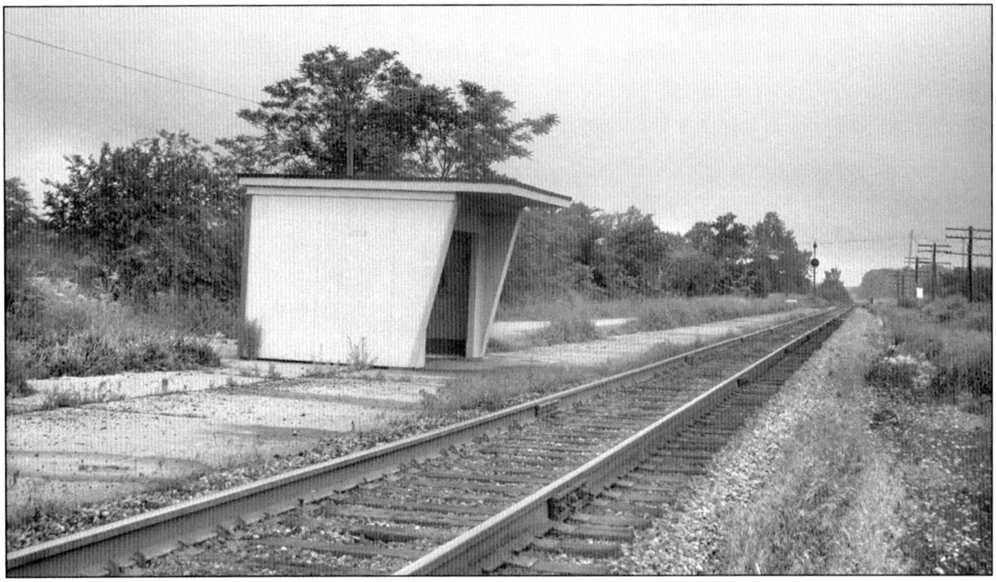

The D&M main line was built a mile east of downtown Piqua in late 1854. The depot was connected to downtown by a hack line or two. By the 1960s, the B&O passenger facilities in Piqua had diminished to this simple shelter. This rather isolated location at the crossing of the PRR became even more desolate when the tracks of the old Columbus, Piqua and Indiana were pulled up in 1985.

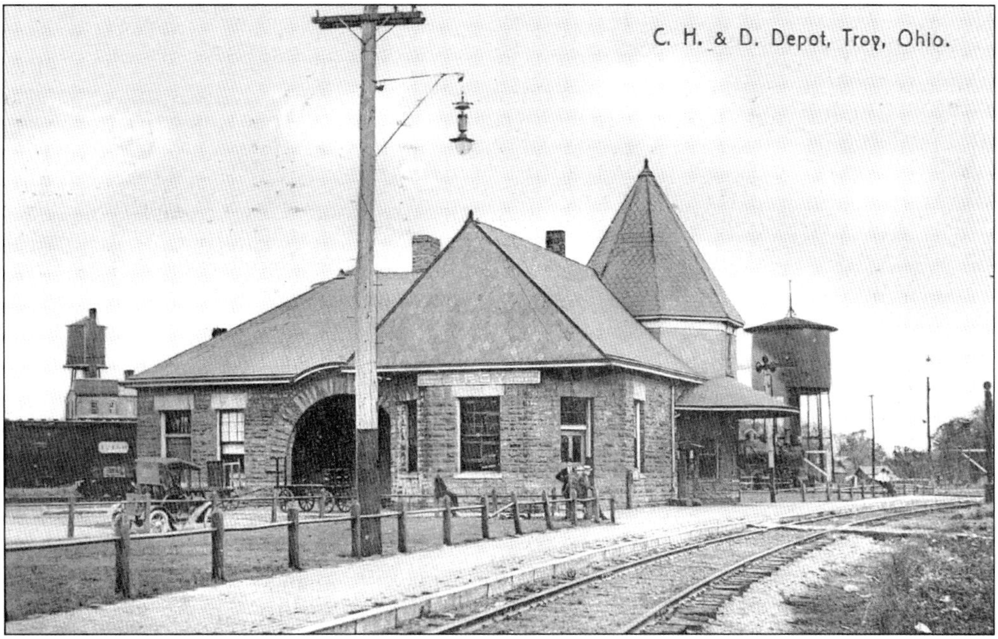

Certainly the most interesting CH&D depot, architecturally, is the still existent CH&D passenger depot at Troy. It was built from stone quarried near Piqua and erected where the Piqua-Troy branch rejoined the main line. This replaced an 1853 D&M brick depot. The Big Four, which maintained its own depot nearby, crossed at this point as well. In the background is a water tank and standpipe for servicing the waiting locomotives. The building is still used by CSX but is surrounded by fence. (Mark J. Camp collection.)

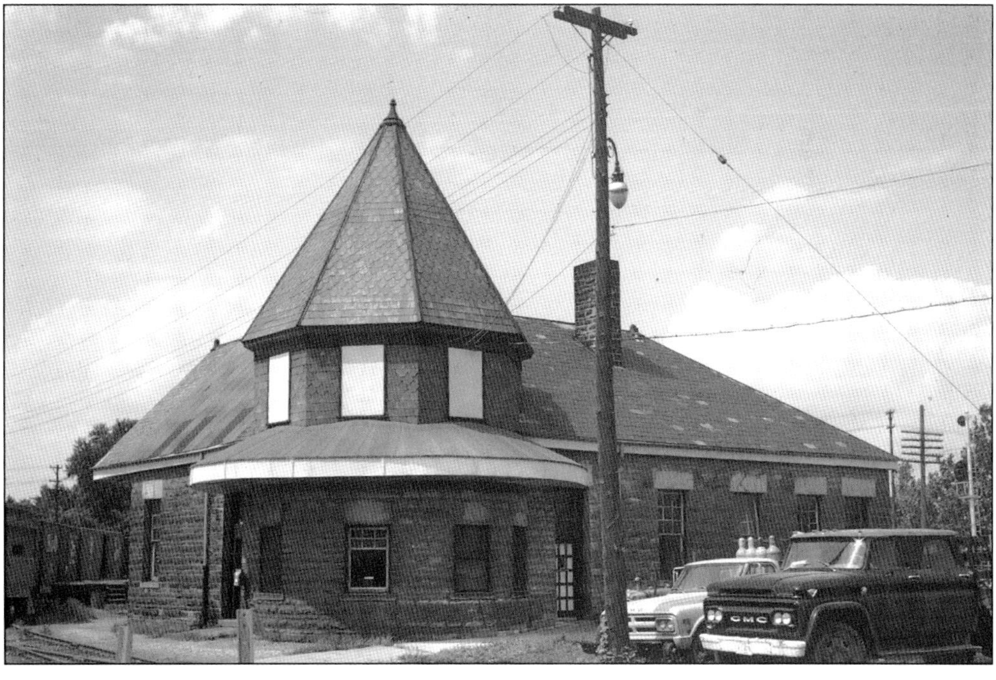

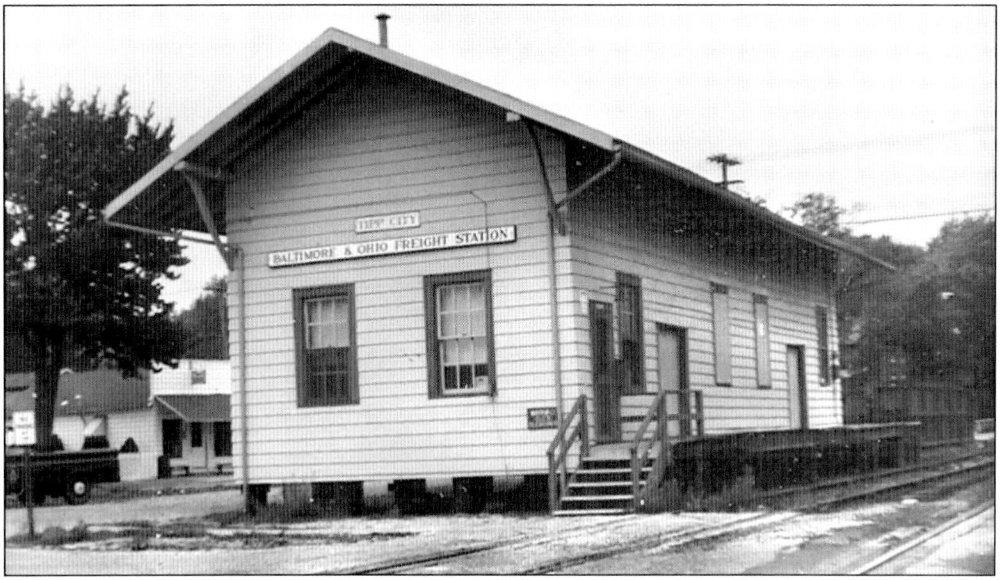

The passenger depot in Tipp City, built around 1890, was reportedly torn down around 1950, but the town still sports this aluminum-sided freight house which was converted to handle the dwindling passenger business. Passenger service ended here in 1969. The depot now has a different paint scheme, but otherwise appears the same today. (William L. Wagner photograph; Mark J. Camp collection.)

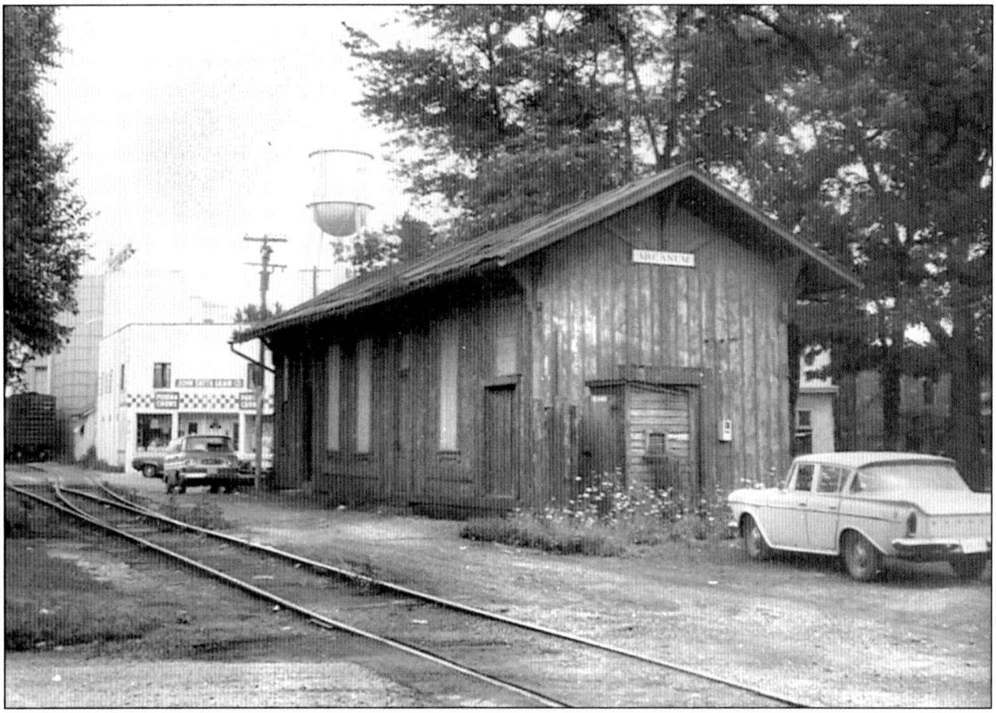

This frame combination depot, photographed in 1969 during B&O ownership, once served the Dayton and Union Railroad in Arcanum. The last passenger train stopped in 1931. It has since been torn down.

Two

The Erie Railroad

The Atlantic and Great Western Railroad, stretching from Salamanca, New York, to Dayton, had its origins in 1853 in northeast Ohio. Construction slowed during the Civil War, and the first train reached Dayton on June 20, 1864, by way of Marion and Urbana. This was a broad-gauge line; the rails were six feet apart. By 1870, financial difficulties arose, as the line lost transfer business with other lines, all built to standard gauge—four feet eight and a half inches. In 1880, the line became the New York, Pennsylvania and Ohio Railroad (NYP&O). In the early morning hours of June 22, 1880, 2,500 workers stretching along the track from Dayton to Leavittsburg, some 325 miles, unspiked one rail and completed the conversion to standard gauge—a remarkable feat, even today.

The year 1871 marks the origin of the Chicago and Atlantic Railway from Hammond, Indiana, to Marion on the NYP&O—an important connection to Chicago. After a number of consolidations and corporate name changes, the first through trains began running in June 1883. Difficulties led to its reorganization in 1890 as the Chicago and Erie Railroad. In 1895, it became part of the Erie Railroad. The Erie merged with the Delaware, Lackawanna and Western in 1960; corporate problems continued, eventually it became part of Conrail, and today only segments of the lines remain in operation.

From the 1890s on, the Erie used a series of standard plans for its depots. Lengths and door and window arrangements varied, but the buildings were very similar. Scalloped boards under the eaves were a characteristic. Most of the depots were combination, but some stations also included freight houses. An elaborate, many-gabled depot was erected at Galion, and union depots were used at Marion, Martel, Ohio City, and Peoria. Today only Kemp, Richwood, and Spencerville remain as examples of Erie standard depots in west central Ohio.

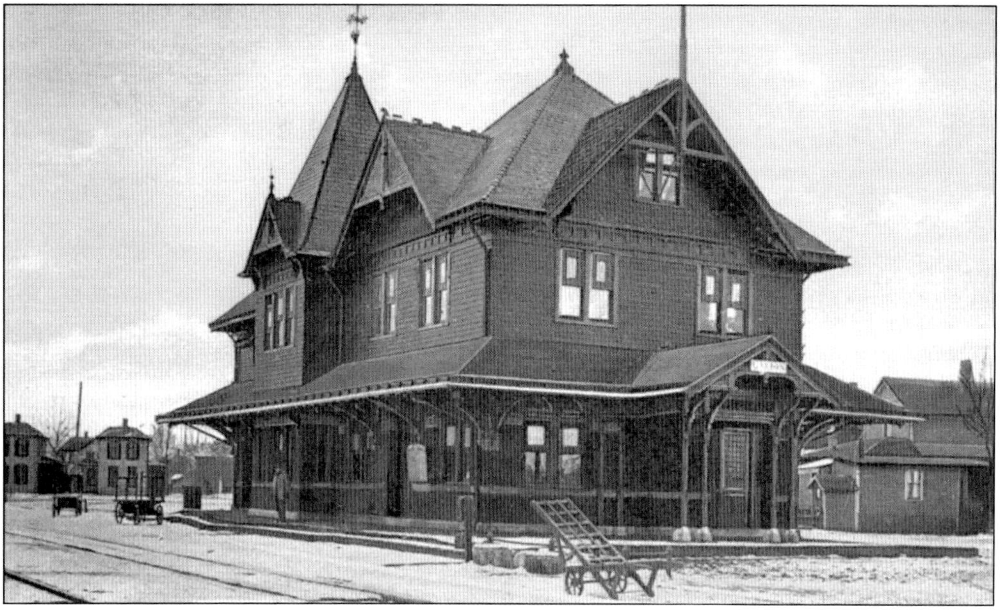

The New York, Lake Erie and Western, which became the Erie in 1895, erected this gabled passenger depot at Galion in 1891 from plans designed in its engineering office. It was certainly an attractive structure, debatably the best on the Erie lines in Ohio. The depot was demolished unannounced in fall 1970. (Mark J. Camp collection.)

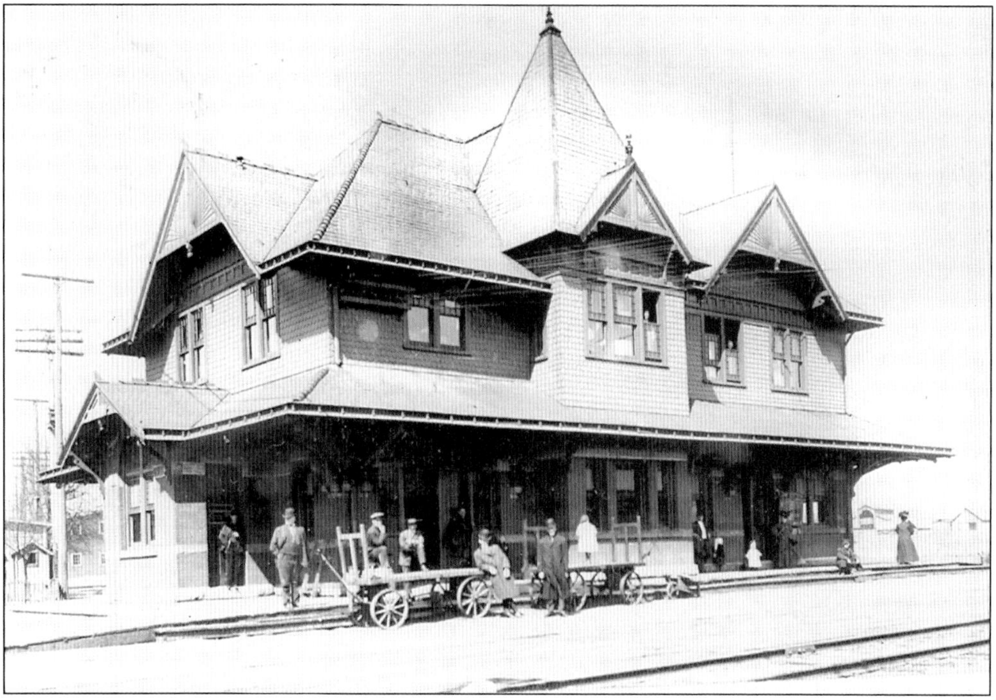

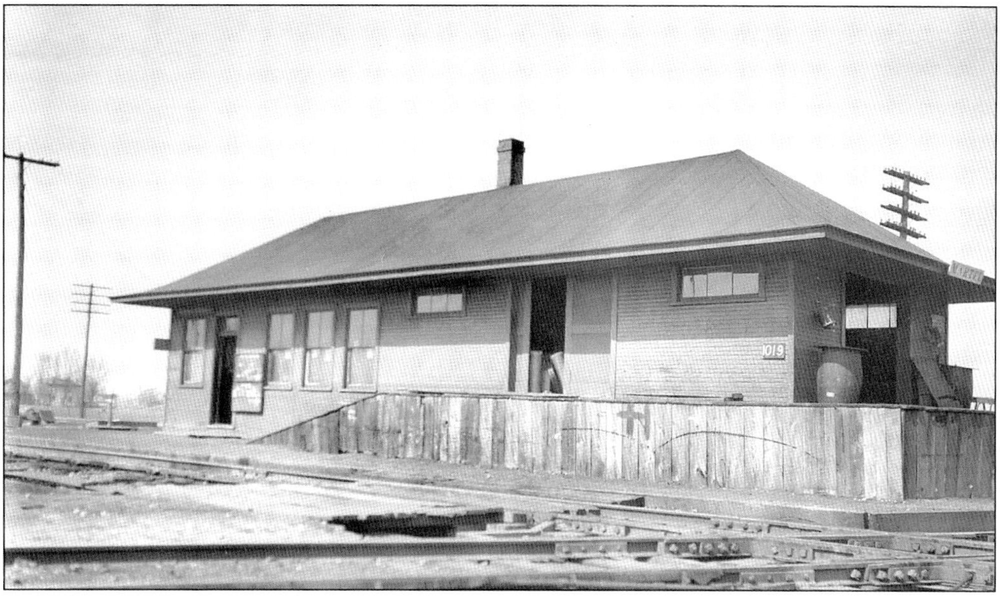

Martel was the crossing of the Erie and T&OC. A combination depot shared with the T&OC and a tower built to T&OC plans were at the diamond. The depot probably dates to 1882 but was removed by the 1960s. (T&OC photograph; Allen County [Ohio] Historical Society collection.)

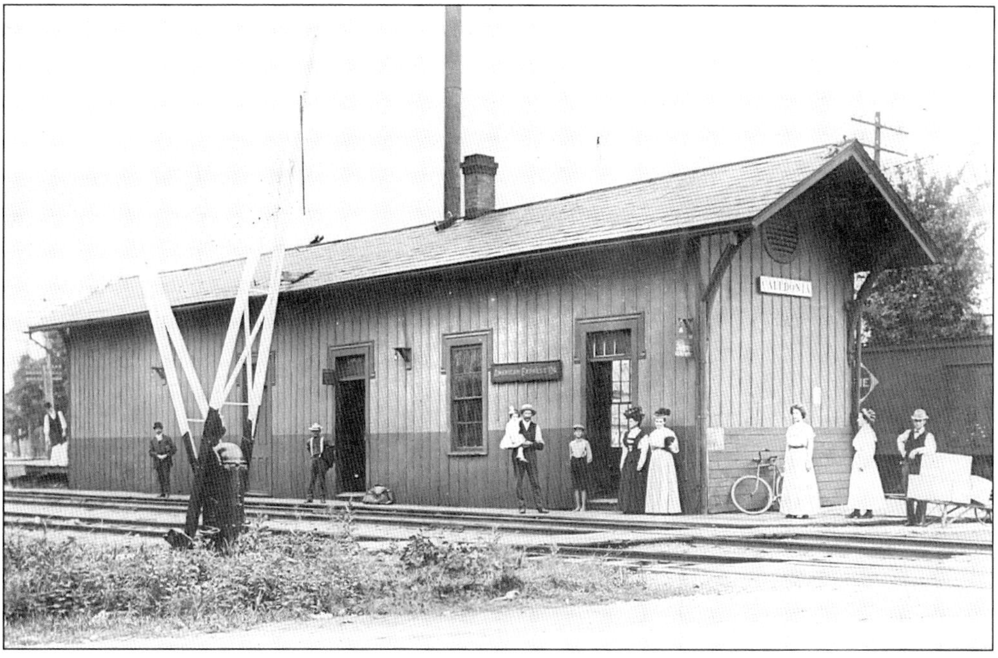

The crossing watchman will soon be lowering the gates adjacent to Erie's Caledonia depot, also used by the Big Four. It is a warm 1913 summer day as passengers await the train. The depot was atypical in having a freight door on the end of the building rather than trackside. Note the plank platform and bicycle for the messenger boy to deliver telegrams. (Mark J. Camp collection.)

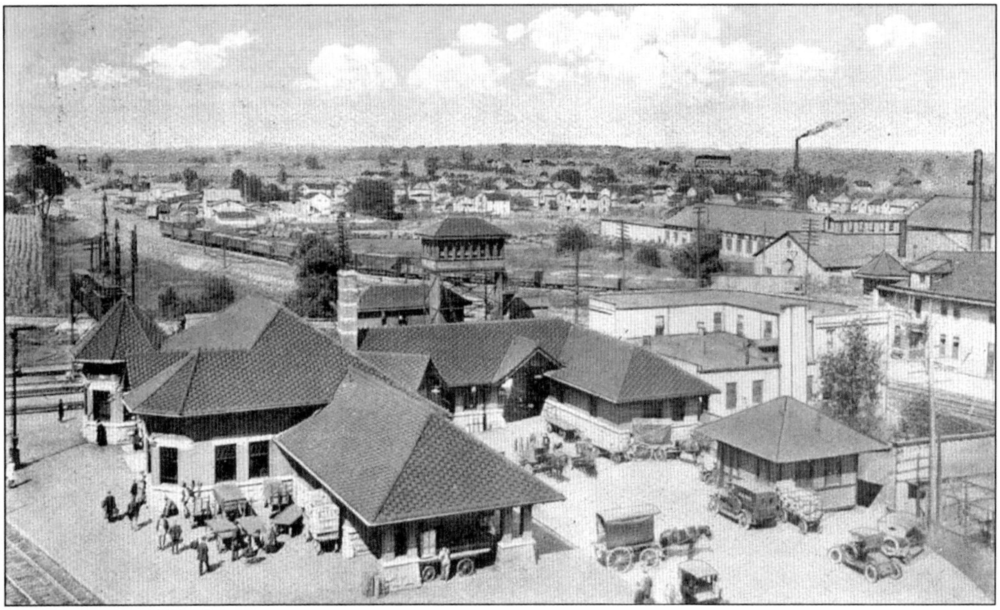

Erie trains used Marion Union Station. This aerial view shows Union Station built in 1901–1902 at the diamond of the Cleveland, Cincinnati, Chicago and St. Louis (CCC&StL) and Erie with the Hocking Valley, to the extreme left. To the right between a couple of hotels and restaurants are the PRR tracks; the PRR had a separate depot, just out of view to the far right. Erie's tall AC tower, in the center, provides unobstructed views along the main line. More than 50 passenger trains per day visited the depot in its heyday. Both Union Station and the interlocking tower have been preserved. (Mark J. Camp collection.)

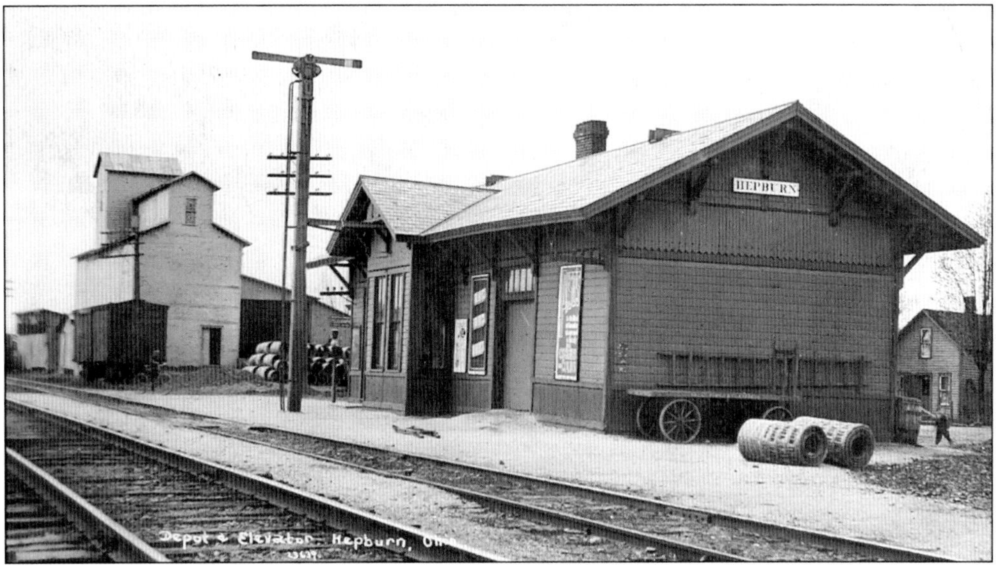

Hepburn was platted and this depot erected in 1882–1883 with the arrival of the Chicago and Atlantic Railroad. Instrumental in establishing this station was the discovery of a thick gravel deposit under a local farm that the line purchased, opened a gravel pit, and ballasted the roadbed for miles beyond. The depot handled a fair number of passengers visiting the summer resort at nearby Spring Lake. (Mark J. Camp collection.)

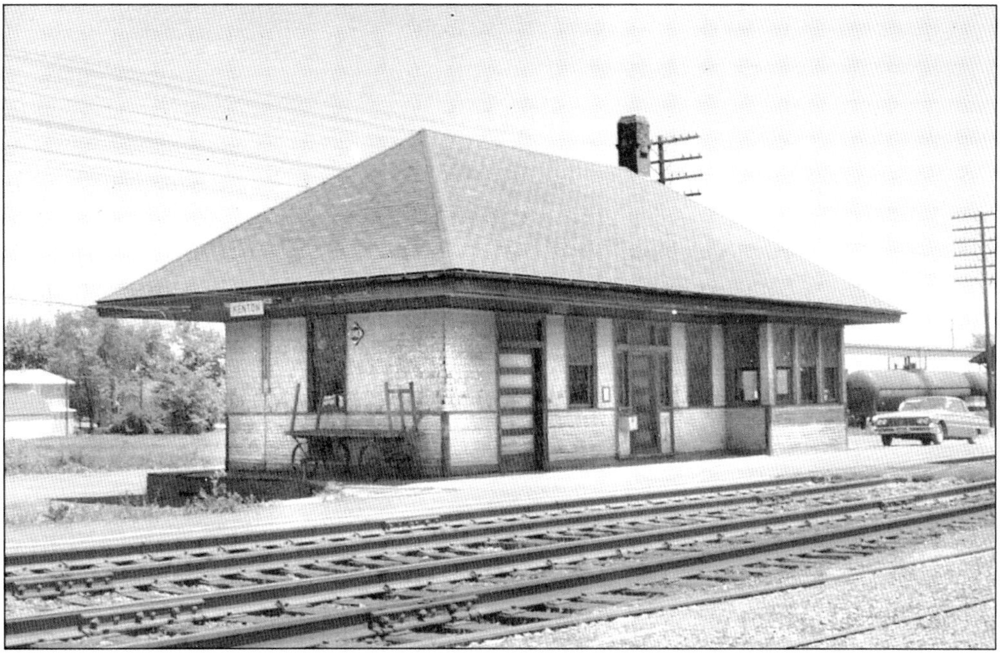

Kenton's Erie facilities included this passenger depot, a nearby freight house and KN tower at the crossing with the Big Four and T&OC. Passenger service was in the waning years in this 1967 photograph. The tower and depots were demolished around 1980. (Charles Garvin photograph; Mark J. Camp collection.)

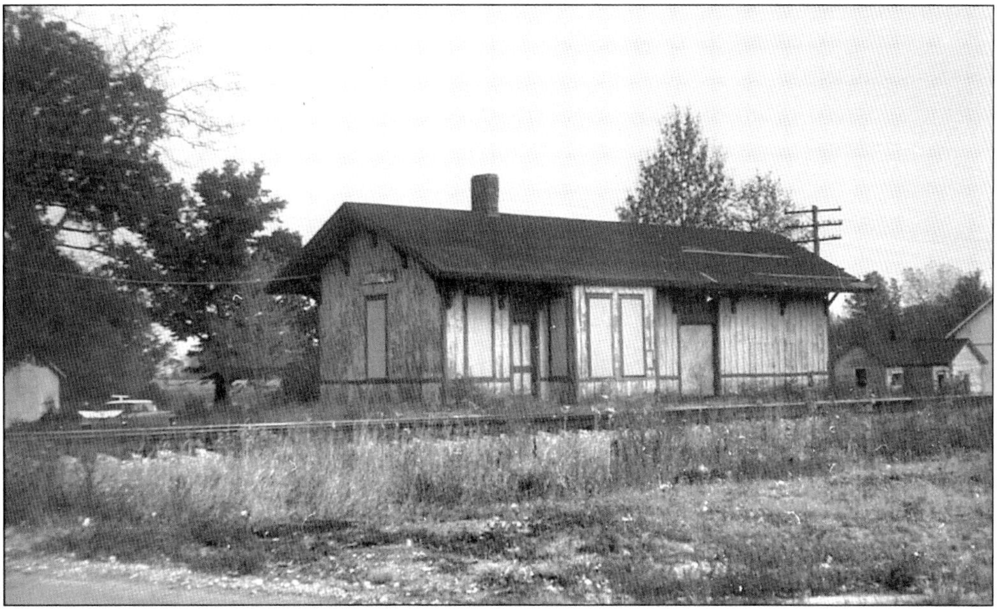

McGuffey depot was built around 1890 with the platting of the community. Located within the Scioto Marsh region, it became a major shipping point for onions. In the early 1900s, the track was lined with large warehouses. By 1959, the agency was closed, and by this 1964 photograph, the depot sat abandoned. Soon it would be torn down. (Charles Garvin photograph; Mark J. Camp collection.)

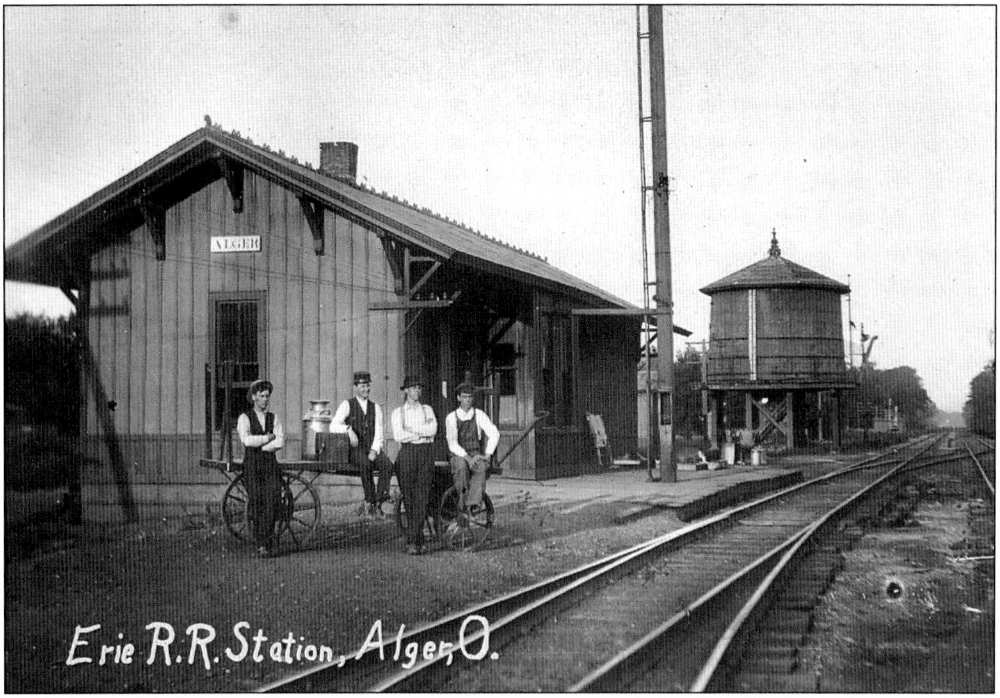

Alger was another onion shipping point, although not evident from this view around 1907. The depot staff poses as they await an approaching train. Water to replenish the steam locomotives was easy to come by since the station was on the west border of the Scioto Marsh. The 1883 depot was relocated slightly around 1928 and torn down in the 1970s. (Mark J. Camp collection.)

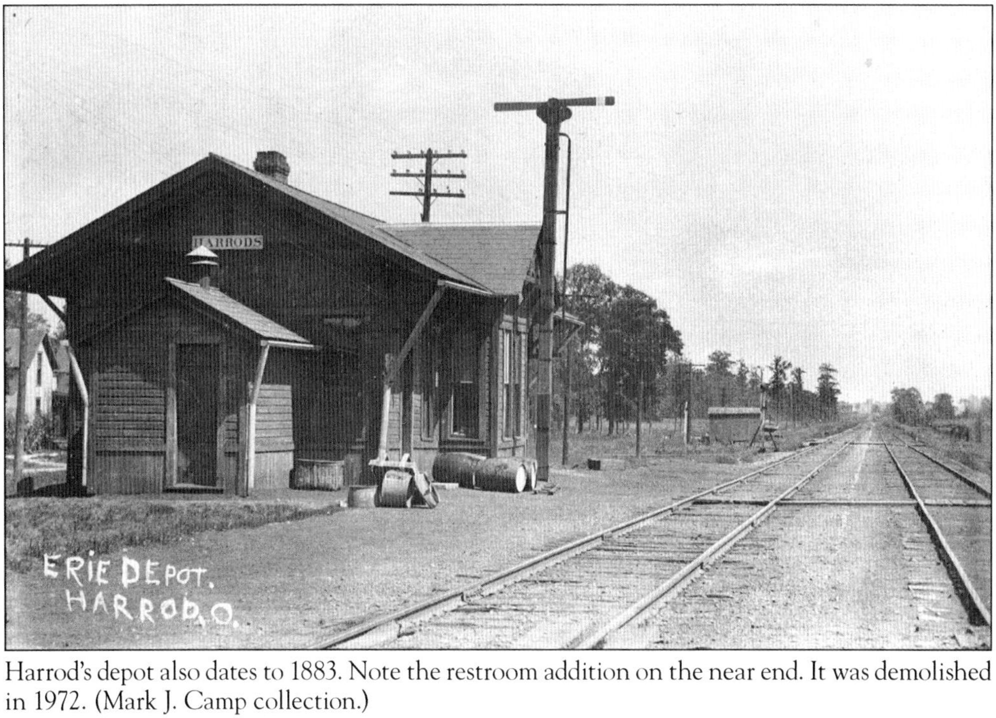

Harrod's depot also dates to 1883. Note the restroom addition on the near end. It was demolished in 1972. (Mark J. Camp collection.)

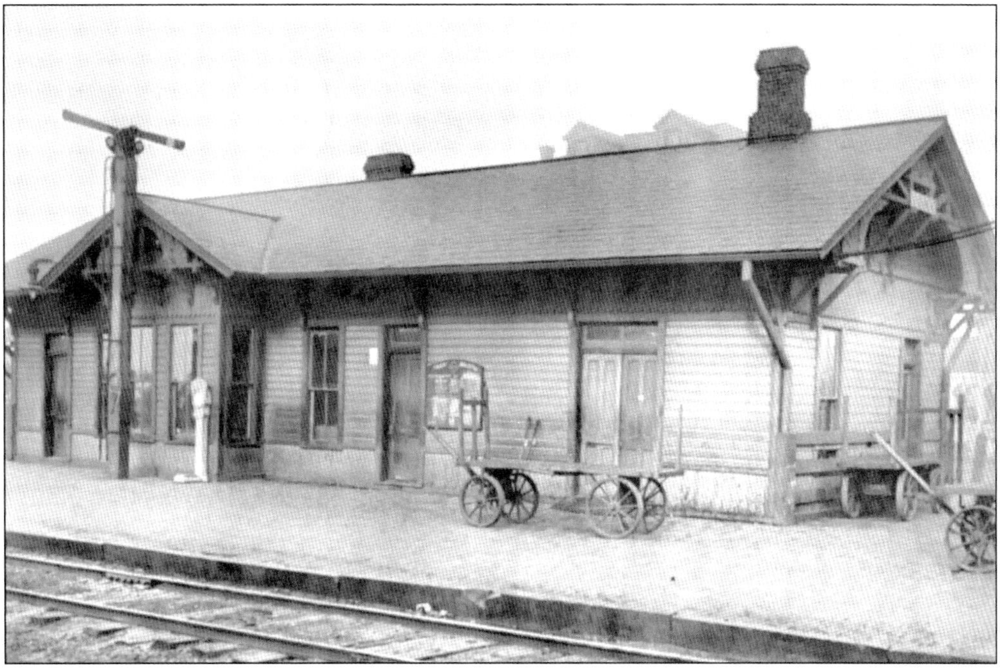

Erie's Lima facilities included this extended version of a standard plan depot with the women's and men's waiting rooms separated by the ticket office and a baggage and express room on the far end. The above view shows the depot around 1910, while the 1967 view below shows a greatly modified version of the same building. The Erie also erected a simple platform shelter across the tracks. Note the smooth-sided part of the modified depot—earlier in 1967, a derailment at the depot sent railroad cars crashing into the building. To the left is the remaining part of LE&W's South Lima roundhouse. None of these structures remain today. (Above, J. E. Bailey photograph; Mark J. Camp collection.)

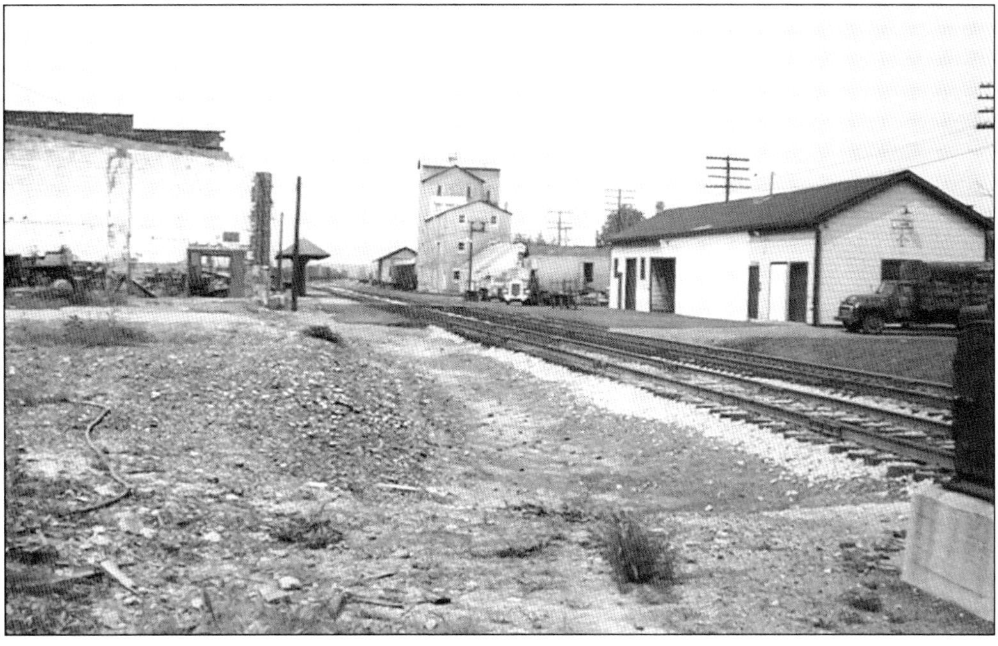

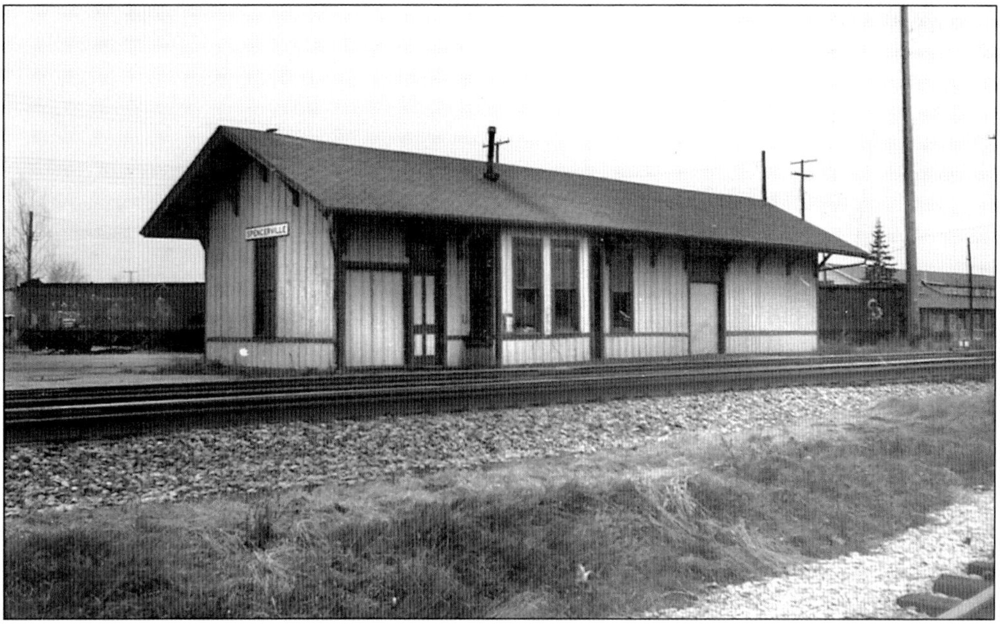

The Erie extended one end of the Spencerville depot to provide additional storage space for freight after its opening in 1883. Spencerville was a water stop, although by the time of this 1967 photograph, the water tank was long gone. On the east edge of town was SU tower. The CH&D once crossed west of the depot. The Spencerville and Elgin used the depot after abandonment by Conrail. Today the depot sits vacant. (Charles Garvin photograph; Mark J. Camp collection.)

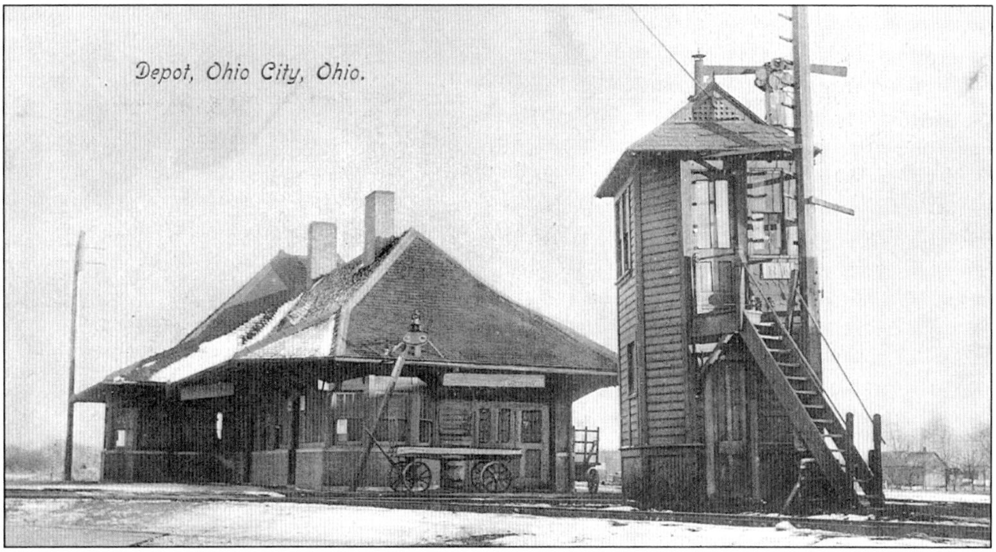

Ohio City, originally Enterprise, had a lot of railroads for a small town. The Cincinnati Northern (CN), Clover Leaf, and Erie crossed at this union depot maintained by the Erie Railroad for many years. The Erie runs behind the tower and past the right side of the depot, the Clover Leaf in front of the tower and past the left side of the depot, and the CN runs between the tower and the depot. Erie's RE tower protected the junction into the early 1900s, but at some point before 1948, it was removed from the diamond and built into the roof of the depot. By the late 1960s, the roof was returned to normal with the removal of the tower. (Mark J. Camp collection.)

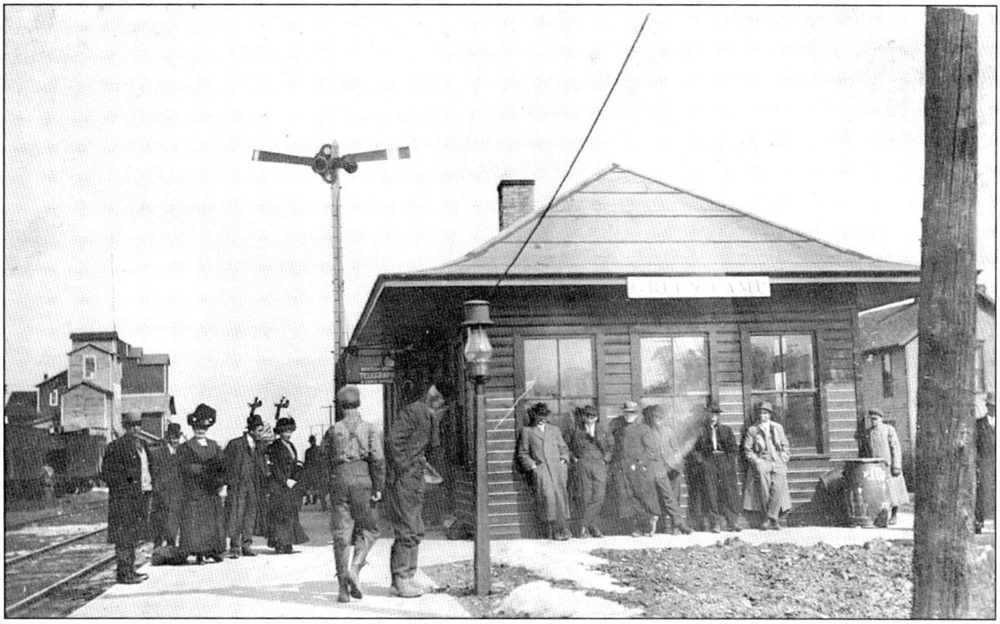

The Dayton branch of the Erie left the main line at Marion. It is a busy day at the newly constructed depot in Green Camp in 1913 as a group waits to depart on a trip to Ora, Indiana. This depot replaced an earlier frame depot. (Mark J. Camp collection.)

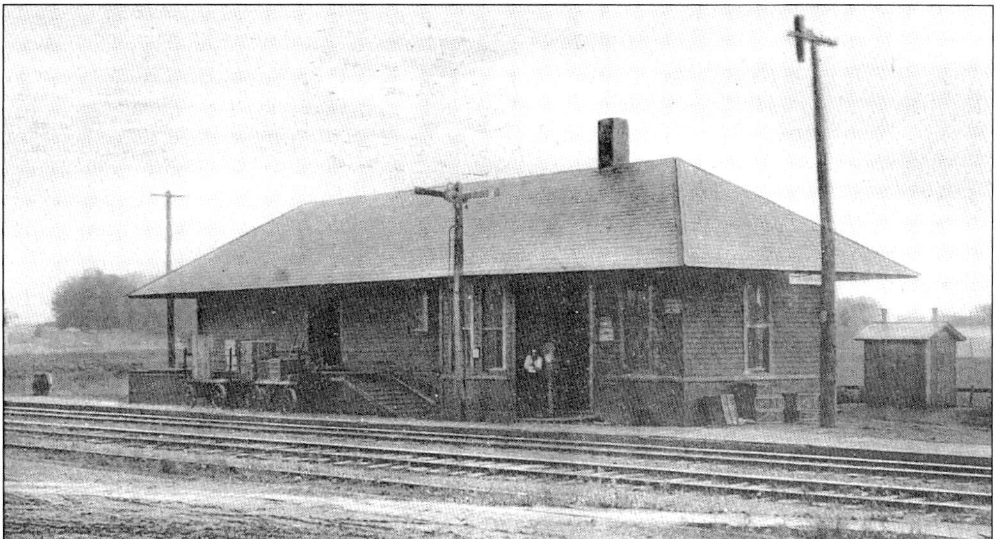

The Richwood depot reportedly was built in 1904 and is a virtual twin of the depot at North Lewisburg. Note the vegetable crates—beans were grown locally. Adjacent is a "two-holer" outhouse. The depot also saw considerable passengers for the local summer resort. It remains on-site in private use; the track is gone. (Mark J. Camp collection.)

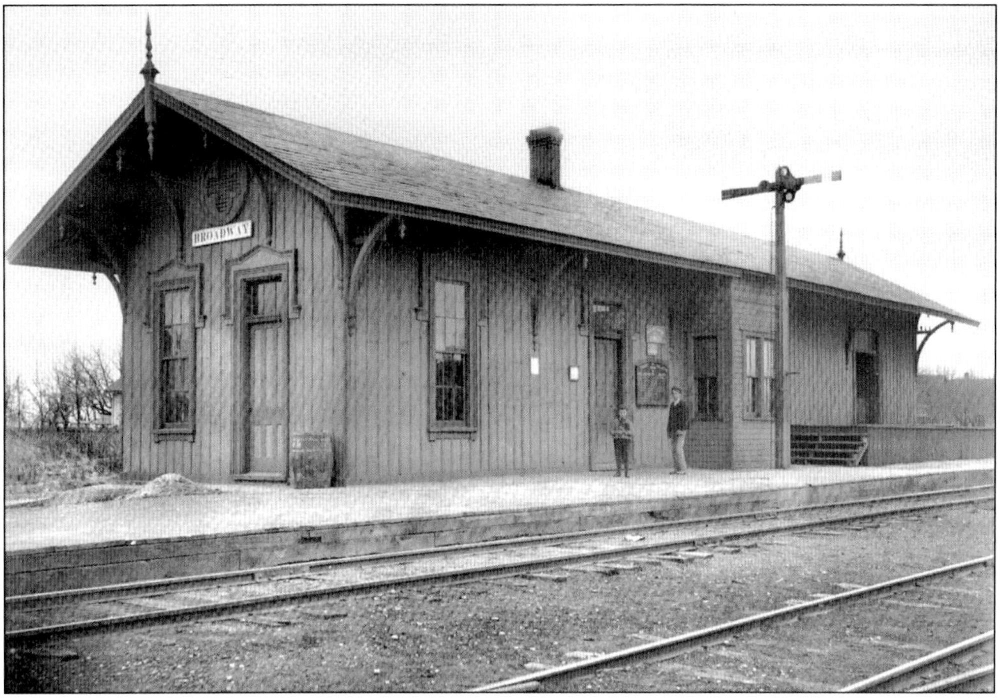

Broadway's depot had adjacent waiting rooms, a central ticket office, and a freight room. The depot was often the gathering spot for local boys. It was demolished before the 1970s. (J. E. Bailey photograph; Mark J. Camp collection.)

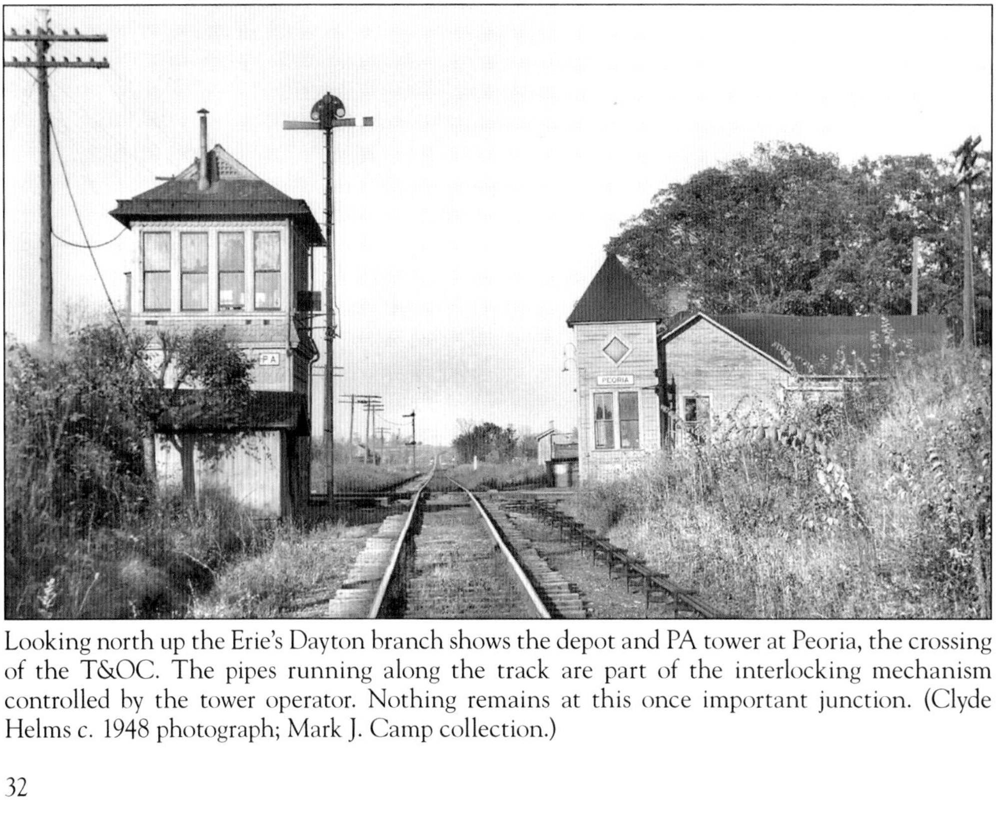

Looking north up the Erie's Dayton branch shows the depot and PA tower at Peoria, the crossing of the T&OC. The pipes running along the track are part of the interlocking mechanism controlled by the tower operator. Nothing remains at this once important junction. (Clyde Helms c. 1948 photograph; Mark J. Camp collection.)

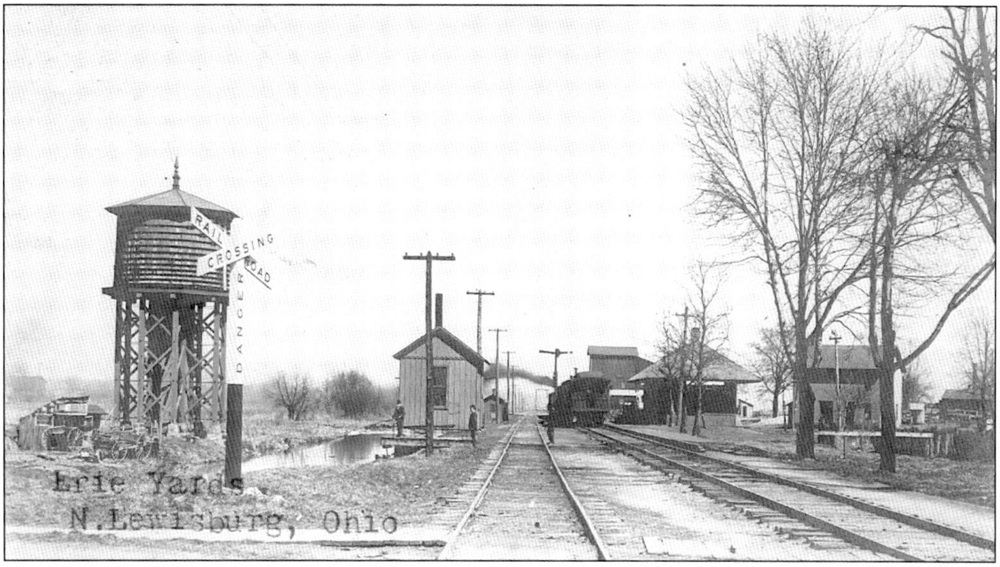

The Erie facilities at North Lewisburg included a combination depot, pump house, and water tank. The agency closed here in 1961; apparently the depot was gone by the late 1960s. (Mark J. Camp collection.)

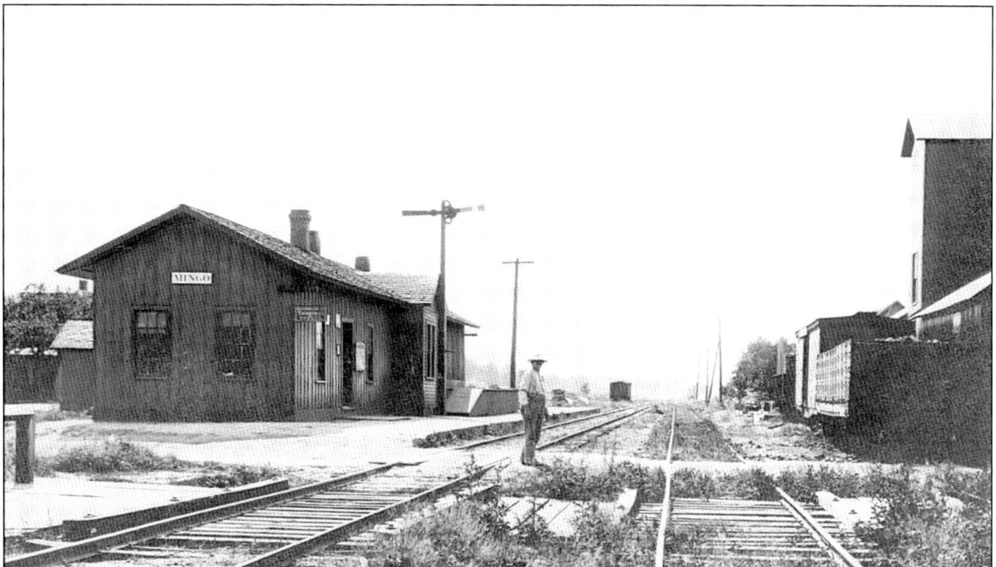

Note the fire barrels on the roof of Erie's Mingo depot. The order board is set to stop approaching trains. Nothing remains at this location today. (Mark J. Camp collection.)

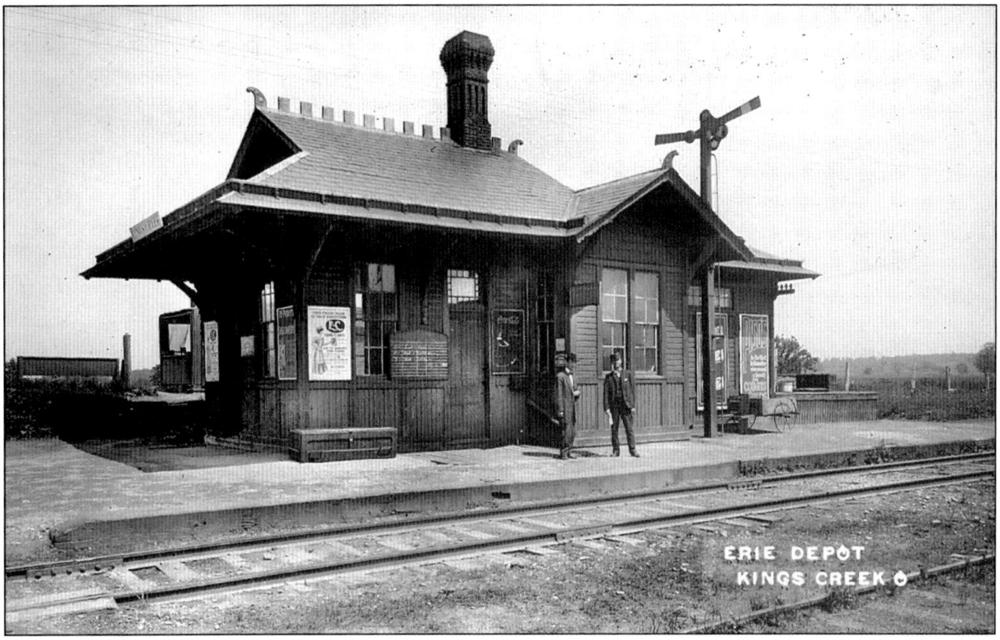

Without a doubt, the Kings Creek Erie depot qualified as the most ornate on the Dayton branch. Broadside advertisements were commonly found plastered to the walls of Erie depots in New York and New Jersey but with the exception of a few locations seem to be rare in Ohio. Unfortunately, this gem disappeared decades ago. (Mark J. Camp collection.)

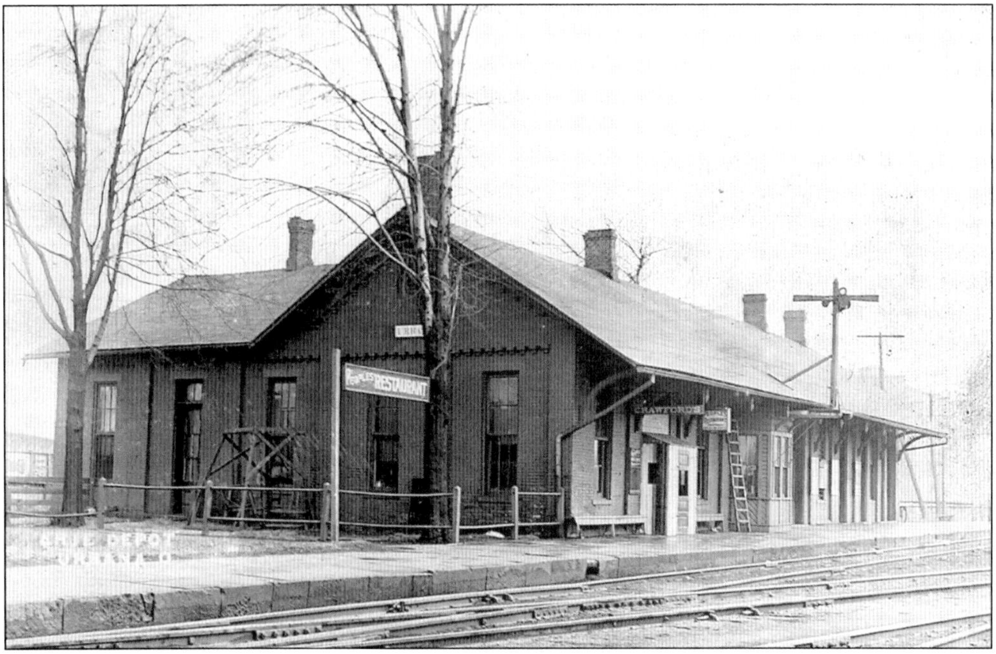

The brick passenger depot in Urbana dates to 1871. Peoples Restaurant advertised "short orders," the 1910 version of fast food. Nearby were depots of the Pennsylvania, Big Four, and Ohio Electric. The depot came down in 1934, and the last passengers boarded from a converted freight house. (Mark J. Camp collection.)

Three

New York Central Lines

The New York Central Railroad (NYC) began acquiring lines in Ohio in the late 1800s, including three that served west central Ohio—the Big Four, Cincinnati Northern, and the Toledo and Ohio Central.

The first tracks to pass through this part of west central Ohio were those of the Mad River and Lake Erie Railroad chartered in January 1832. The Mad River line laid its rails 4 feet 10 inches apart since that was the gauge of its first locomotive, originally built for an eastern rail line. After reaching Tiffin from Sandusky in 1841, track laying progressed southwestward, reaching Kenton in August 1846, Bellefontaine in July 1847, and eventually Dayton in 1851. A branch line from Carey to Findlay was taken over in 1853. After a number of reorganizations and name changes, the line became part of the Cleveland, Cincinnati, Chicago and St. Louis Railway in 1890, which became known as the Big Four Railway.

In 1845, the dormant charter of the Cleveland, Columbus and Cincinnati Railroad (CC&C) was reinvoked, and trains began running between Cleveland and Columbus in February 1851. In 1848, the Bellefontaine and Indiana Railroad was chartered to build a line between Galion, on the CC&C, and Union City, the eastern terminal of the Indianapolis and Bellefontaine Railroad, an Indiana line. Construction began in 1852 east and west from Bellefontaine. Service opened to Sidney in March 1853, and Union City in July 1853.

The Big Four gained control of the Cincinnati Northern Railway (CN) in 1902. The CN began in Franklin in Warren County and built northward through Ansonia, Celina, and Van Wert, eventually terminating in Jackson, Michigan. The route was built as the Cincinnati, Jackson and Mackinaw Railway in the 1880s. The last passenger service was on February 1, 1938. Except for a few short stretches at interchanges, the tracks are gone.

Connecting the southeast Ohio coalfields with Toledo were two lines that became the Toledo and Ohio Central Railroad (T&OC). The Ohio Central Railroad opened between Toledo and Middleport in 1882, passing through Fostoria and Bucyrus. It became the Toledo and Ohio Central in 1885. The Toledo and Indianapolis Railway built between Findlay and Dunkirk by 1889, reorganized as the Toledo, Columbus and Cincinnati (TC&C), and completed track into Kenton in 1892. The next year, the T&OC absorbed the TC&C and completed the line to Columbus and a junction with the old Ohio Central. In 1901, the T&OC also took over a short-lived branch of the Detroit and Lima Northern (D&LN), from Peoria to St. Marys.

Depots on these New York Central lines were mainly inherited from predecessor lines. Standard designs are most evident along the Big Four; depots remain at Ansonia, Belle Center, Carey, Galion, Kenton, Sidney, Versailles, West Liberty, and Wharton. CN depots remain at Celina, Coldwater, and New Weston. T&OC depots remaining are from Bucyrus, East Liberty, McCutchenville, New Winchester, Raymond, St. Marys, Spore, Wapakoneta, and Williamstown.

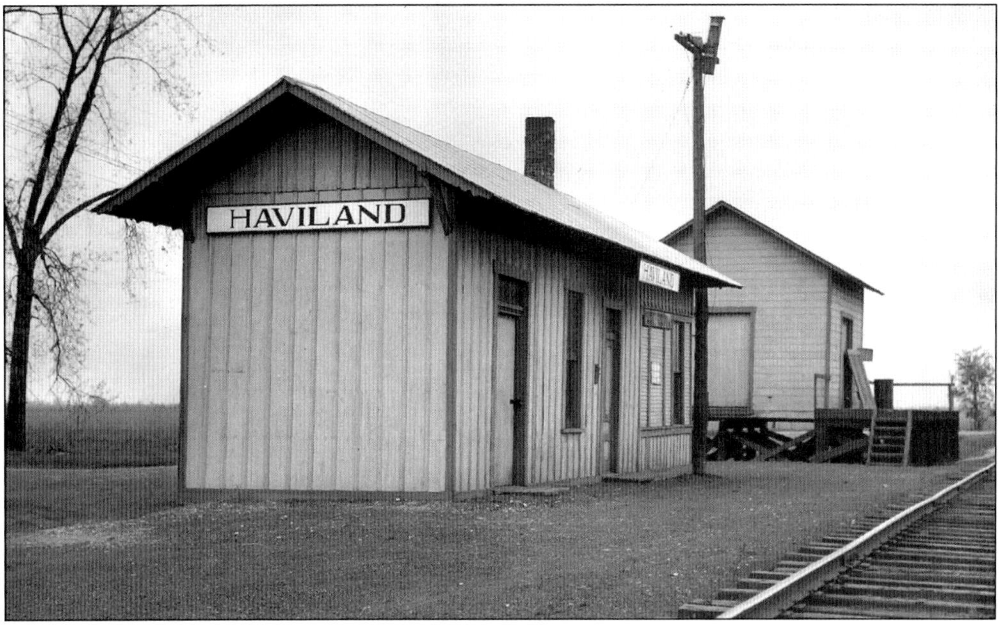

The FFW&W crossed the CN at Haviland. Here are the passenger and freight depots around 1947. Note the nonstandard order board and absence of a bay window. A brick and tile plant provided considerable business for the freight agent. The depot closed by the 1940s and was gone by the late 1960s. (Clyde Helms photograph; Mark J. Camp collection.)

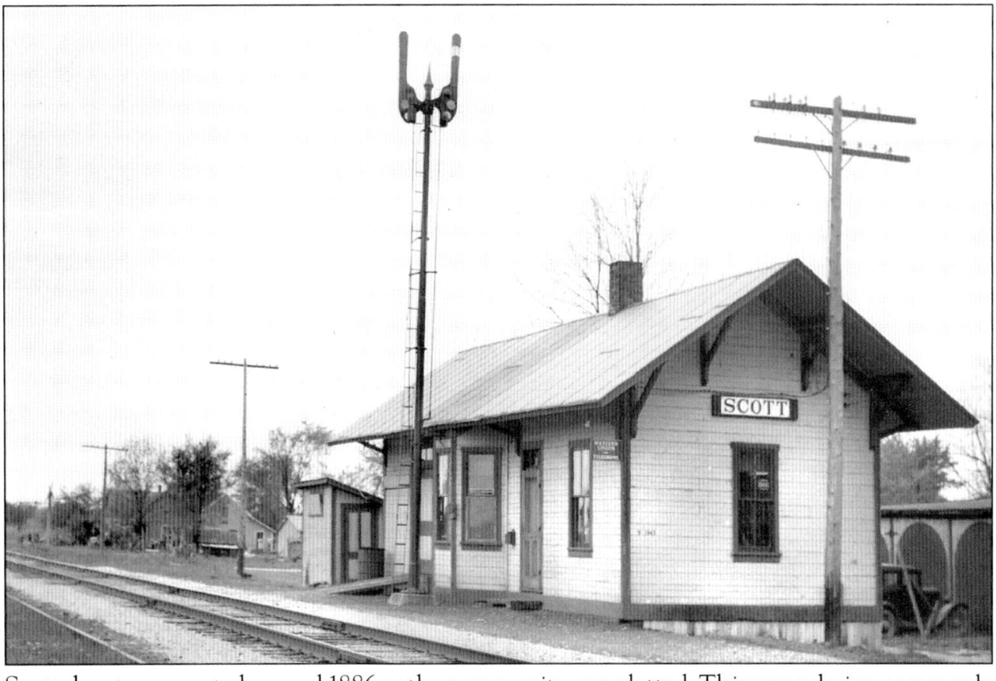

Scott depot was erected around 1886 as the community was platted. This was a design commonly used by the CN. Scott handled the business from Haviland and Cavett after those agencies closed. The agents at Scott handled stone shipments from a nearby quarry for many years. (Clyde Helms c. 1947 photograph; Mark J. Camp collection.)

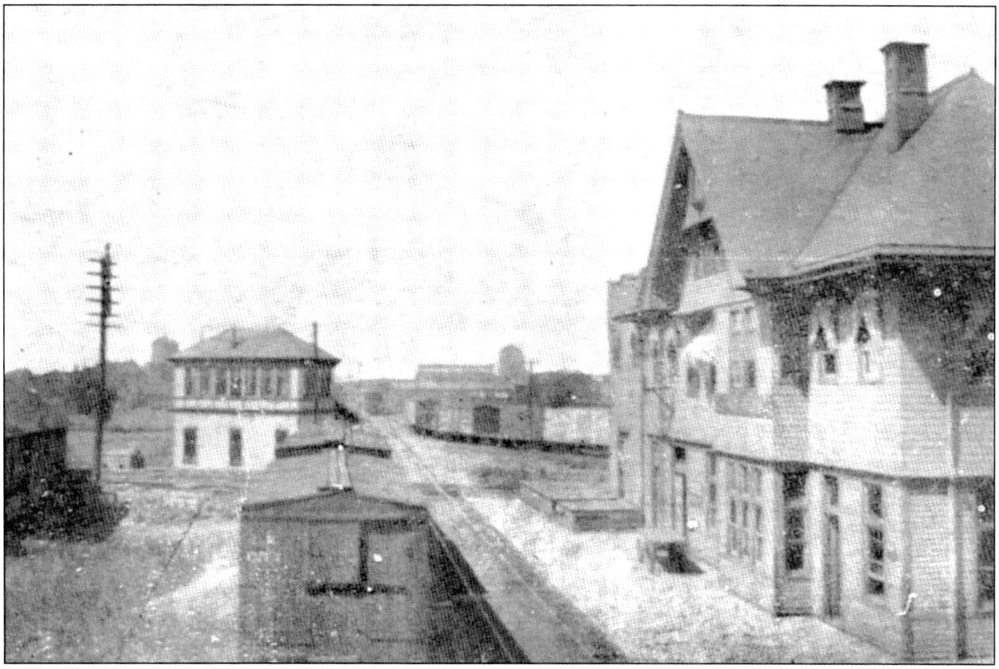

Although Van Wert was a terminal and location of the main offices of the CN, few photographs seem to exist of its large 1893 frame depot. The railroad had offices on the second floor and a restaurant, waiting rooms, and ticket office on the first. Interchange took place with the PRR, which crossed at PRR's Estry tower in the background. Northeast of the PRR diamond was a large freight house. The main CN shops were located about four blocks north of the depot. The passenger depot came down in September 1939, and Estry tower was toppled in May 1985. Only a solitary brick shop building remains as a legacy of the now gone line. (Mark J. Camp collection.)

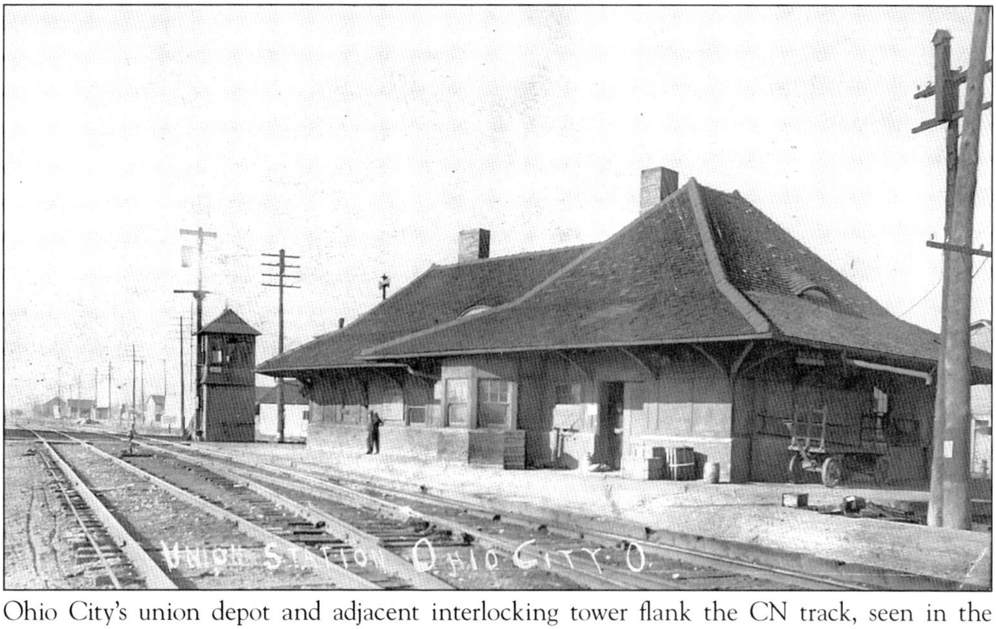

Ohio City's union depot and adjacent interlocking tower flank the CN track, seen in the background of this photograph from around 1912. (Mark J. Camp collection.)

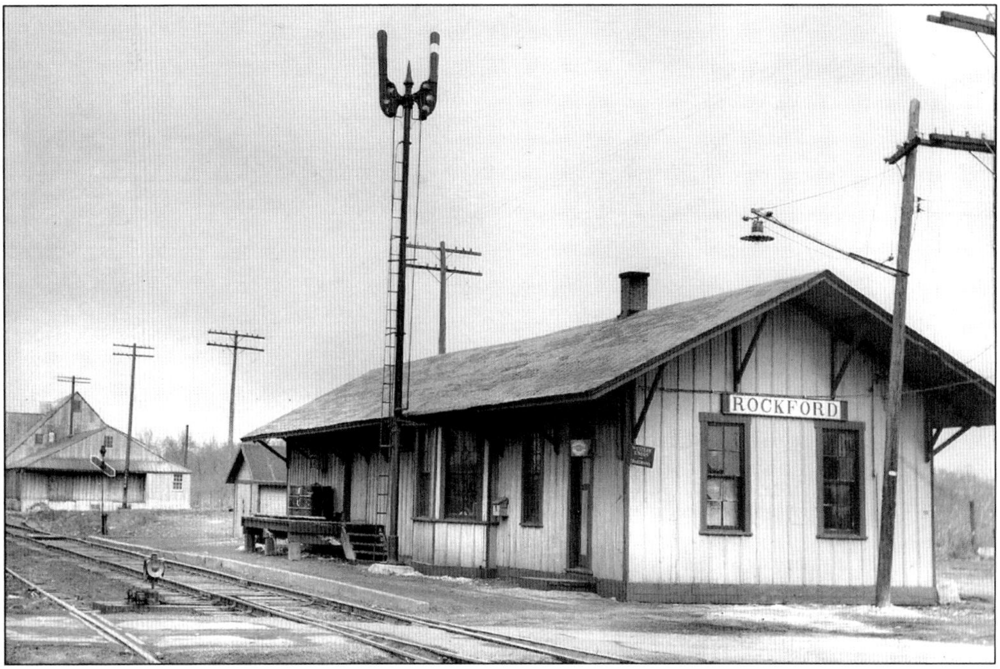

Rockford was an important shipping and debarking point for northern Mercer County folks. The c. 1884 depot was built when the town was called Shane's Crossing. This standard plan was repeated at a number of stations on the CN. It is now gone. (Clyde Helms c. 1947 photograph; Mark J. Camp collection.)

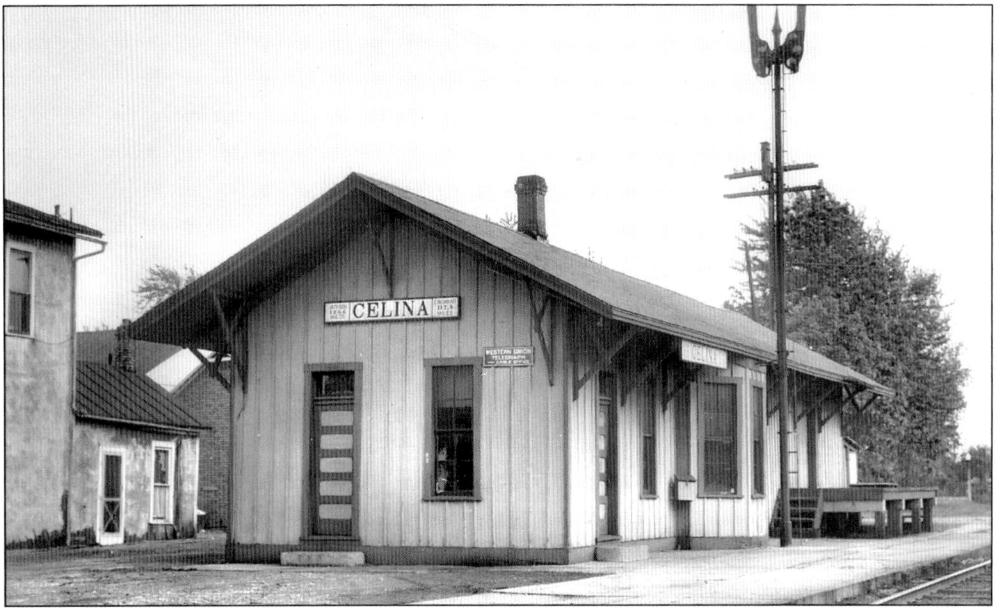

Celina's c. 1884 depot was similar to Rockford's except for a change in roof brackets, window and door placement, and a switch of waiting and freight room locations. Nearby was a water tank. In its early days, the depot served many passengers arriving to visit Grand Lake spas and resorts. The slightly modified depot remains by the abandoned right-of-way in private use. (Clyde Helms c. 1947 photograph; Mark J. Camp collection.)

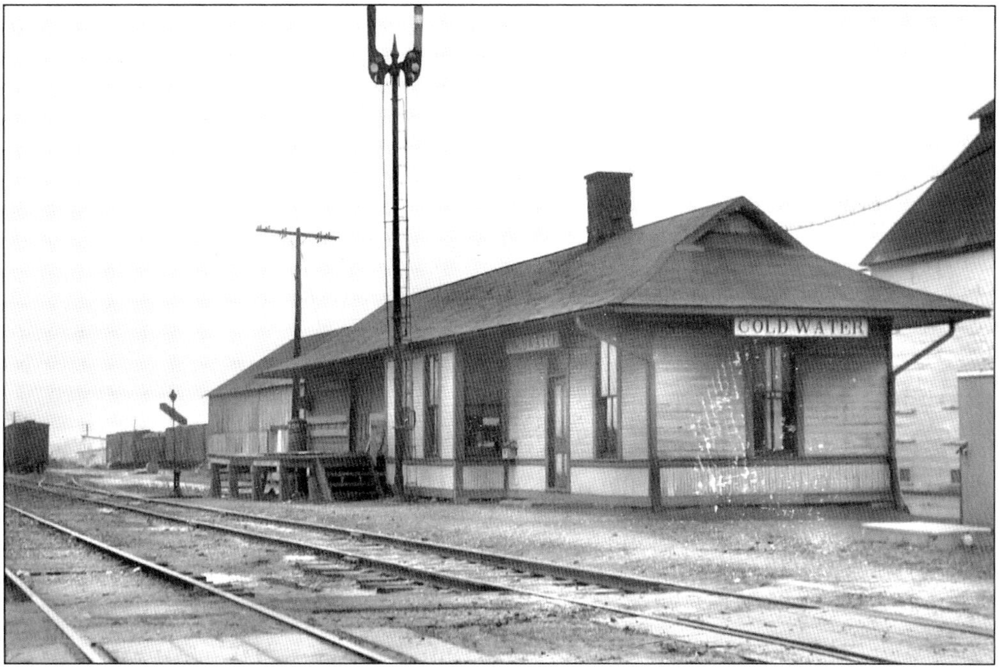

Yet another CN depot plan is present at Coldwater. The depot dates to the 1880s. It remains as a residence. (Clyde Helms c. 1947 photograph, Mark J. Camp collection.)

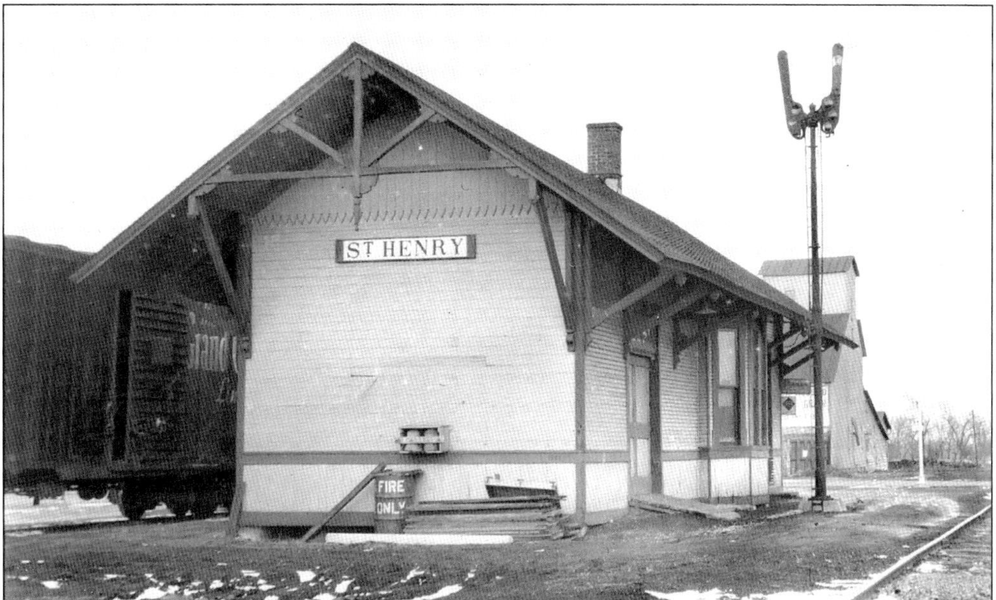

The first train chugged into St. Henry three days before Christmas in 1883. This is not the depot that witnessed that event, since a fire destroyed the original depot on February 15, 1906. A CN construction crew was on the scene shortly, erecting this depot, which opened April 20, 1906. A boxcar temporarily served as the depot. Unfortunately, the depot was demolished in 1965. (Clyde Helms c. 1947 photograph; Mark J. Camp collection.)

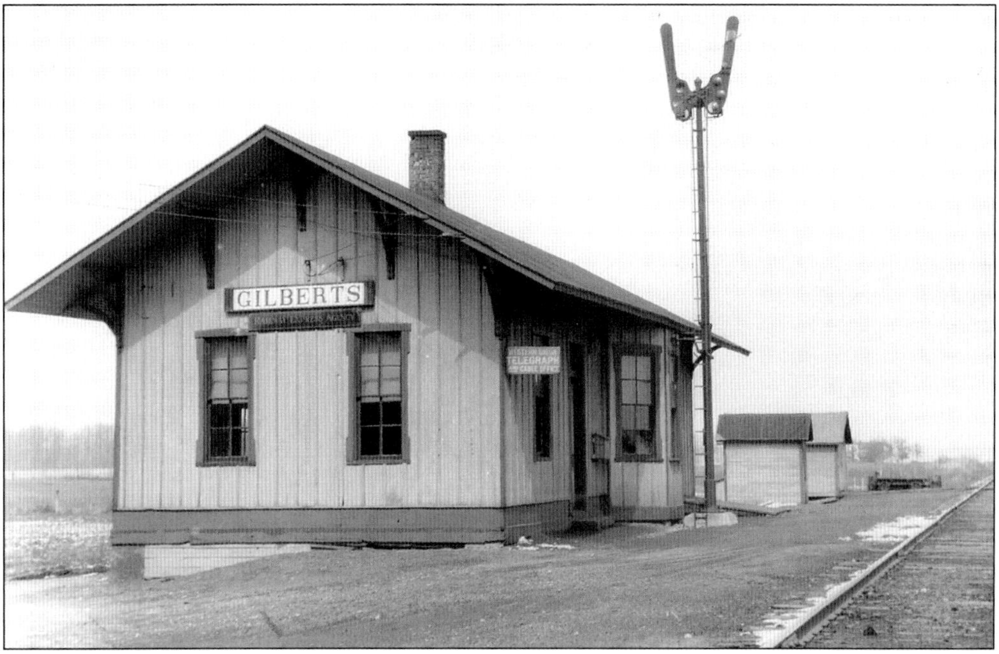

Similar to Rockford and Celina, the Gilberts depot seems deserted on this cold March day of 1947. The agency shut down around 1959. This depot is long gone, but the nearby New Weston depot still remains in private use. (Clyde Helms photograph; Mark J. Camp collection.)

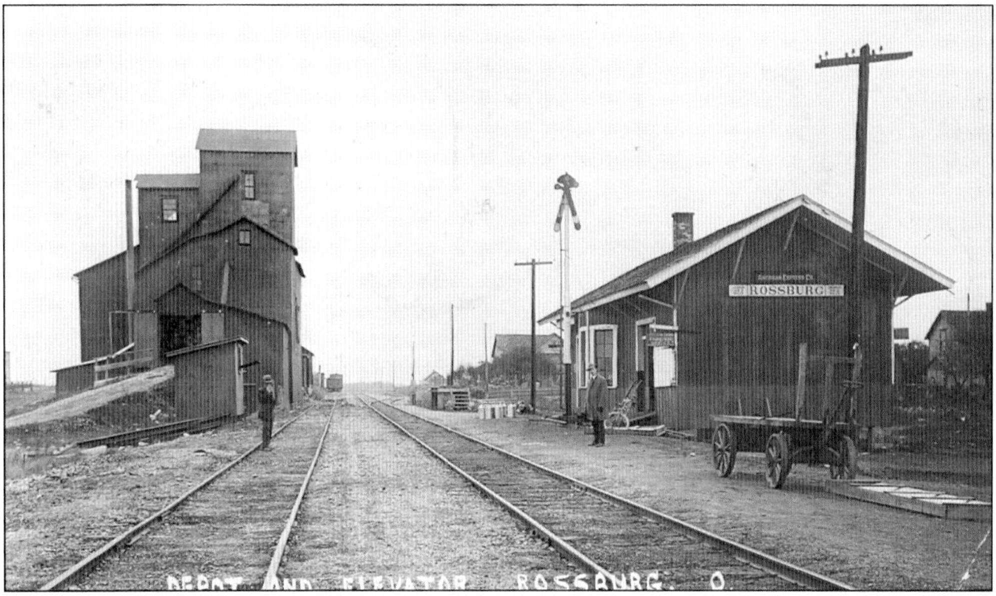

Typical of many small farming communities along the CN was Rossburg with the combination depot and ever-present grain elevator. In this c. 1910 view, a single passenger awaits a train on the platform. The depot has since been removed. (Mark J. Camp collection.)

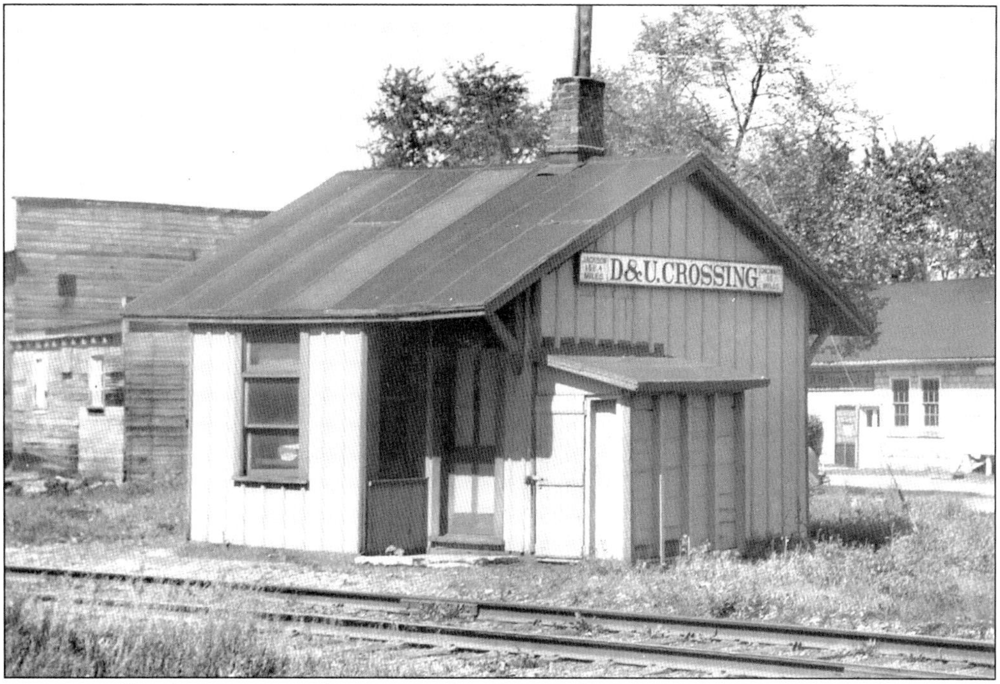

In Greenville, the Dayton and Union Railroad (D&U) crossed the CN. This small depot sat to the southeast of the diamond. The interlocking was controlled by the D&U. (Eldon Neff photograph; David P. Oroszi collection.)

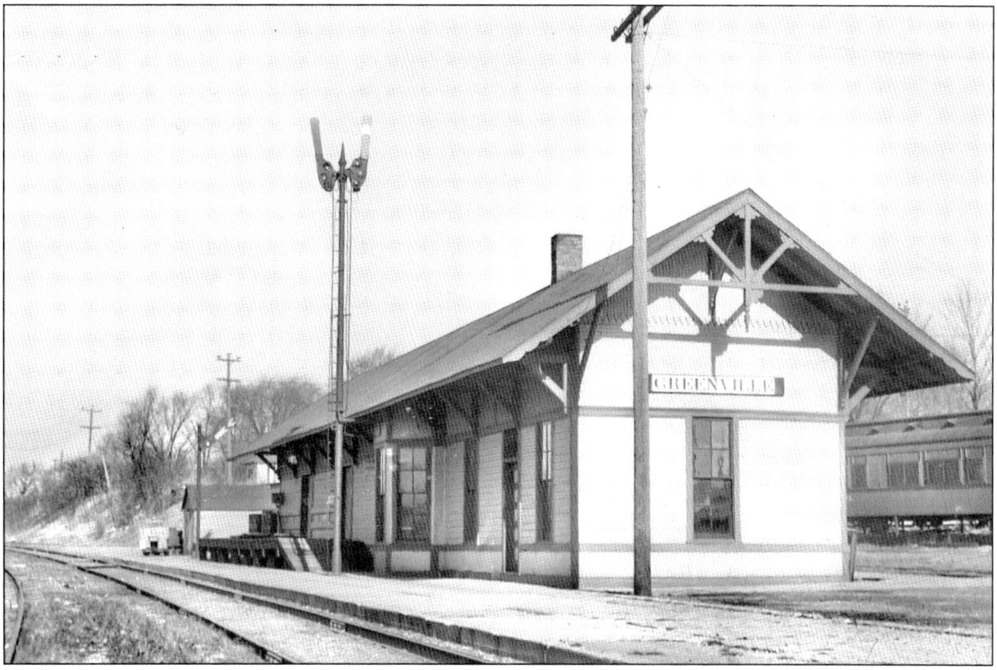

This was the main CN depot in Greenville, photographed around 1947. Passing sidings were on either side of the depot. Interchange with the PRR and D&U provided the freight agent with plenty of paperwork. The depot remains. (Clyde Helms photograph; Mark J. Camp collection.)

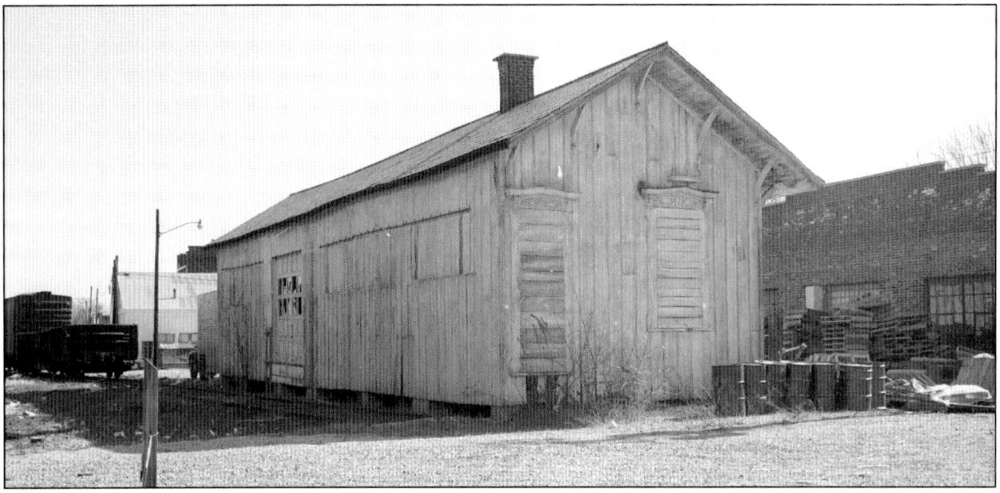

Findlay completed a railroad connection to the MR&LE at Carey in November 1849. The MR&LE assumed operation of this line in 1853. The stub end terminal in Findlay included this freight house and a passenger depot supposedly built around 1890 when the Big Four took over the line. The passenger depot was moved away from trackside after the 1930s and served as a residence for many years until being torn down a few years ago. The freight house remained on site but unfortunately burned down August 10, 1990, just as it was in the early stages of restoration as a museum. There is a historical plaque marking the site today. The only other depot on the branch was a small frame building at Vanlue. (Charles Garvin 1968 photograph; Mark J. Camp collection.)

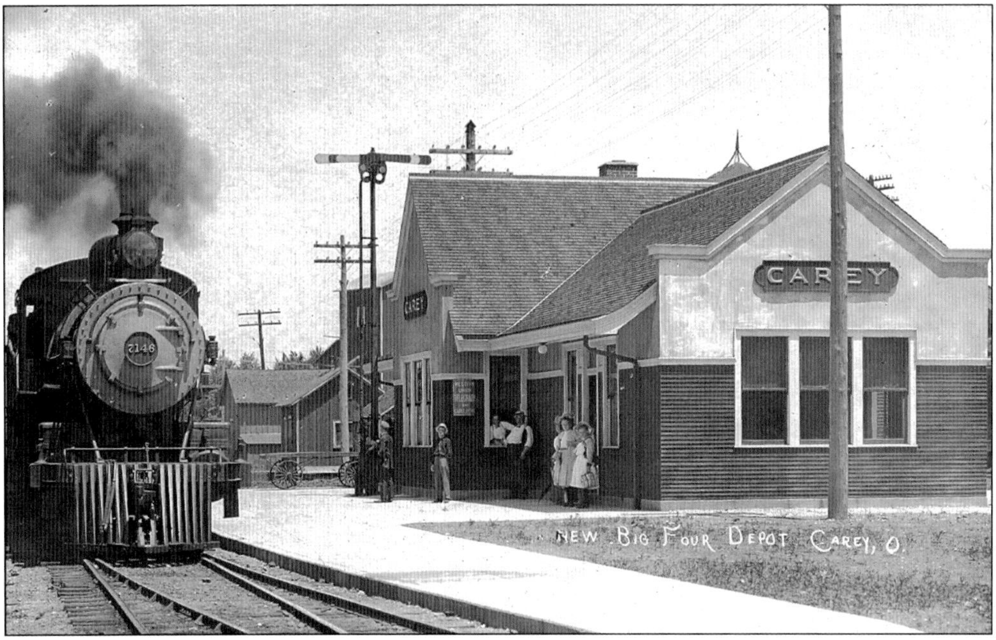

The CCC&StL used the old frame MR&LE depot in Carey after taking over the line in 1890. This handsome depot was built around 1908, a one-of-a-kind structure. Most likely materials for the stucco upper walls were provided from the local stone quarries. Behind the depot on a siding was a frame freight house. The passenger depot now serves as a community center along a trackless right-of-way; the freight house is gone. (Mark J. Camp collection.)

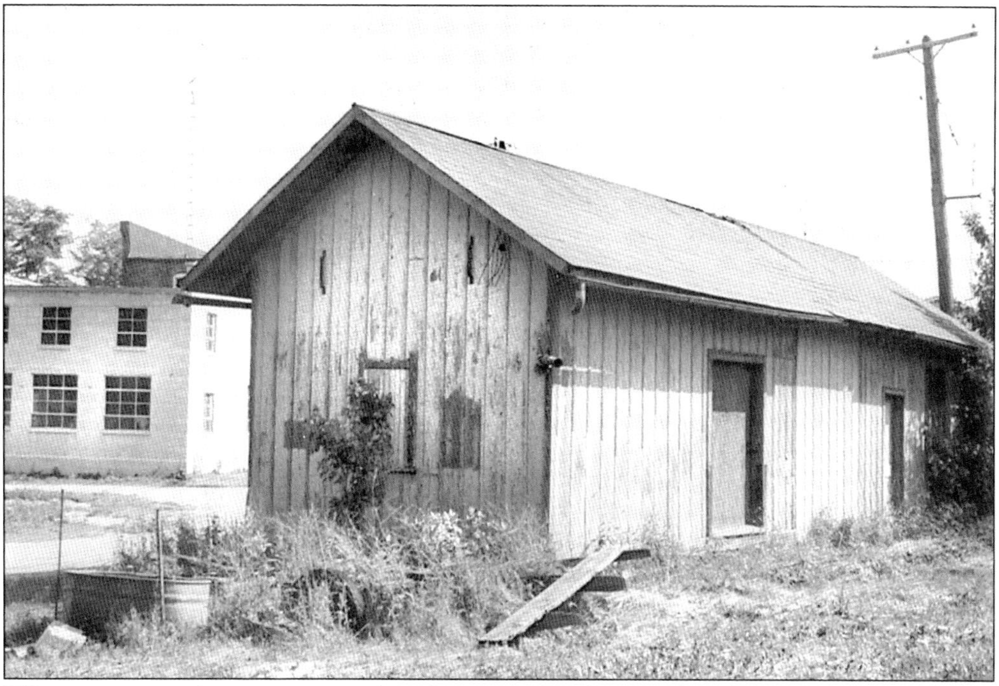

Wharton was another community platted in 1848 after the arrival of the railroad. Its CCC&StL combination depot, shown here in 1968, was converted to storage and business use.

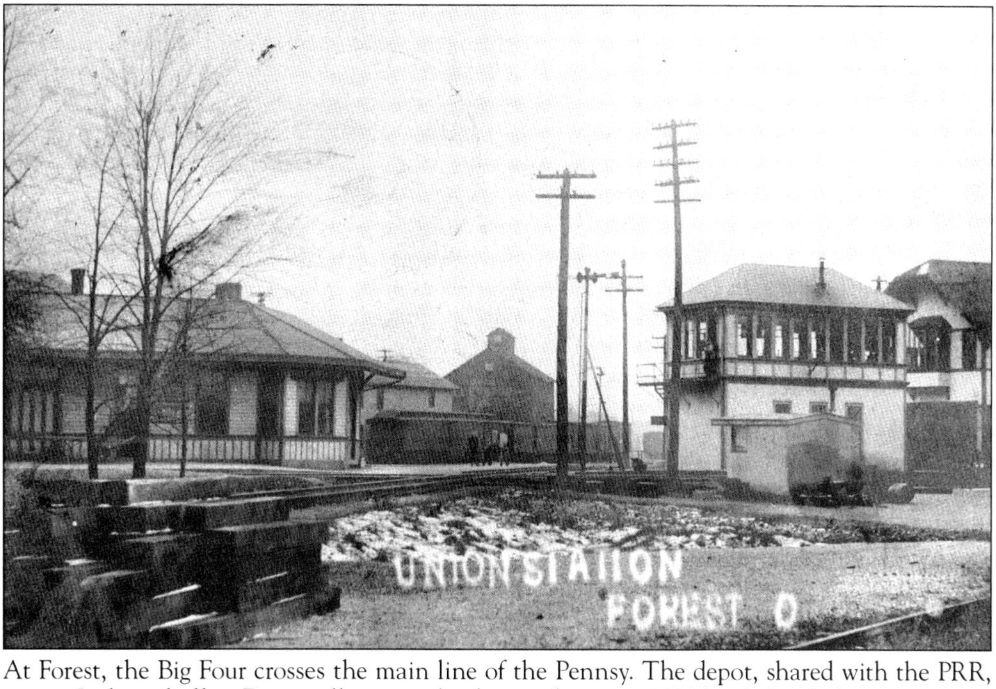

At Forest, the Big Four crosses the main line of the Pennsy. The depot, shared with the PRR, was an L-shaped affair. Diagonally across the diamond was a c. 1890 brick freight house, not seen in this view, and to the right is PRR's Forest interlocking tower. Only the freight house remains, which is now the town library. (Mark J. Camp collection.)

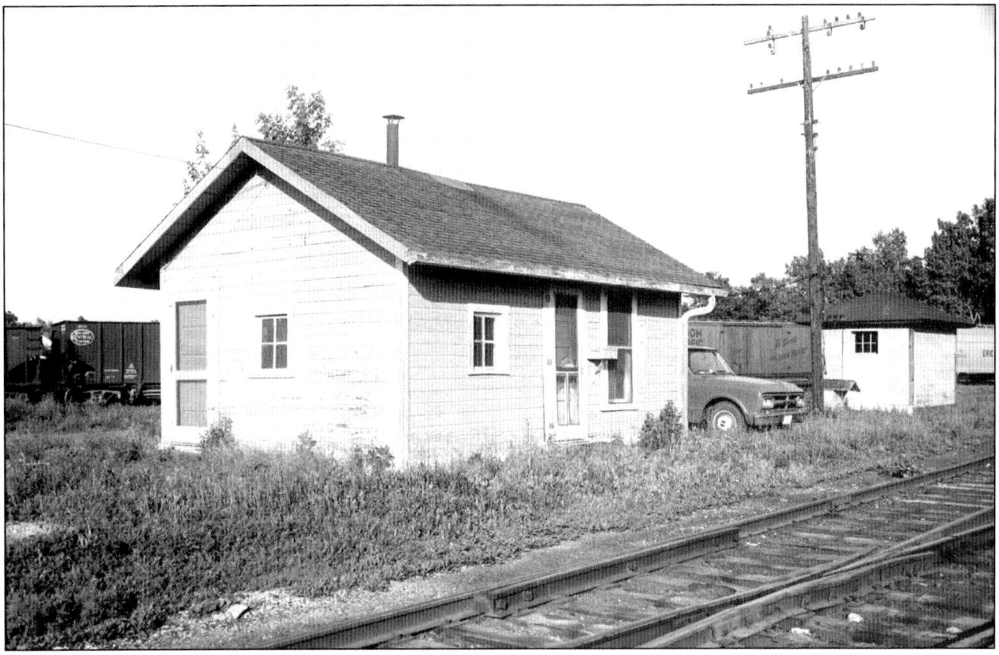

This building served as the CCC&StL and later NYC depot at McVitty's until the 1970s. A coaling station was located at Grants between McVitty's and Kenton. (Charles Garvin photograph; Mark J. Camp collection.)

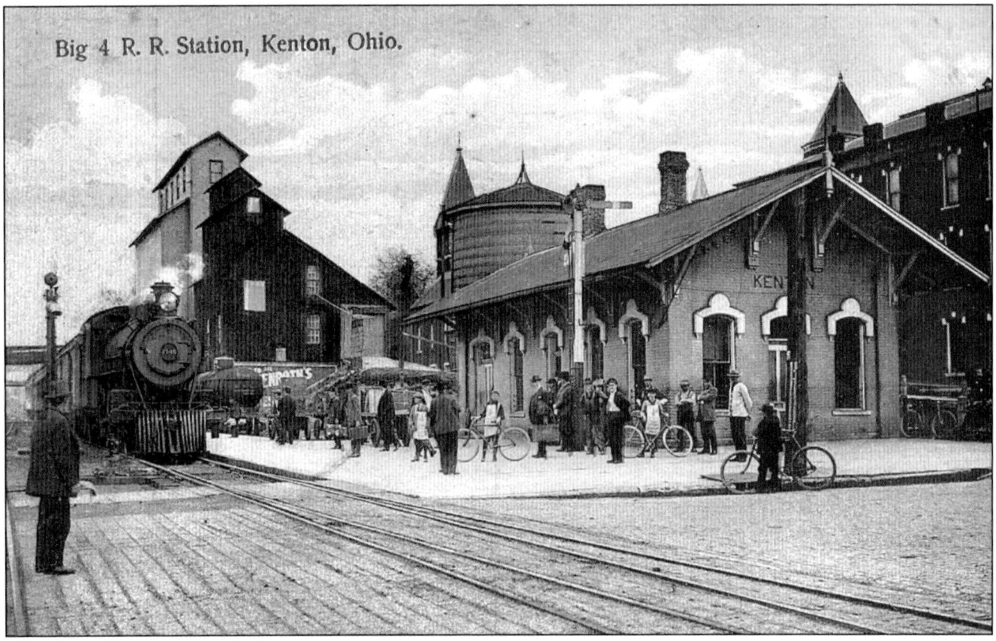

The Mad River line reached Kenton in 1846. The earliest depot was a frame structure that reportedly was replaced by this brick structure in 1882. The train from Sandusky has just pulled in around 1908. Note the water tank behind the depot and the water plug next to the locomotive. The depot remains along a trackless roadbed; it is now a small office building, nicely restored and with a historical plaque. (Mark J. Camp collection.)

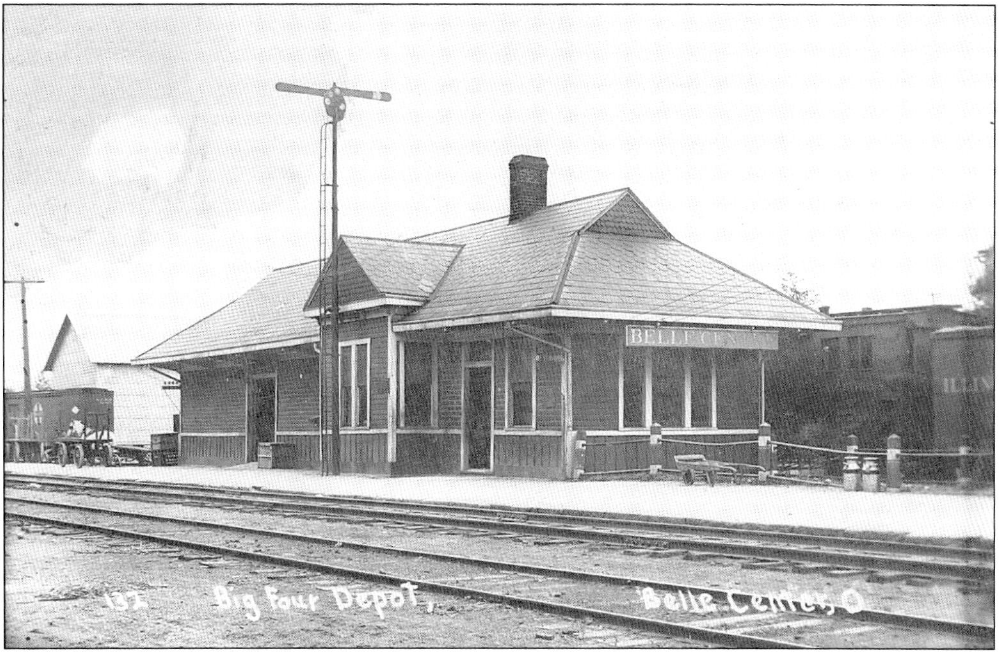

Belle Centre came into existence as a water stop on the MR&LE. This depot, erected in the 1890s by the CCC&StL, replaced an earlier MR&LE structure in Belle Centre, now Belle Center. The agency closed around 1959, but the depot remains along the abandoned right-of-way. (Mark J. Camp collection.)

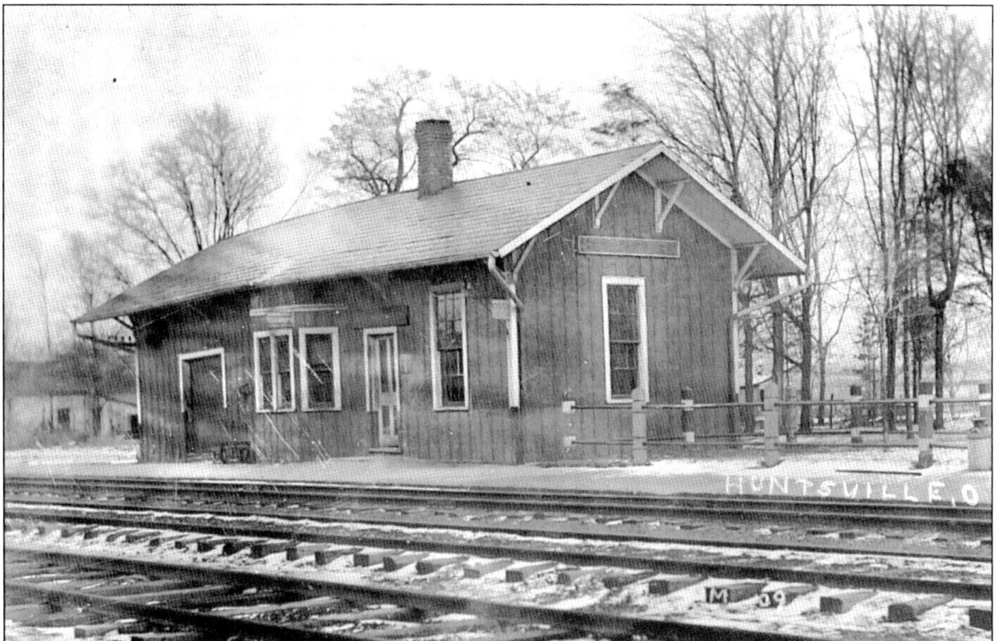

Huntsville's combination depot was built to a plan repeated often along the Big Four lines. The town dates to 1846 when the MR&LE was surveyed through the township. After serving the railroad for many years, it was moved and converted to a residence. (Mark J. Camp collection.)

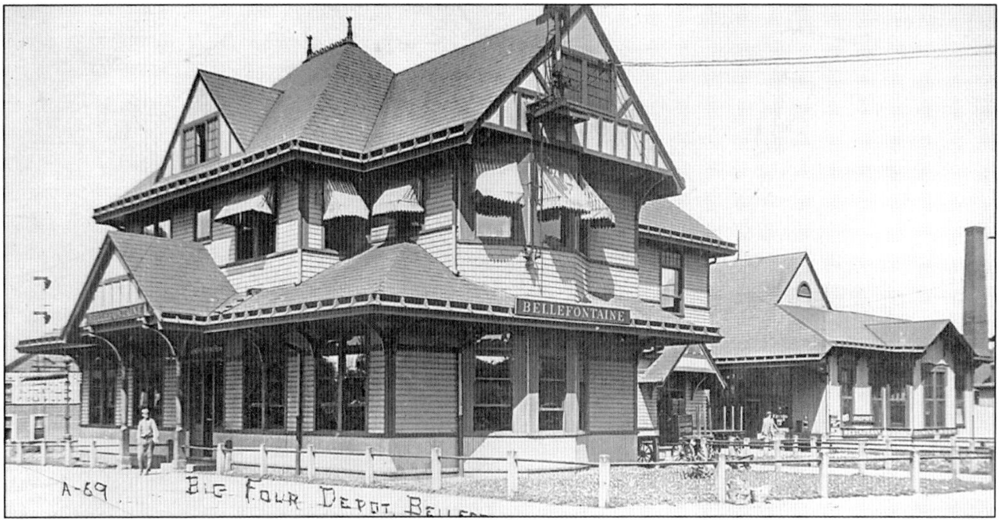

The Sandusky (MR&LE) and Indianapolis Divisions of the CCC&StL crossed at Bellefontaine and originally had separate depots dating to the predecessor lines. The Columbus and Northwestern, later the D&LN and T&OC added their track in 1897. On the morning of April 12, 1892, the old MR&LE structure caught fire but was saved by the quick actions of the operator. The townsfolk were ready to lynch him, for they wanted a new depot more representative of 1890s Bellefontaine. The old depot was repaired, and the building of a new union depot was delayed for a couple years. There are conflicting reports on the fate of the old depot—one calls for it to be moved to Forest and rebuilt as the depot at that point; the other reports that it was torn down and hauled away in May 1899. The depot on the Indianapolis line was reportedly to be moved into the yards and used as a telegraph office. The new two-story depot was erected between the divisions in 1898. The second floor originally had offices for the trainmaster, road foreman, and police department and two rooms for layover crew use. A large waiting room, ticket office, newsstand, and restrooms were on the first floor. To the rear of the depot stood a one-story dining hall. The depot soon became the hub of activity in Bellefontaine. The depot was remodeled in 1927; significant changes were made to the old dining hall. Fire swept through the depot on the evening of September 20, 1946, and it was not rebuilt. The above view shows the depot around 1908 with the dining hall behind the main depot. The view below shows the depot just before its fiery demise. The Sandusky Division (old MR&LE) wraps to the left; the Cleveland Division to the right. (Above, Mark J. Camp collection; below, Logan County Historical Society collection.)

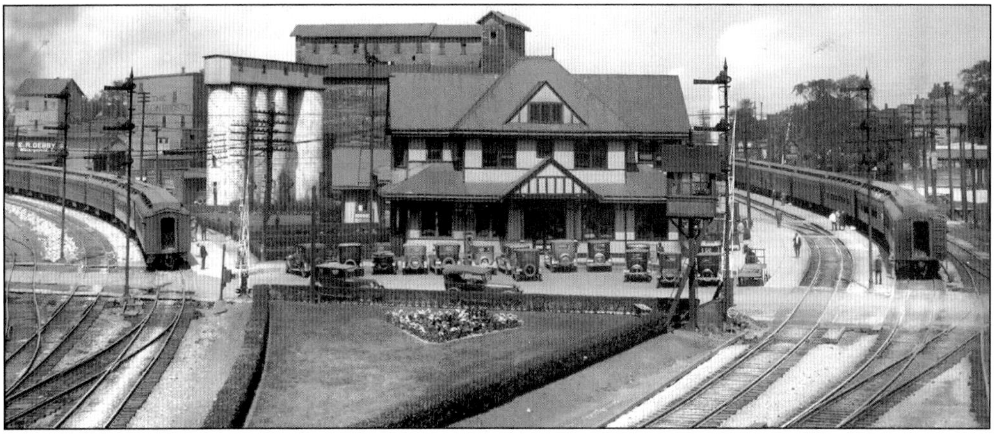

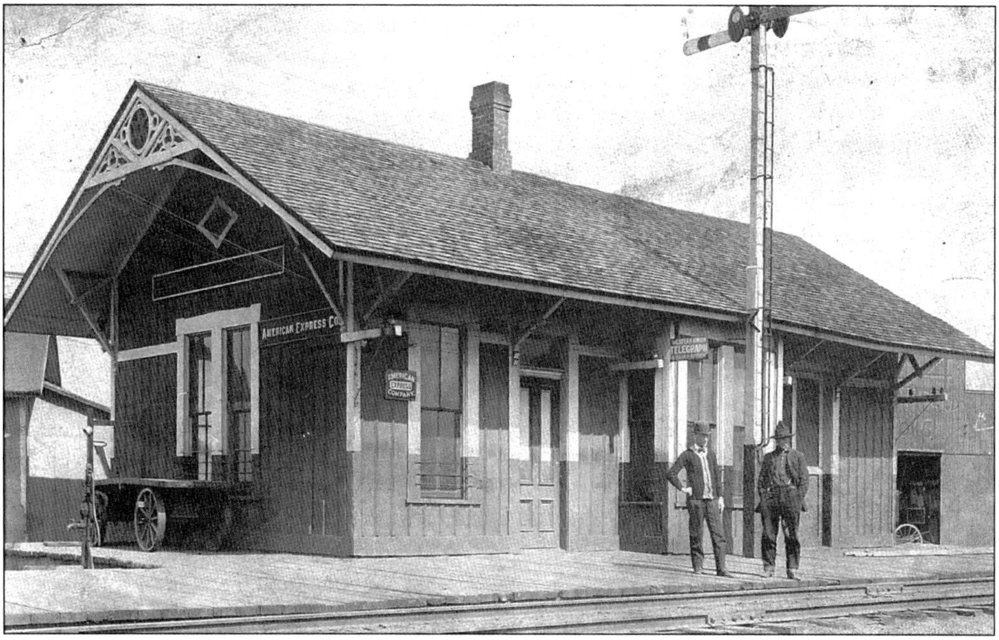

The first depot in West Liberty was of MR&LE origin, a simple frame structure. This view shows the second Big Four depot, which probably dates to the 1890s. This particular design was employed at many sites in Ohio and Indiana. In the mid-1920s, the Big Four rerouted its track about a mile west and constructed a new depot in 1926. This is the only depot that remains. It has been relocated as a candy store on U.S. 68. (Mark J. Camp collection.)

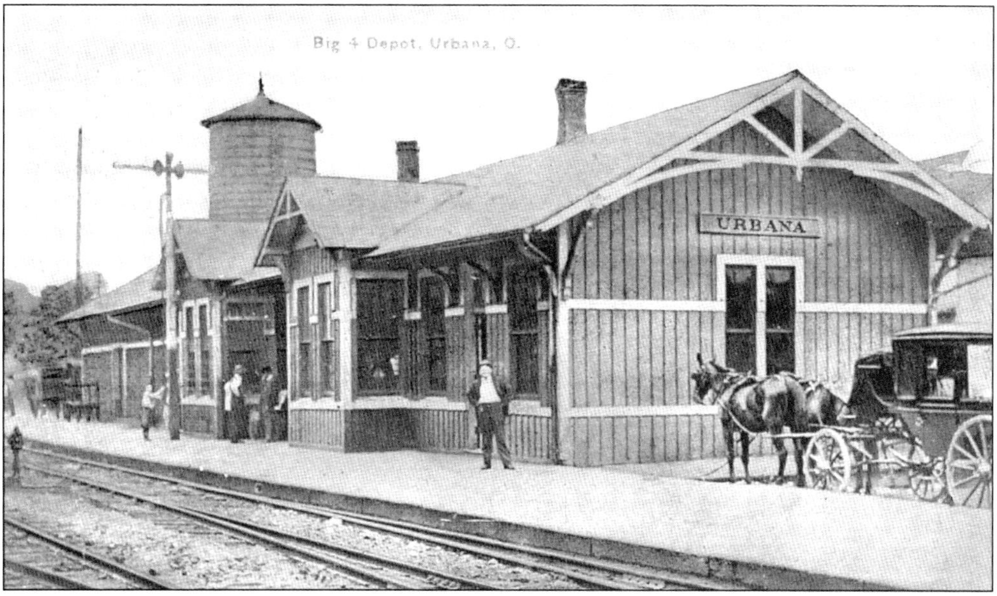

This is the original Big Four passenger depot on the old alignment through Urbana. Interesting is the presence of two bay windows due to the fact that the PCC&StL shared this depot in the early years. A train is due soon, as the waiting hotel hack suggests. In the mid-1920s, the line was elevated through town and a new brick passenger depot erected. Only a freight house remains. (Mark J. Camp collection.)

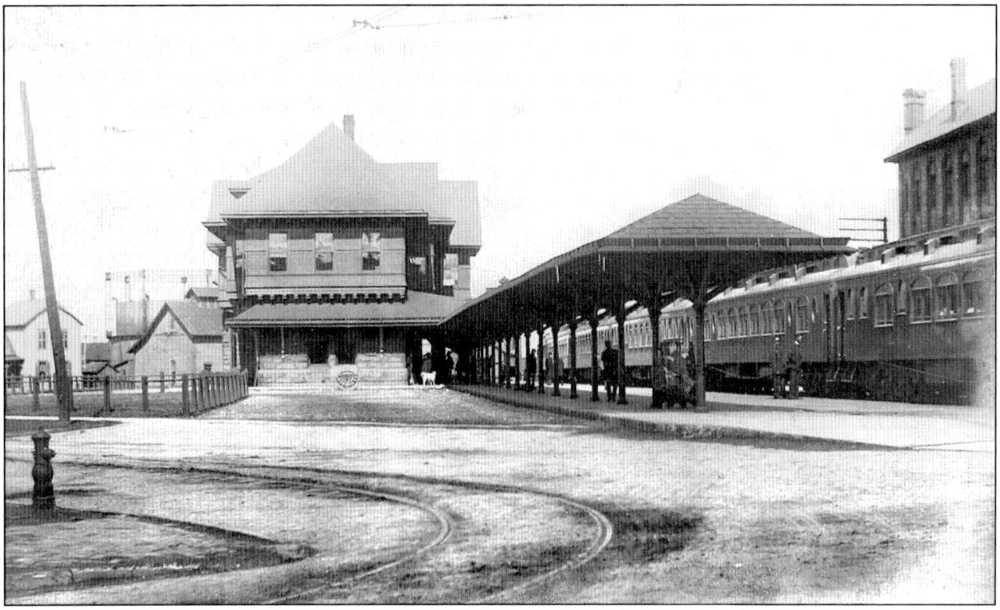

The Cleveland, Columbus and Cincinnati Railroad reached Galion in 1851, a frame barnlike depot, built around 1856, served the community in the early years. In December 1900, the Big Four opened the doors to this two-story depot. The second floor housed division offices. When the New York Central took over the Big Four in 1929–1930, the division offices were moved to Bellefontaine. The ticket office relocated to the Galion yards in 1964, and the last railroad use of the building took place in 1969. After vandalism almost led to its demolition in the mid-1980s, the depot was restored as a series of shops for a while and vacated once again. The city purchased the depot in 2000 and is returning it to its former glory. Above, one of nearly 30 daily passenger and mail trains loads in 1908. Below, the mail must go through no matter the weather conditions. (Mark J. Camp collection.)

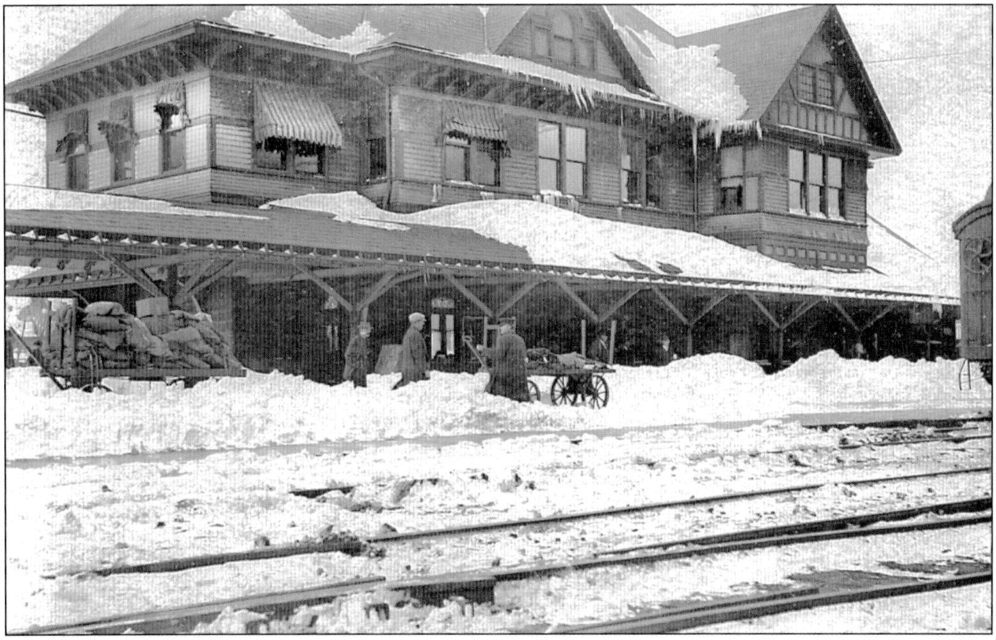

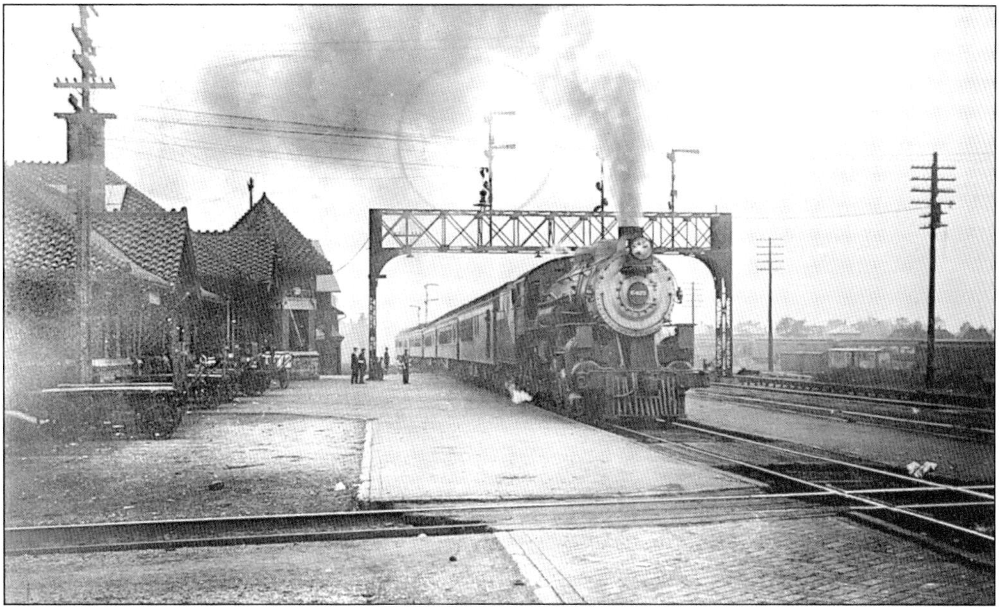

The CCC&StL parallels the Erie and crosses the PRR and Hocking Valley at 1902 Marion Union Station. Around 1911, an eastbound passenger train approaches the PRR diamond. Just behind the signal bridge is the Hocking Valley crossing. The last passenger train on the Penn Central left this depot in 1971, and the depot was closed before the year's end. The depot is currently under restoration. (Mark J. Camp collection.)

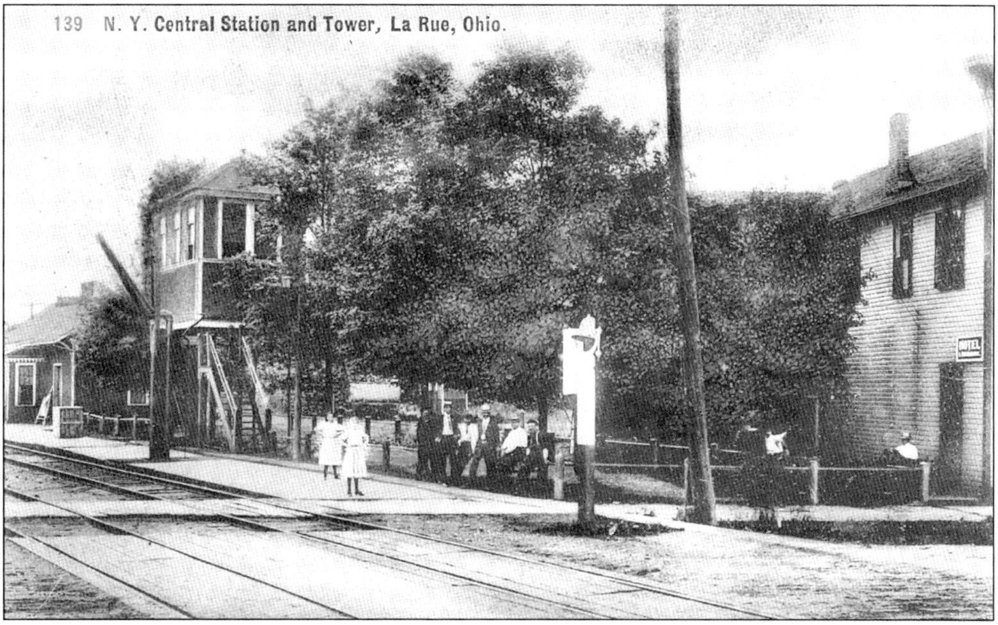

LaRue was platted in 1851 as a watering station on the Bellefontaine and Indiana (B&I). Later the CCC&StL maintained a combination depot and telegraph/signal tower at LaRue, shown here around 1908. The depot dates to 1879. To the right is a railroad hotel. Note the warning bell at the road crossing. The agency closed around 1959. The depot and tower are now gone. East of LaRue, the village of Agosta once had a depot of similar design. (Mark J. Camp collection.)

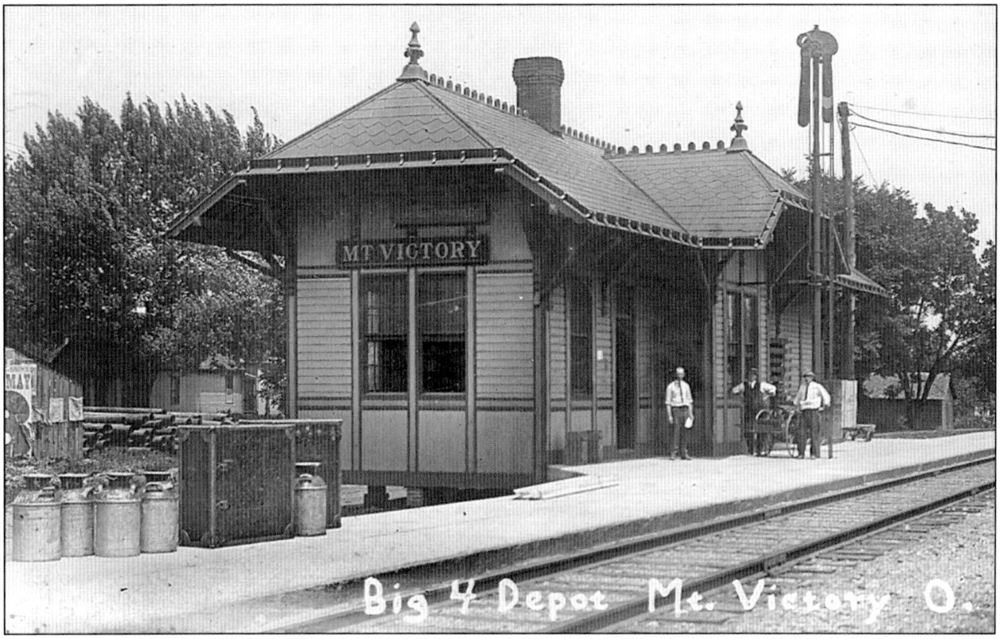

Mount Victory also came into existence with the construction of the B&I. The staff at Mount Victory's Big Four combination depot around 1907 is ready for the next train. The roof finials, dental work, and hipped roof and bay made this an attractive design of the CCC&StL engineering office. Unfortunately, the depot was gone by the late 1960s. (Mark J. Camp collection.)

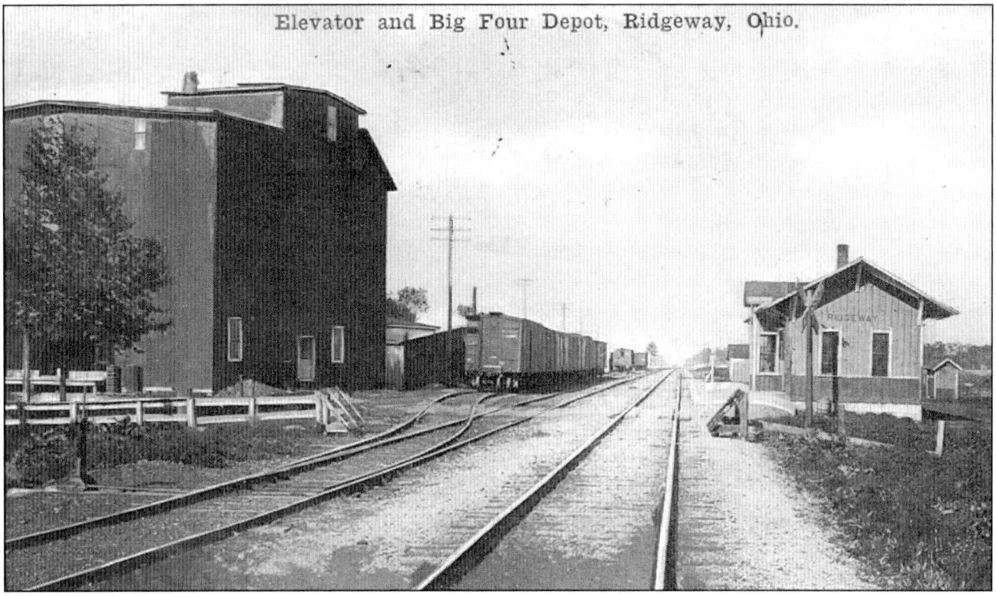

Ridgeway, like Mount Victory, was laid out with the coming of the railroad in 1851. In the early 1890s, the T&OC built through town, necessitating the construction of an interlocking tower from which this picture was probably taken. It was rumored in 1900 this depot was haunted by the ghost of a man killed on the nearby tracks. A door reportedly would rattle or fly open and shut each evening at the time the accident had occurred. The depot was dismantled in July 1967; Ridgeway tower was torn down later. (Mark J. Camp collection.)

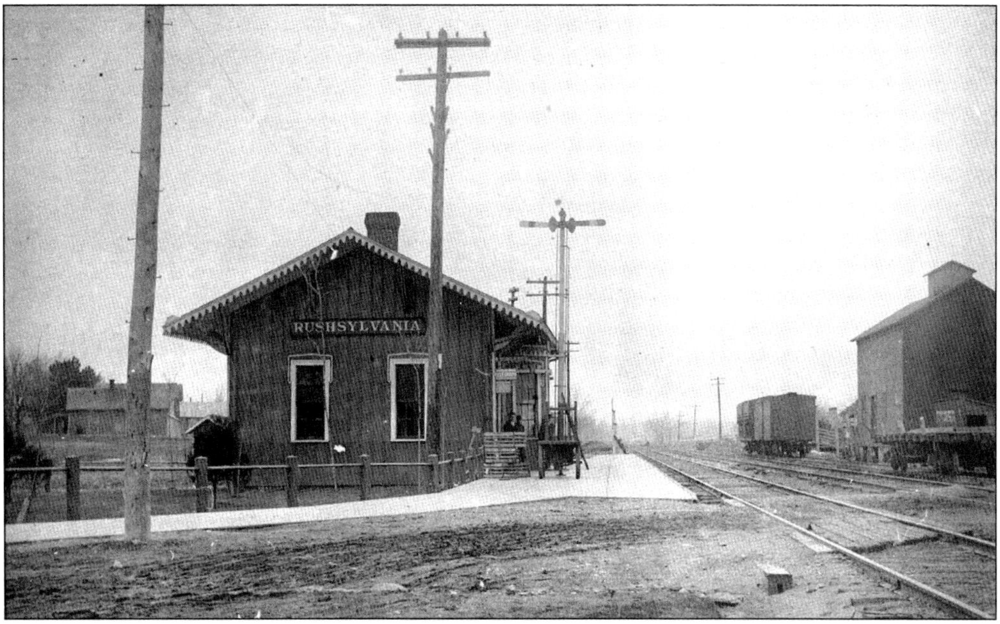

Another attractive depot design on the CCC&StL is exhibited by the Rushsylvania depot. By the late 1940s, the frills were removed in remodeling. The structure was gone by the 1960s. Between Ridgeway and Rushsylvania, the CCC&StL maintained a standard design combination depot at Big Springs that closed in the late 1920s. About a half mile from Big Springs was a telegraph tower, pump house, and water tank. (Mark J. Camp collection.)

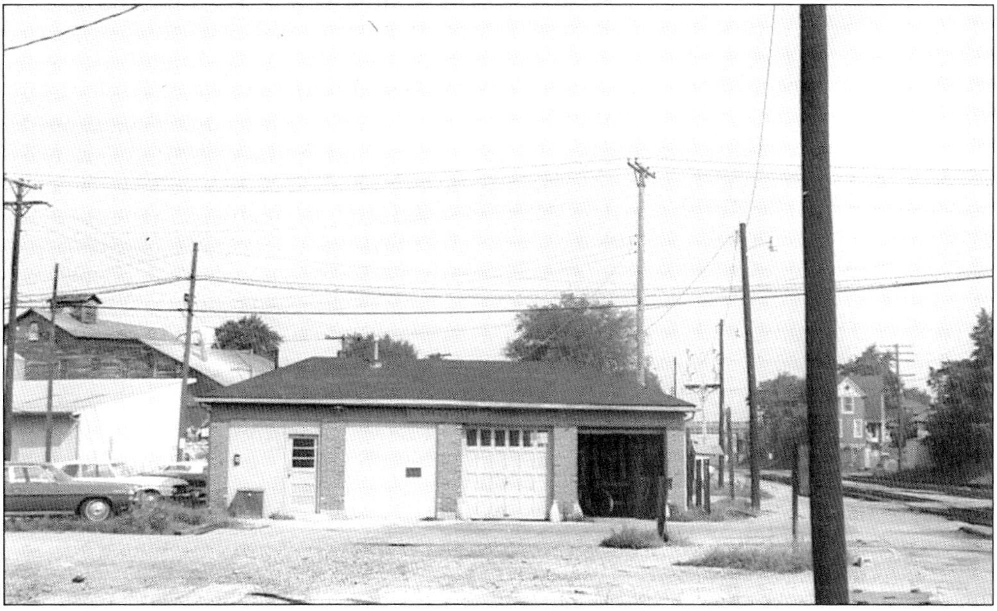

After fire damage forced the demolition of Bellefontaine's Big Four passenger depot, the NYC elected to landscape the former site of the depot and use a small frame depot to serve passengers. The brick building shown here was built around 1950 to shelter baggage carts. In the 1960s, the frame depot was gone, and this building was serving as the passenger facility until the end of service in 1969. Only the lower portion of former BS tower remains near the depot site today.

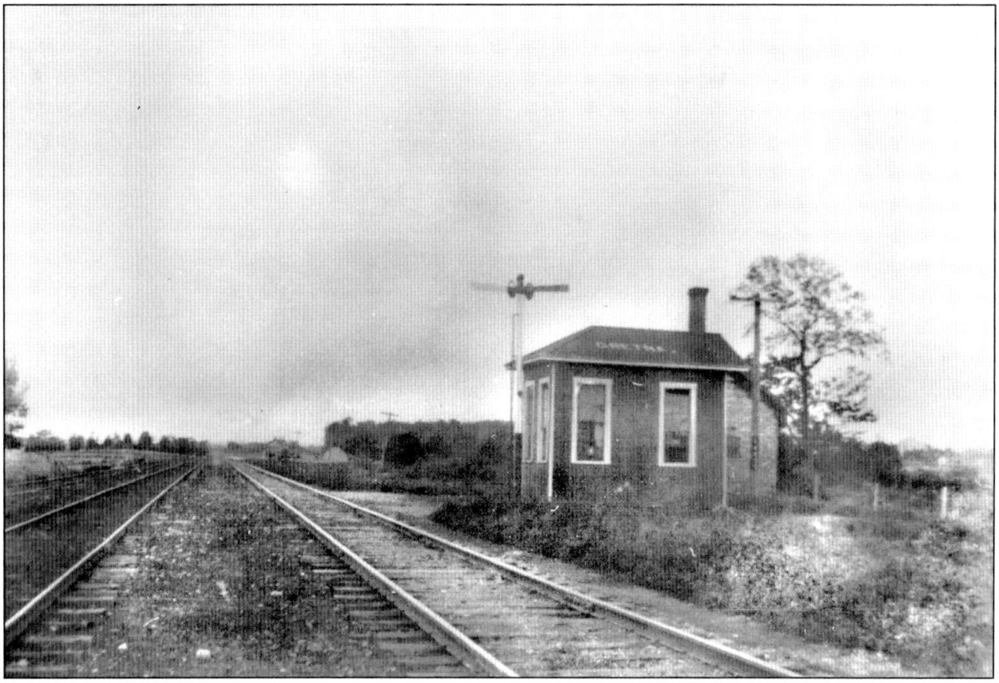

The small building at Gretna never served many passengers and was mainly a telegraph office. (Logan County Historical Society collection.)

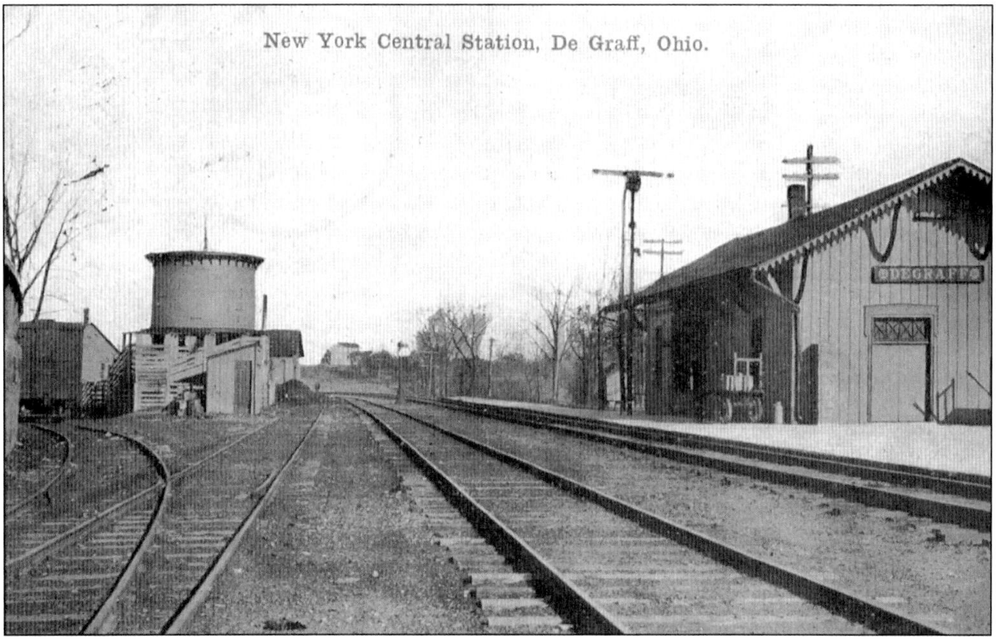

DeGraff's facilities around 1910 included a combination depot, nearly identical to Rushsylvania, a water tank, pump house, and water standpipe. By the mid-1960s, the depot was heavily modified. It has since been removed. (Mark J. Camp collection.)

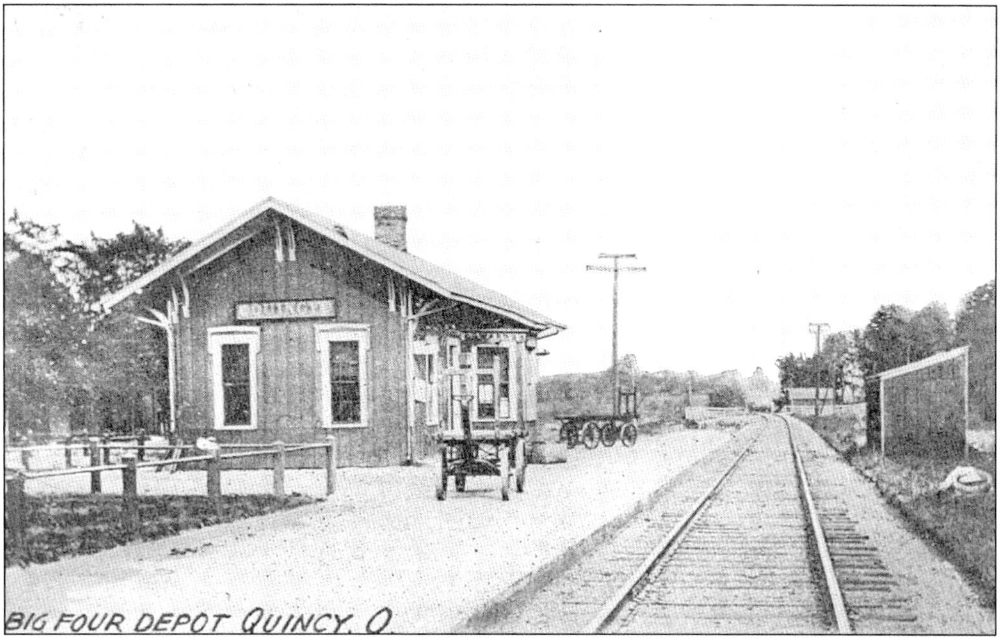

Built to the same design as DeGraff, the CCC&StL's Quincy combination depot sat near the crossing with the DT&I. This depot was gone by the 1960s; only a DT&I depot remains. (Mark J. Camp collection.)

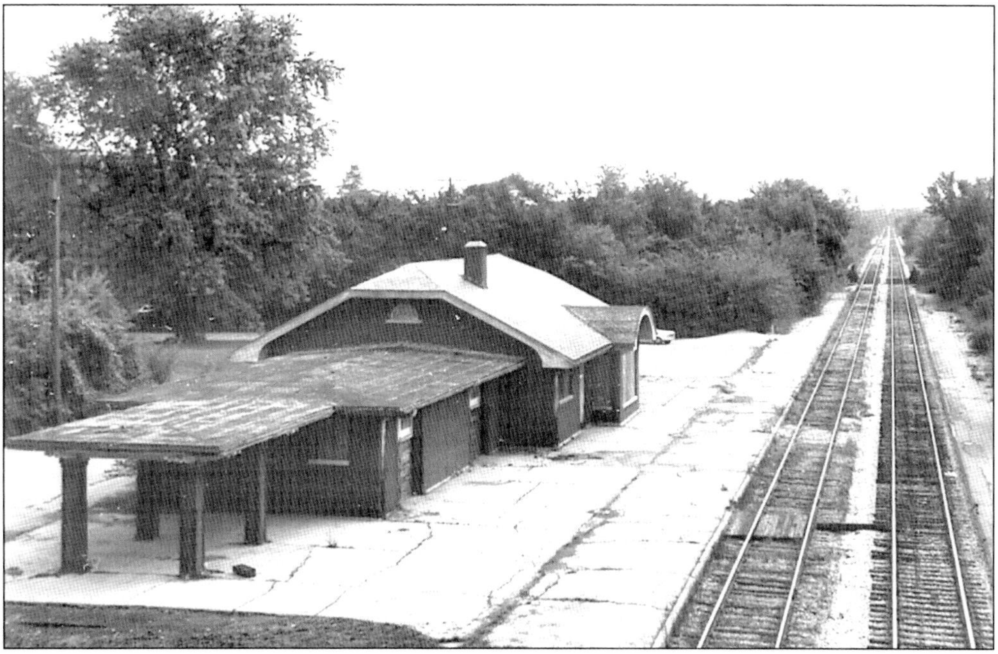

The Big Four built a bypass around downtown Sidney sometime between 1922 and 1925, abandoning its downtown passenger depot and transferring business to this newly constructed (1923) brick depot on the south edge of town. Across the tracks, a shelter served passengers. Near the depot, a high concrete arch viaduct spans the Great Miami River valley. The last passenger trains left in 1966. In recent years, the local model railroad club has used the building.

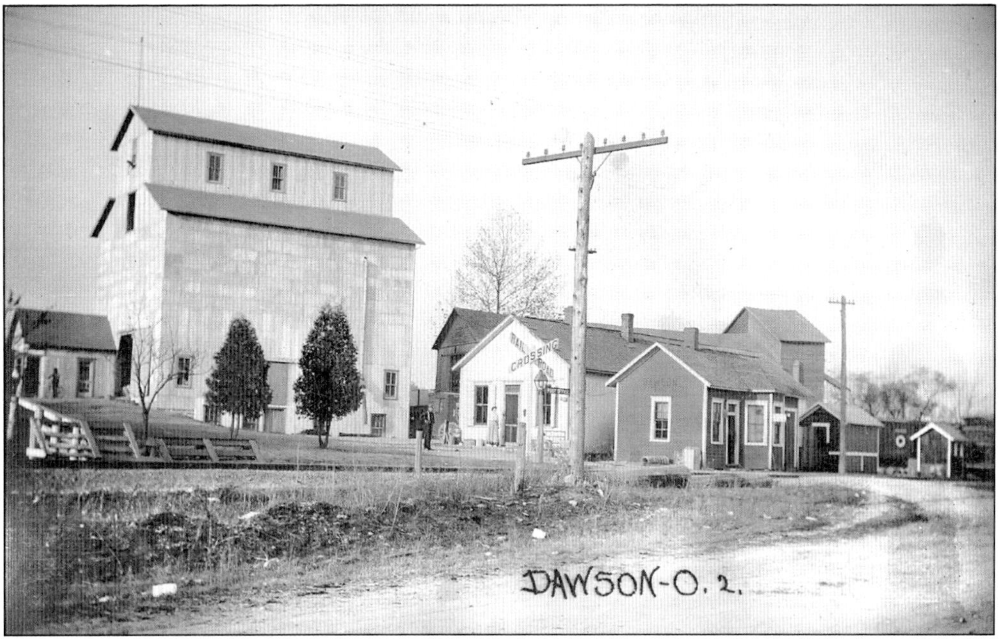

The engineering office used the same floor plan for the depots at nearby towns of Dawson (above) and Houston (below), but made each unique by a different bay window design. Note the Dawson depot has the town name stenciled on the end wall rather than the usual town board. The Houston depot seems to lack any identification. The occasion of the crowd remains unknown. Both depots have been gone for some time. (Mark J. Camp collection.)

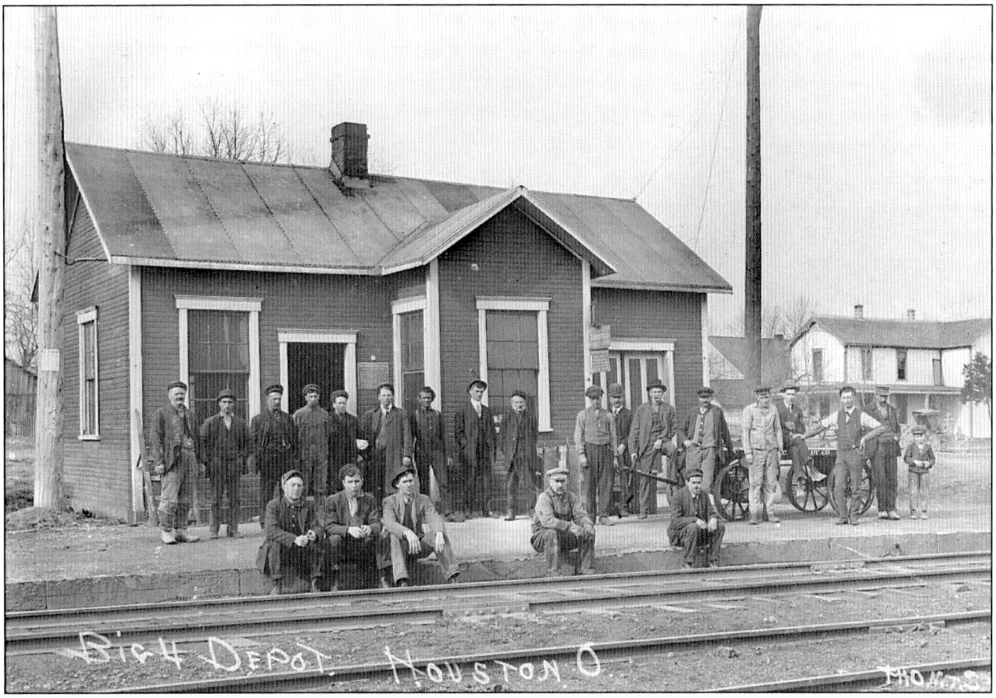

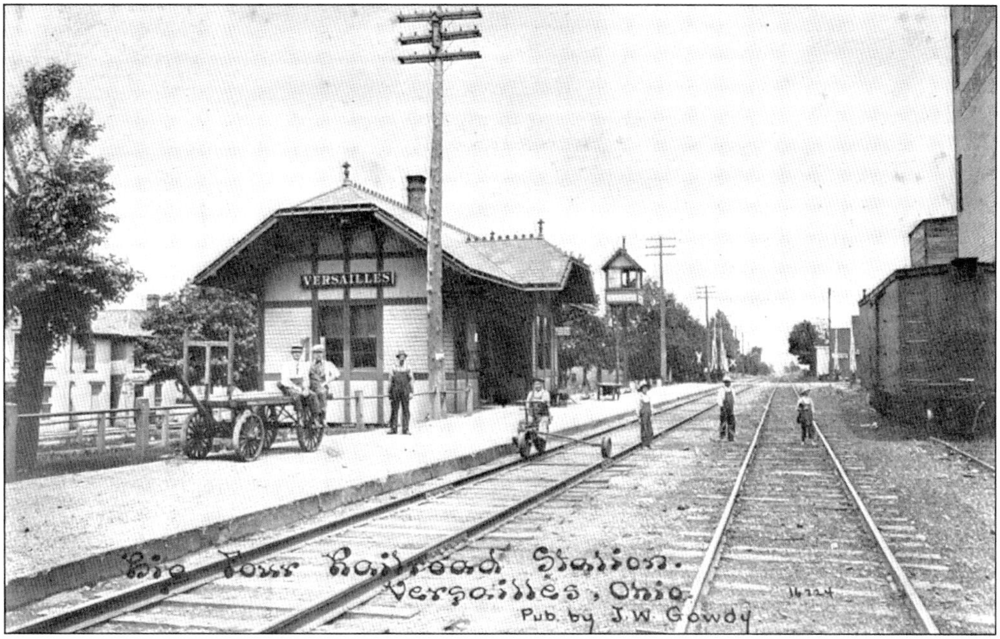

Versailles's depot was identical to one at Mount Victory. Note the gate tower just east of the depot. From this lofty perch the operator could raise and lower the gates at the nearby road crossing. By the 1950s, the NYC redesigned the roof, windows, doors, and siding of the depot and took down the tower. The depot was moved in the early 1970s and converted to office use. (Mark J. Camp collection.)

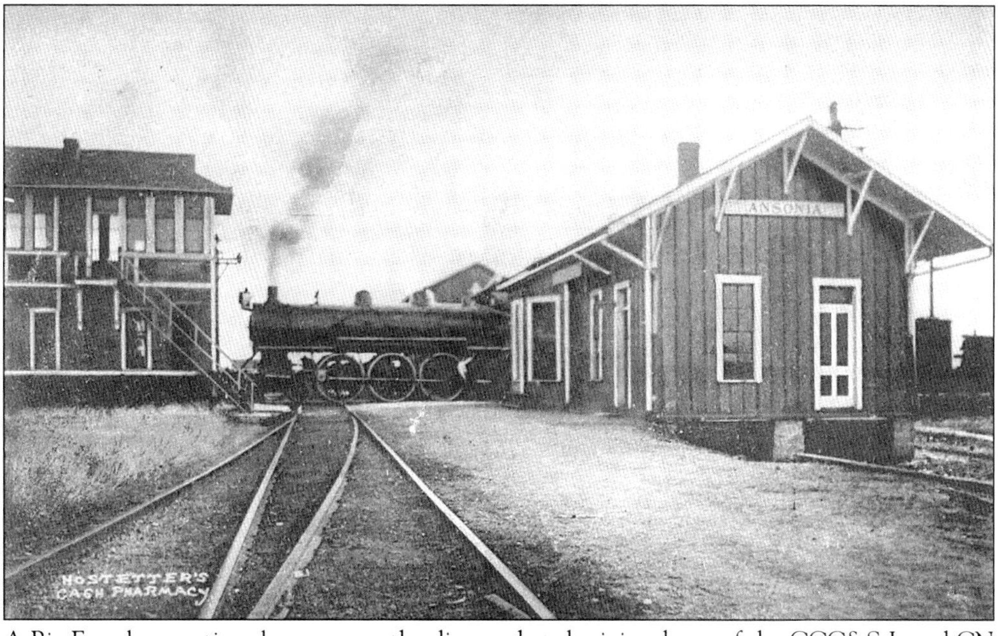

A Big Four locomotive clangs across the diamond at the joint depot of the CCC&StL and CN at Ansonia, past the interlocking tower around 1910. The NYC remodeled this depot, much like Versailles, by the 1950s, again changing the roofline and door and window arrangement. The depot still serves the railroad, but the tower is gone. (Mark J. Camp collection.)

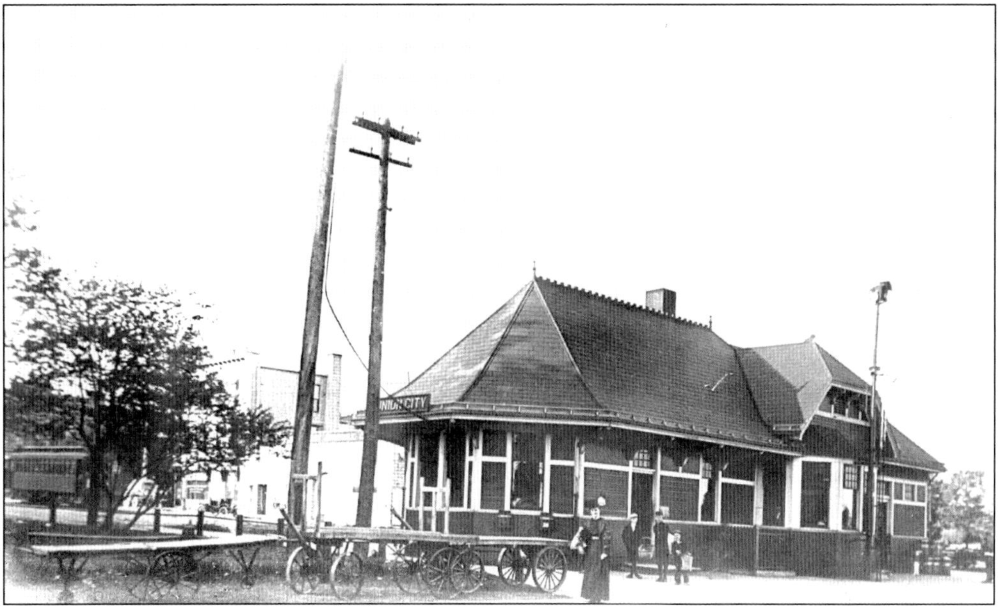

Union City had three depots in the early 1900s, including this CCC&StL structure. The depot follows the same blueprint as Mount Victory and Versailles, but the angled waiting room end and fancy dormer over the bay window gave it a unique appearance. The depot was a busy place in the early 1900s with as many as 14 passenger trains daily. Note the interurban that took passengers to a number of Indiana towns. The only depot surviving in Union City is the former PCC&StL depot. (Mark J. Camp collection.)

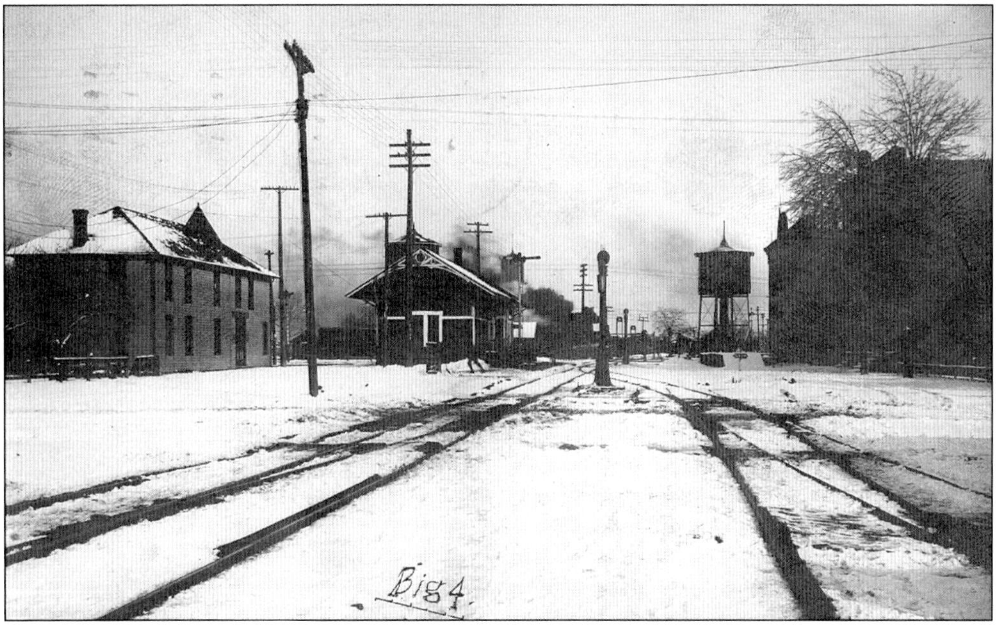

The Big Four passenger depot in Troy was within walking distance of the CH&D depot (the tip of its turreted office just shows above the hotel to the left). The Big Four reportedly built it in 1882. The siding to the right leads to the freight house, behind the photographer. Passenger service ended around 1950, but the depot lasted until 1985. (Mark J. Camp collection.)

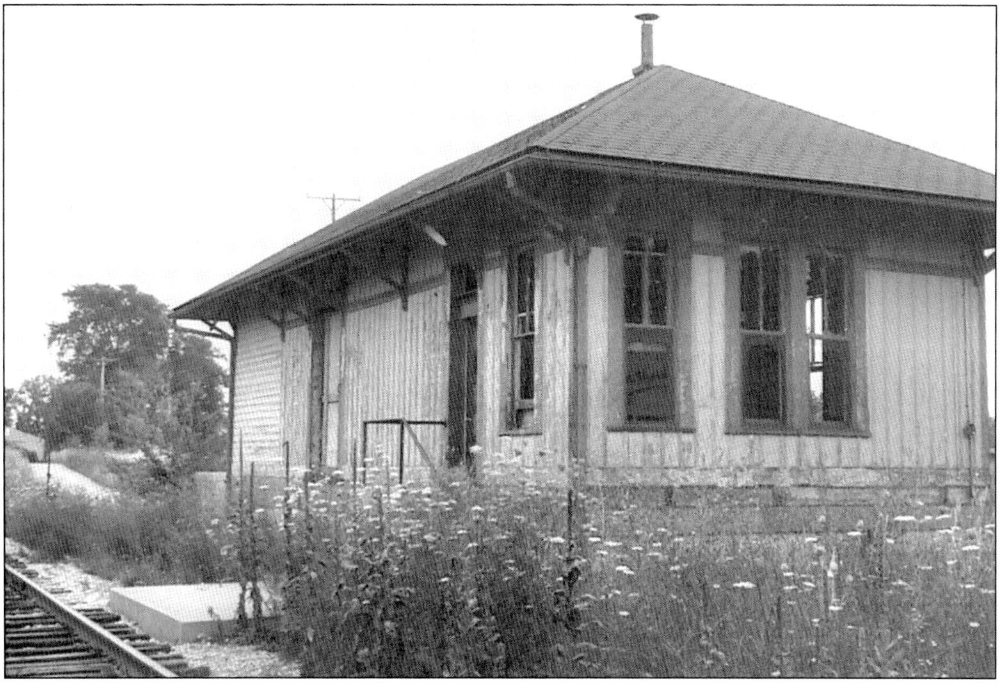

When the standard design CCC&StL depot at Ludlow Falls was demolished in a train derailment in the early 1950s, the then unneeded Kessler depot was moved in to replace it. By the late 1960s, it sat abandoned and vandalized. Around 1972, it was moved again and converted to business use.

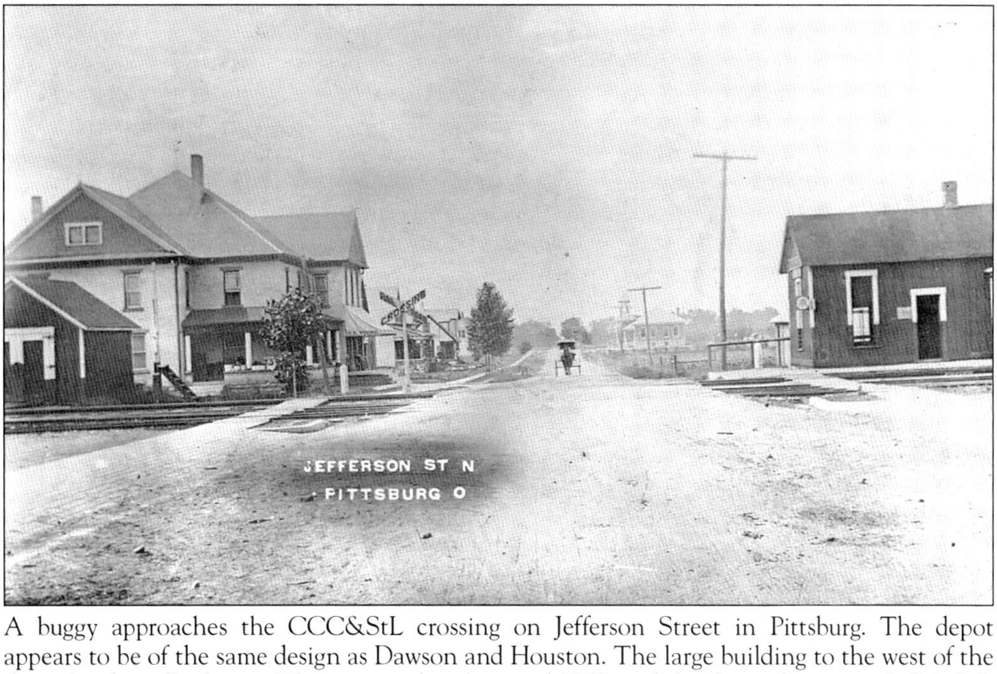

A buggy approaches the CCC&StL crossing on Jefferson Street in Pittsburg. The depot appears to be of the same design as Dawson and Houston. The large building to the west of the depot is a boardinghouse. The agency closed around 1959, and the depot disappeared. (Mark J. Camp collection.)

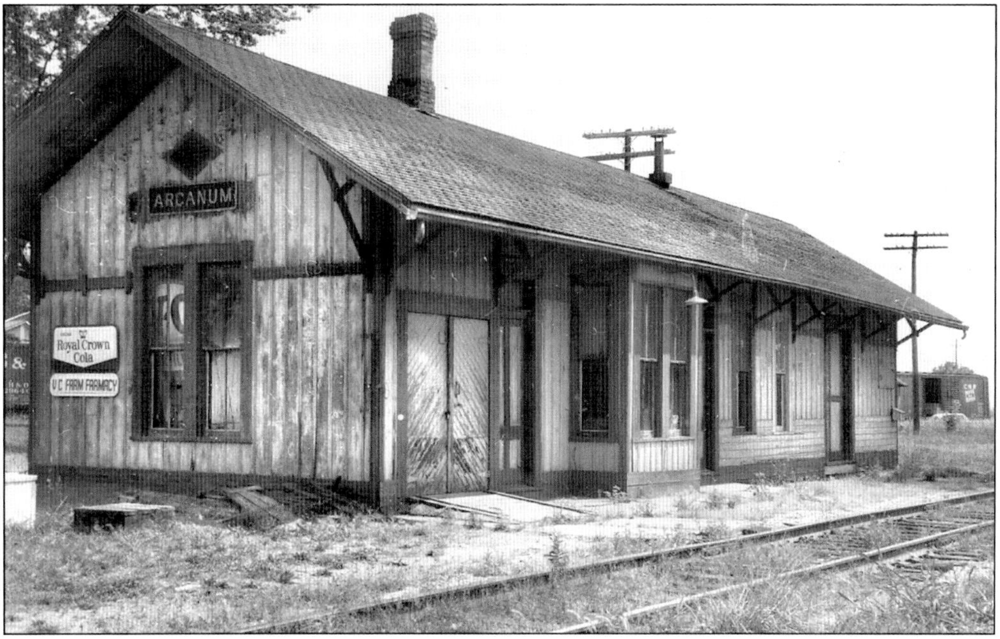

This 1960s view of the Big Four depot in Arcanum shows a building of similar design to Troy. Note the cast-iron town boards, a symbol of NYC depots in the 1950s and 1960s. (Mark J. Camp collection.)

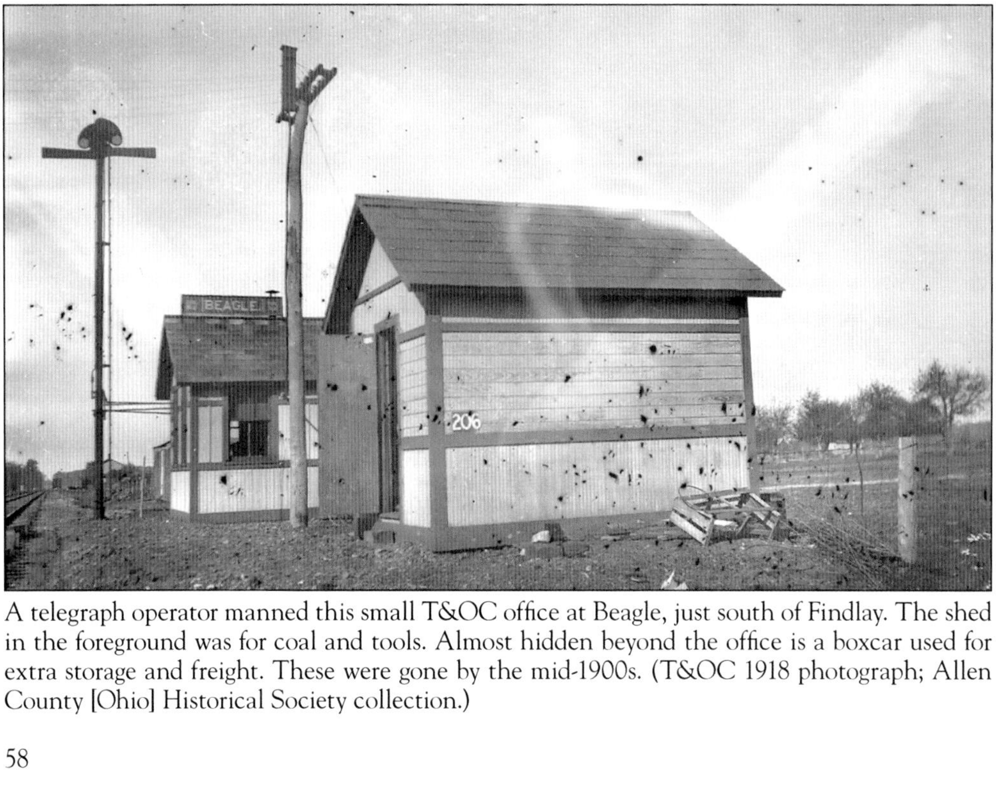

A telegraph operator manned this small T&OC office at Beagle, just south of Findlay. The shed in the foreground was for coal and tools. Almost hidden beyond the office is a boxcar used for extra storage and freight. These were gone by the mid-1900s. (T&OC 1918 photograph; Allen County [Ohio] Historical Society collection.)

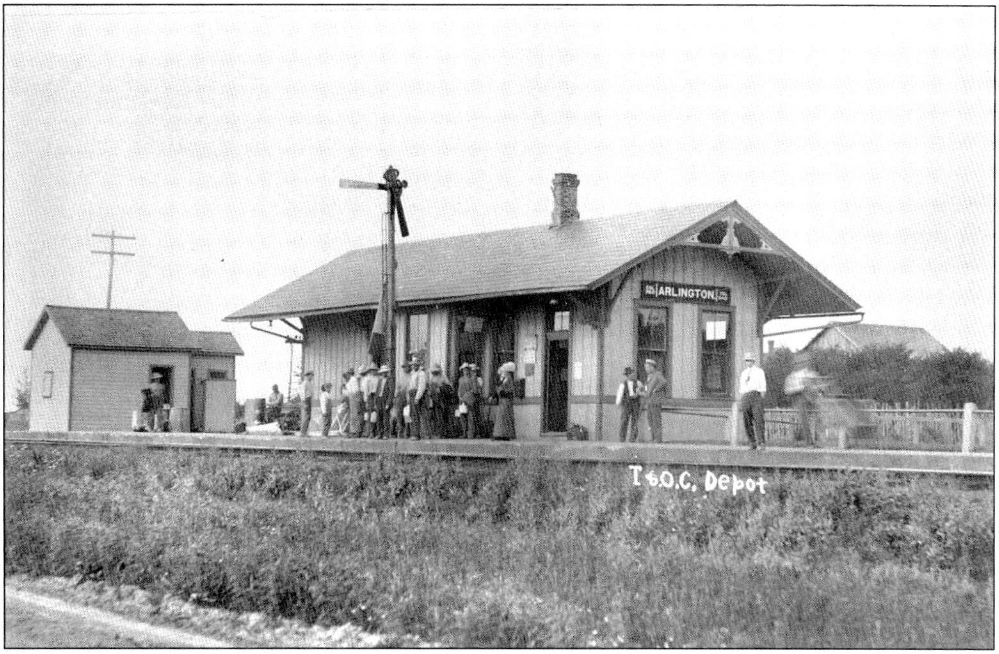

A crowd awaits the next train at Arlington. In later years, the NYC added cast-iron town boards. One remains in the town park as of 2003. The depot, probably built around 1890, was closed around 1959 and was reportedly torn down in 1966. (Mark J. Camp collection.)

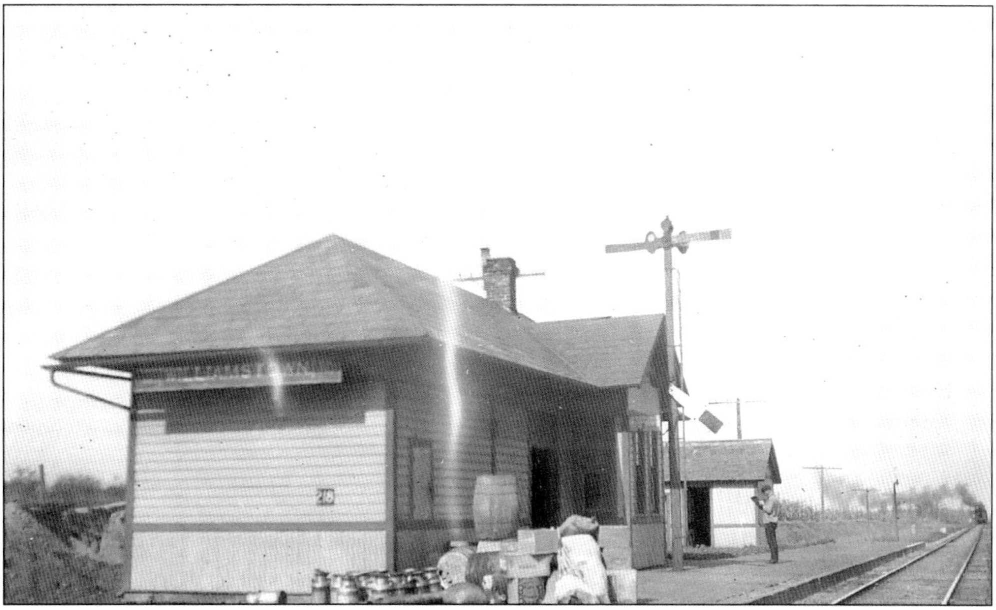

A few T&OC depot plans called for hipped roofs, including this one at Williamstown. The man recording notes is with the property evaluation team surveying the structural holdings of the T&OC. Many of the photographs taken during this evaluation appear on the following pages. Williamstown's *c.* 1890 depot was relocated in town where it rested many years as an outbuilding. In 2002, it was relocated between Wapakoneta and Botkins and restored. (T&OC 1918 photograph; Allen County [Ohio] Historical Society collection.)

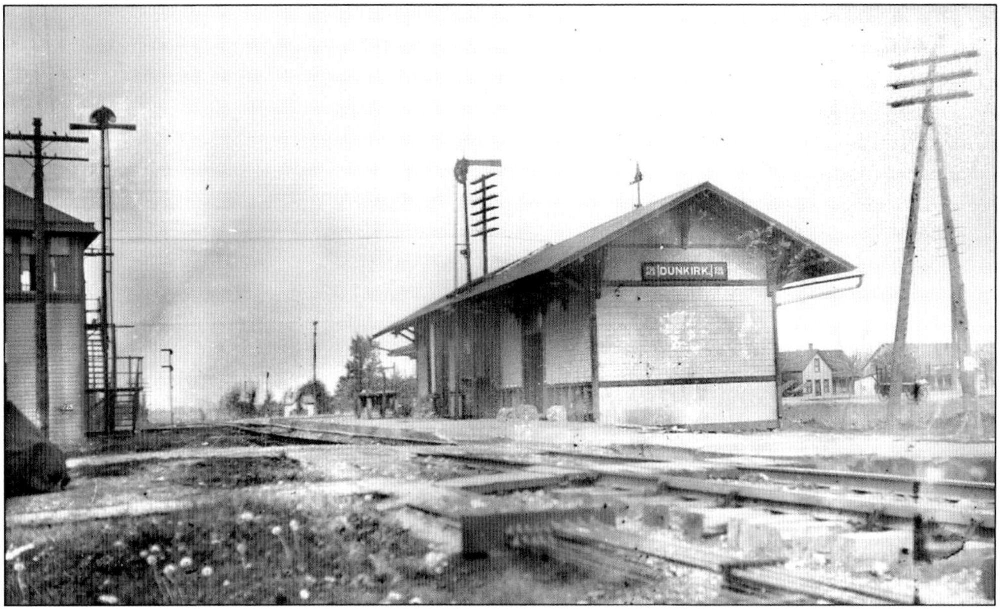

The T&OC crossed the PRR main line at Dunkirk. Here is the *c.* 1889 T&OC combination depot looking north to Findlay. To the right is the old PRR interlocking tower. Just an edge of the roof of the PRR's brick passenger depot shows behind the T&OC depot. The NYC cast-iron town boards from this depot, reportedly closed in 1959, marked the town limits on U.S. 68 for many years. All that remains is a later PRR brick interlocking tower. (T&OC 1918 photograph; Allen County [Ohio] Historical Society collection.)

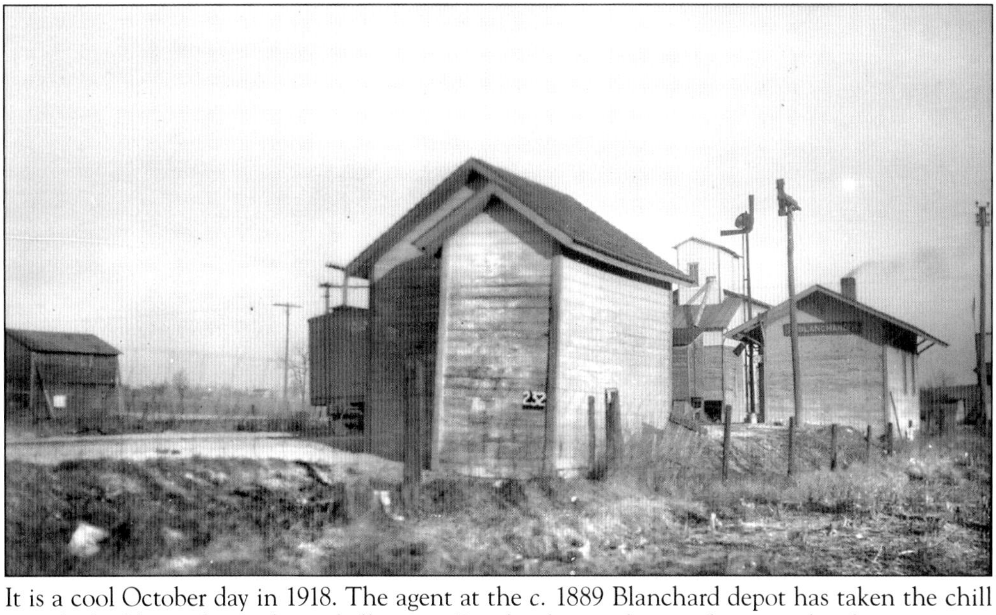

It is a cool October day in 1918. The agent at the *c.* 1889 Blanchard depot has taken the chill away by building a fire in the potbelly stove. Besides the usual grain elevator, a local stone quarry provided considerable freight business. This depot appears to have been gone by the 1960s. (T&OC 1918 photograph; Allen County [Ohio] Historical Society collection.)

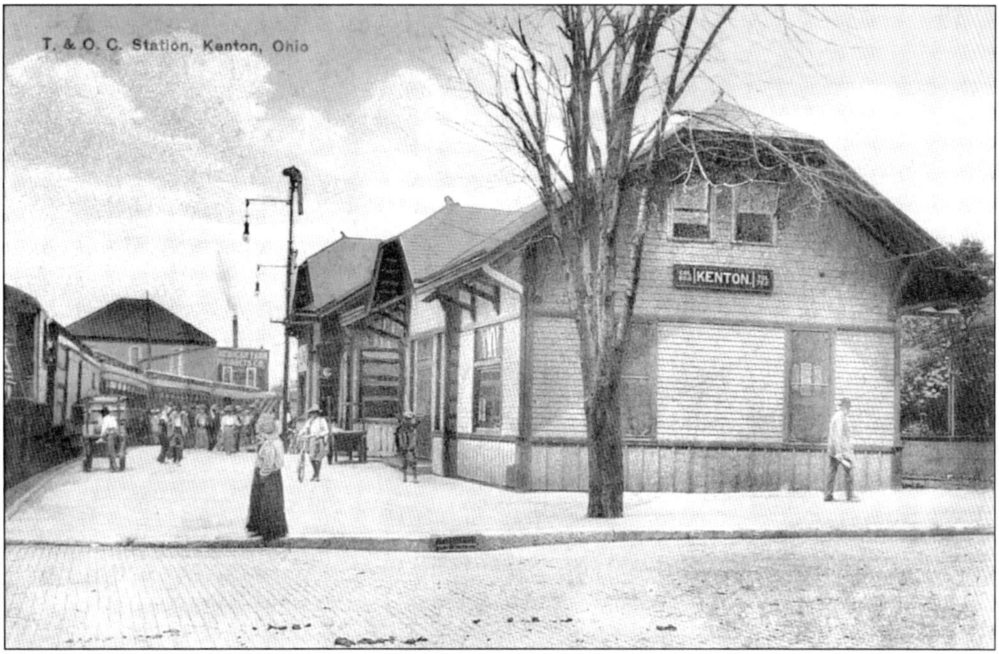

The Hardin County seat of Kenton was always an important stop on the T&OC. The passenger depot and baggage building were commonly alive with activity and date to about 1892. The T&OC also employed around 165 workers in 1910 at its 1892 Kenton shops. The shops were closed down by the 1930s. Except for a shop building, nothing but memories remain of the T&OC's presence in Kenton. (Mark J. Camp collection.)

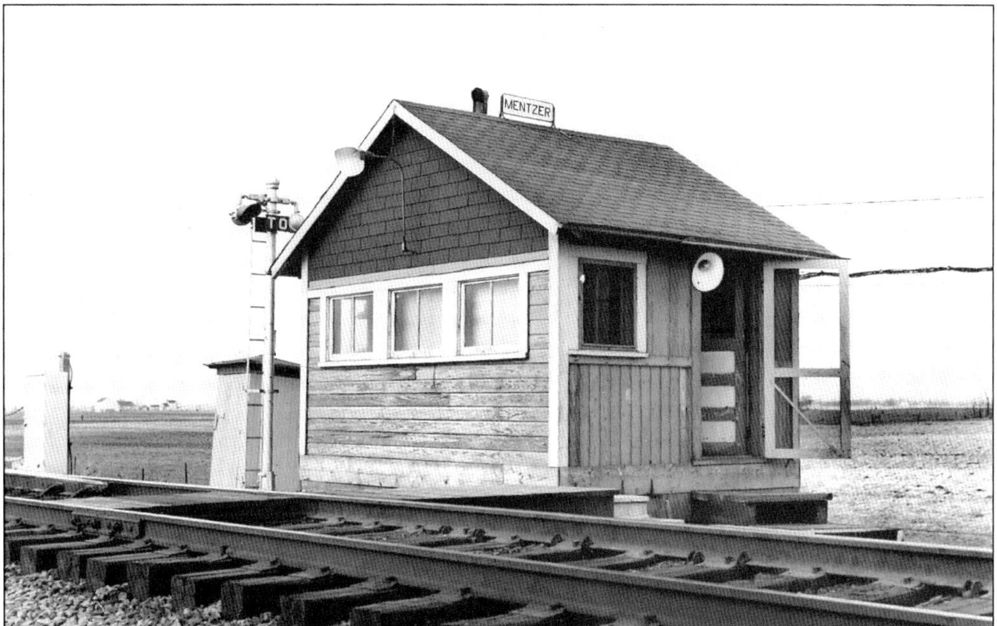

The former telegraph office at Mentzer, south of Kenton, had received some modernizations by this early 1960 view. Farther south the T&OC crossed the Big Four at Ridgeway. (Bob Lorenz photograph.)

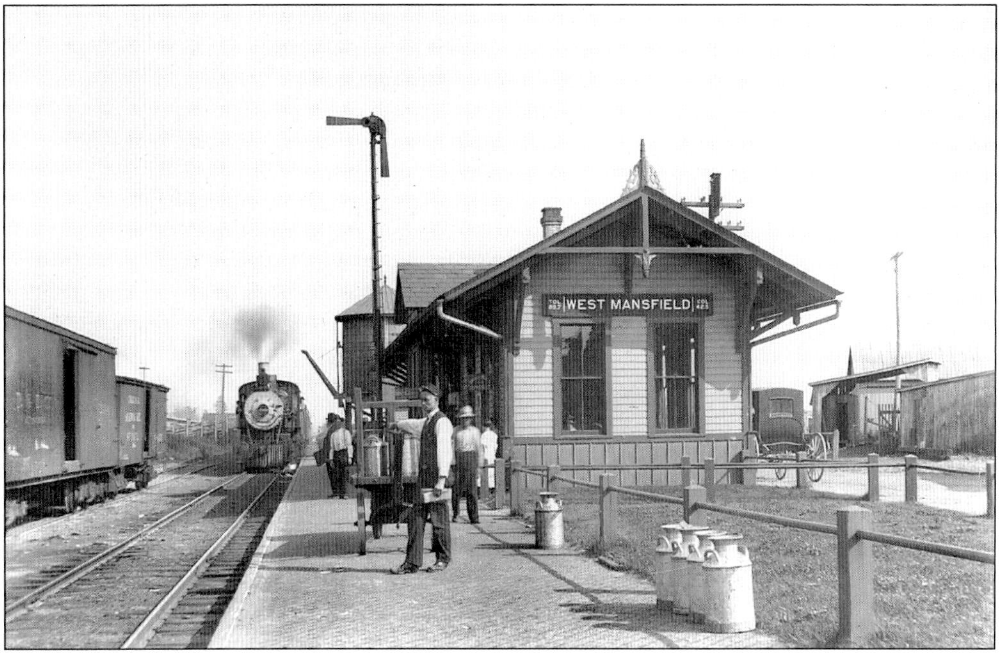

Train time at West Mansfield was a beehive of activity in the early 1900s. Behind the 1894 depot, a hack, the 1900 version of a taxi, waits to take people to the local hotel. The depot lasted until 1968. (Mark J. Camp collection.)

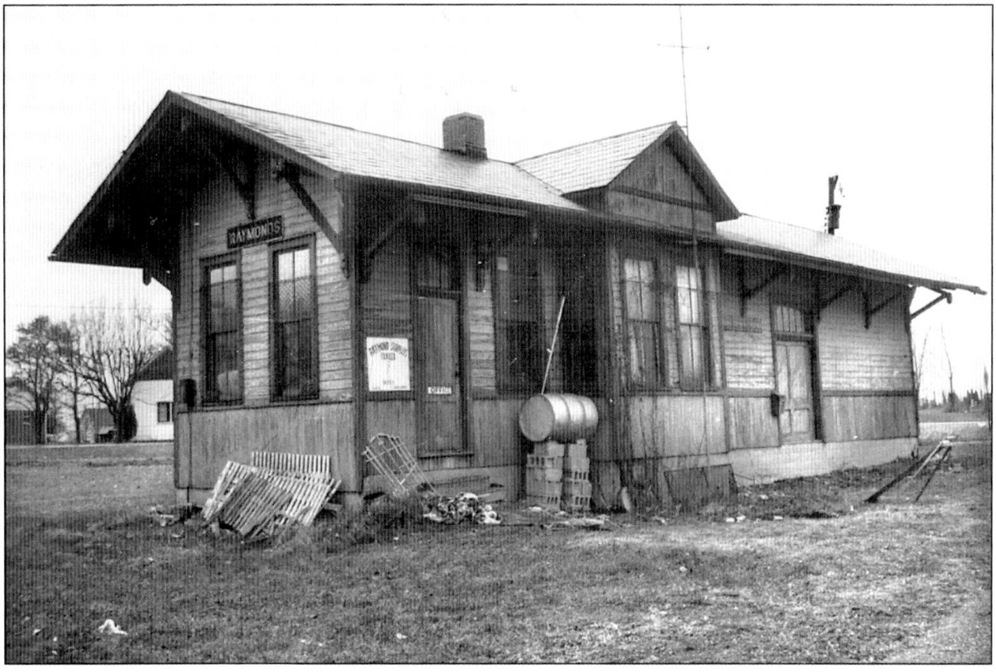

At Raymonds, the waiting and freight rooms were reversed, but the depot was built to the same plan as West Mansfield. The depot operated from 1894 to 1950. By the late 1960s, the depot had been relocated in town as shown here. It remains a residence. (Charles Garvin 1969 photograph; Mark J. Camp collection.)

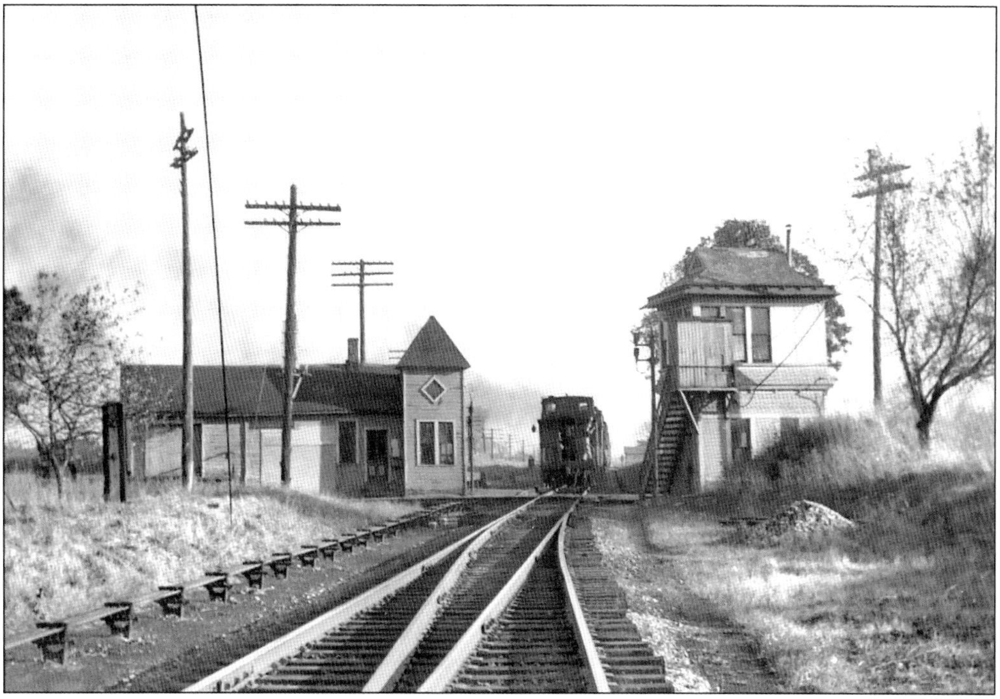

Looking along the T&OC at the Erie crossing in Peoria around 1947 shows the joint depot of Erie design and tower of T&OC design. Nothing remains at this always remote location. (Clyde Helms photograph; Mark J. Camp collection.)

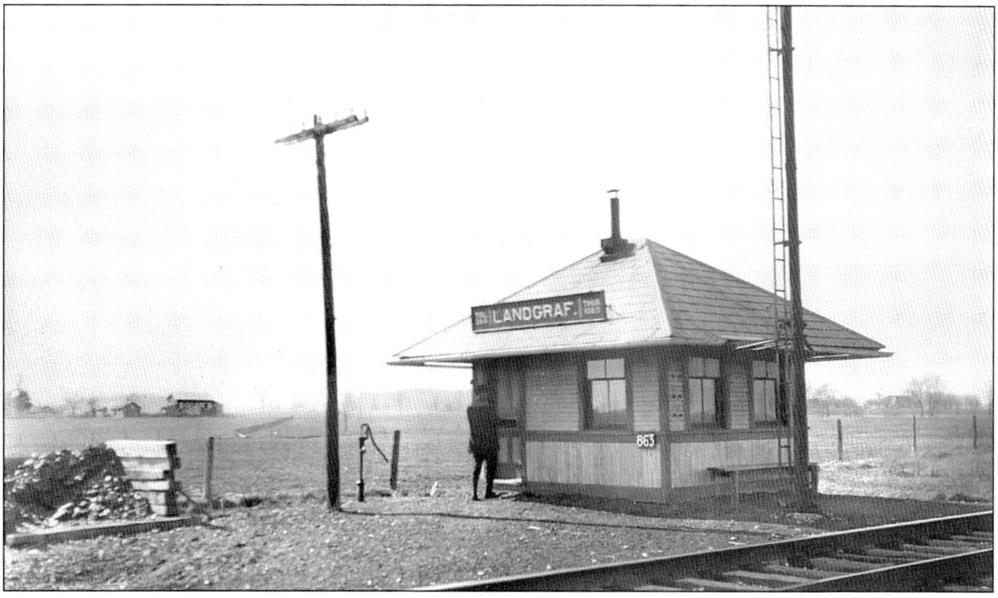

Landgraf was the first station south of Fostoria on the original Ohio Central. It was basically a train order station and not equipped to handle passengers or freight. The building probably dates from 1885 to 1889. It was closed around 1956. (T&OC photograph; Allen County [Ohio] Historical Society collection.)

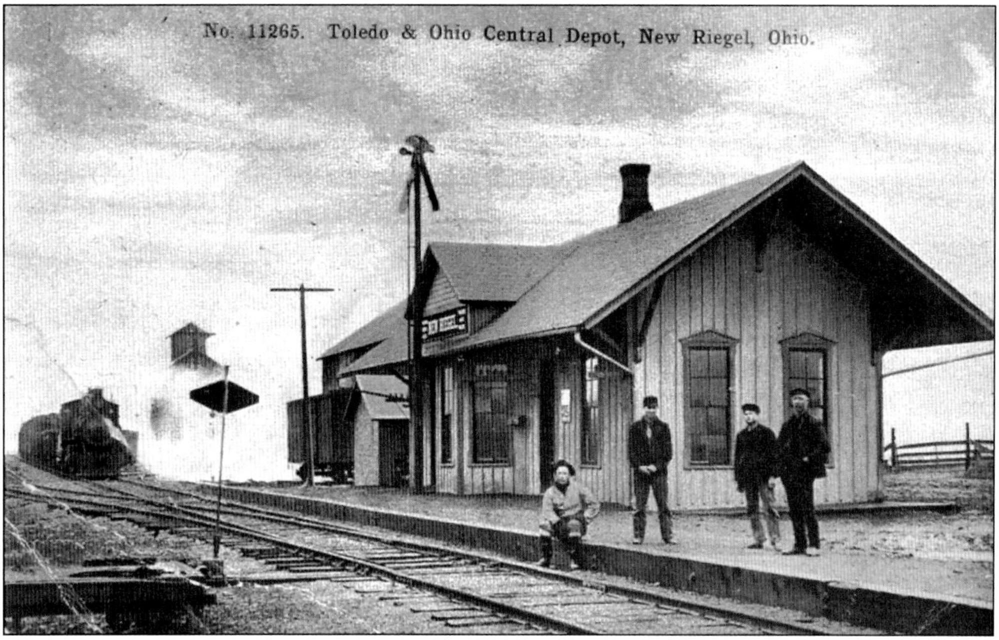

New Reigel's combination depot was of standard Ohio Central or T&OC design and probably dates to somewhere between 1882 and 1885. After the agency closed, the depot was moved off the tracks and used for storage by the late 1960s. It has apparently been torn down. (Mark J. Camp collection.)

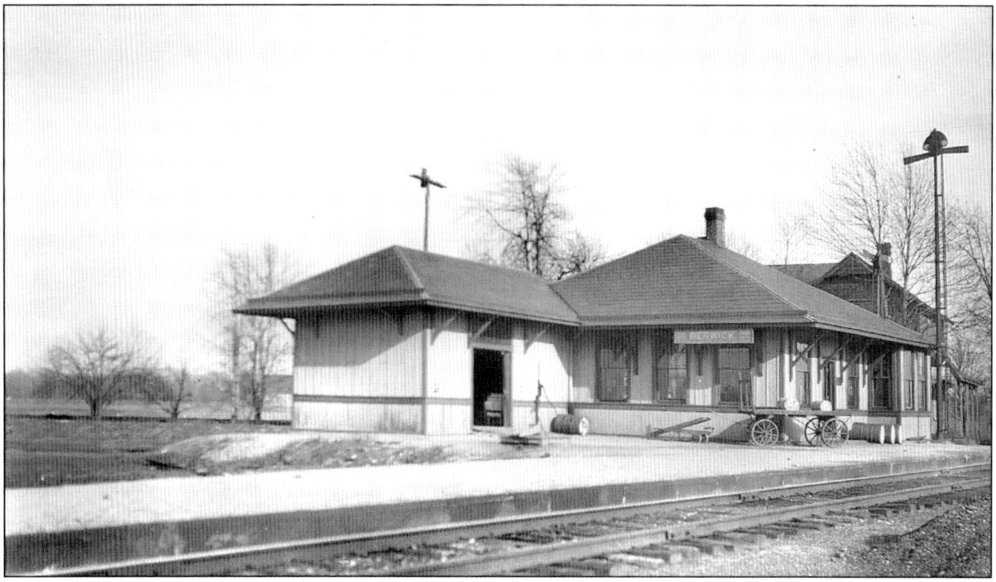

The Ohio Central crossed the former MR&LE at Berwick. This joint depot replaced the earlier MR&LE depot probably between 1882 and 1885 and served both the T&OC and soon the Big Four. It was a busy spot in the early days. Around 1957, the agency was closed. There are reports that part of this depot survived, but they have not been confirmed. (T&OC 1919 photograph; Allen County [Ohio] Historical Society collection.)

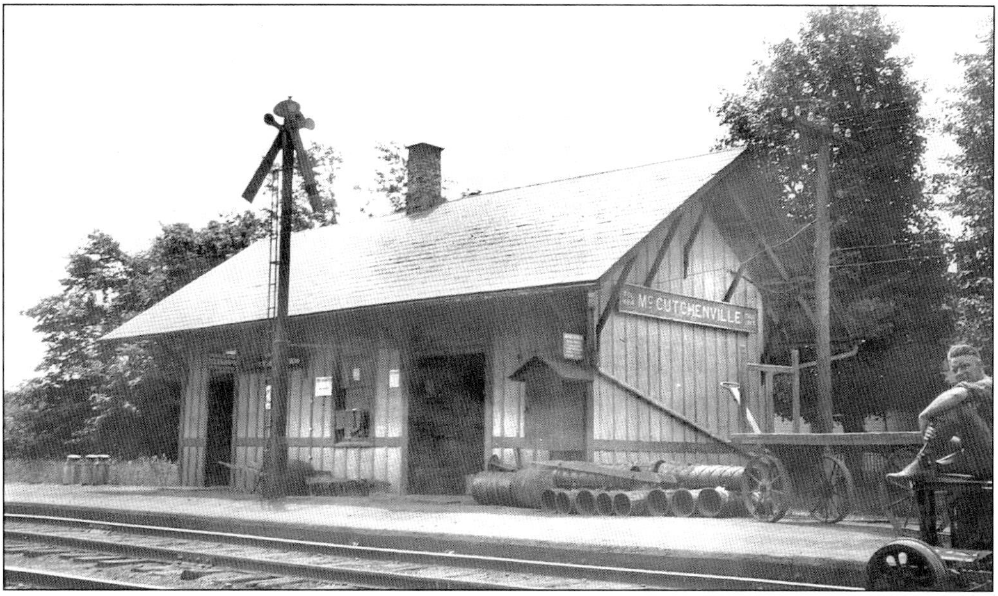

The Ohio Central or T&OC built a small combination depot in McCutchenville between 1882 and 1885, a design that was repeated at many other stations. Later it was moved, remodeled, and exists today as a residence. (T&OC 1919 photograph; Allen County [Ohio] Historical Society collection.)

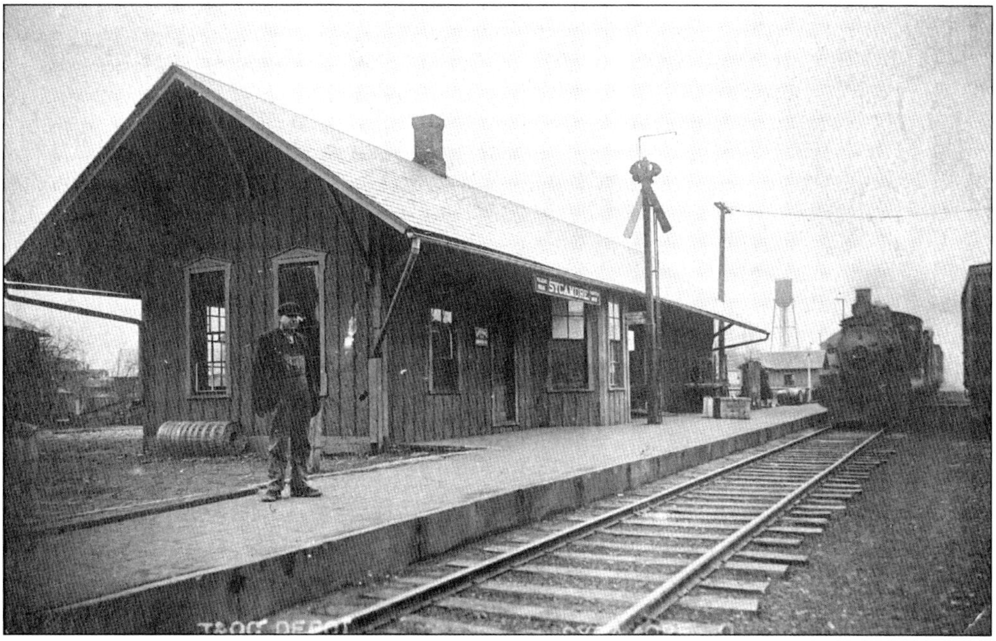

A much larger depot was needed in Sycamore, so the railroad built an extended version of the New Reigel structure minus the dormer over the bay window. It probably dates to 1882. The agency closed in 1967, and the building was dismantled two years later. (Mark J. Camp collection.)

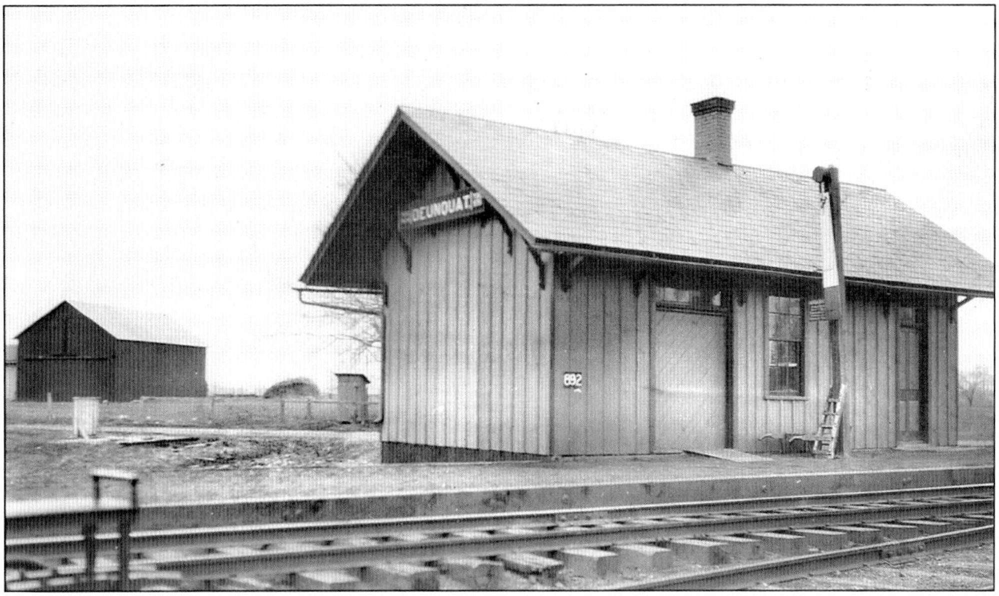

The T&OC depots at the small communities of Deunquat and Lemert demonstrate well the modifying of a standard plan to get two different-looking depots. Deunquat and Lemert have similar board and batten siding, but Deunquat lacks a bay window. Both date to the 1880s. Lemert served a grain company in the 1960s, but no longer exists. Deunquat has been gone for years. (T&OC 1919 photographs; Allen County [Ohio] Historical Society collection.)

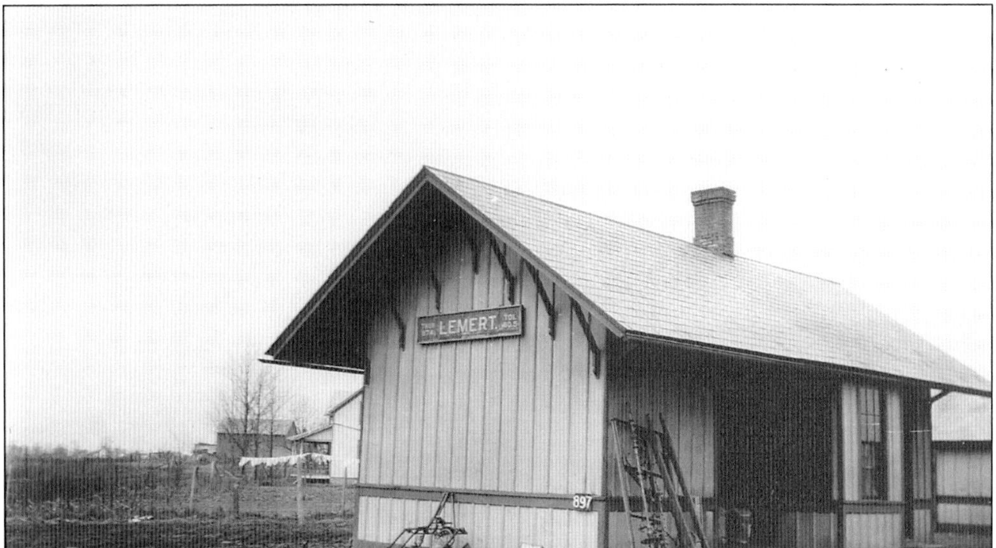

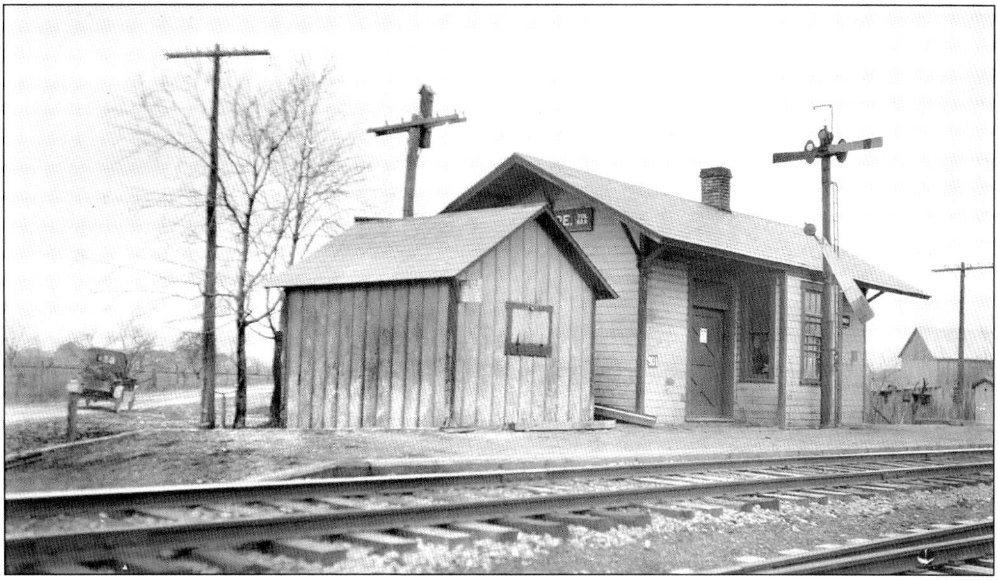

Spore's depot was similar to Deunquat and Lemert but had horizontal plank siding. It closed in 1956, was relocated, and survives as a house. (T&OC 1919 photograph; Allen County [Ohio] Historical Society collection.)

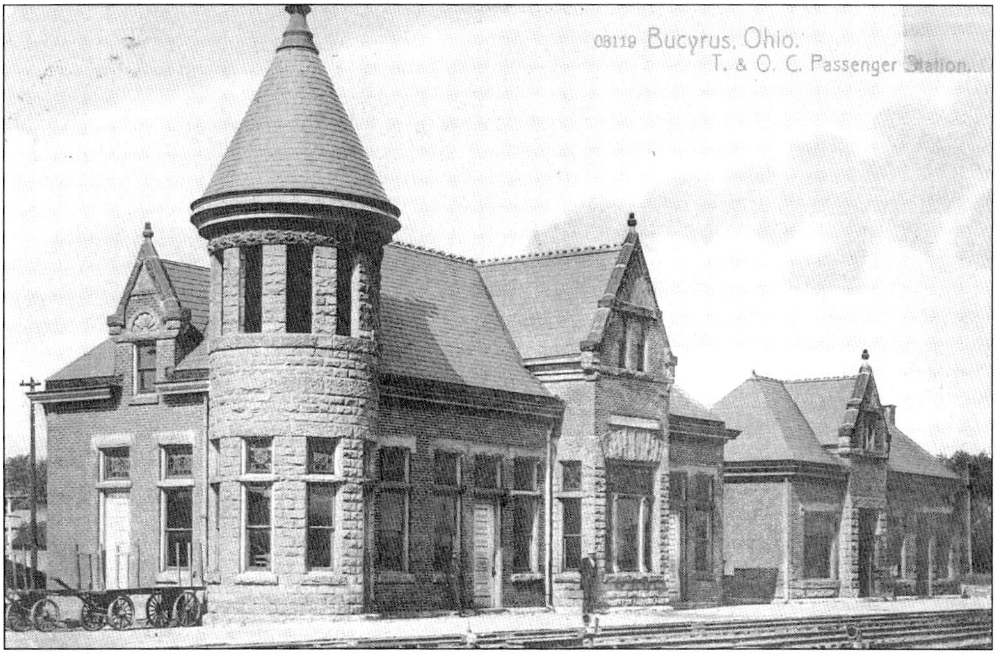

The T&OC built one of its greatest depots in the Crawford County seat of Bucyrus. This stone and brick passenger depot and adjacent baggage building was erected in 1892, replacing an earlier frame depot. The depot was alive with activity in the early 1900s, as were the nearby T&OC shops. Unfortunately, use of the depot declined through the years, and it was eventually vacated. The depot later became a workshop. (Mark J. Camp collection.)

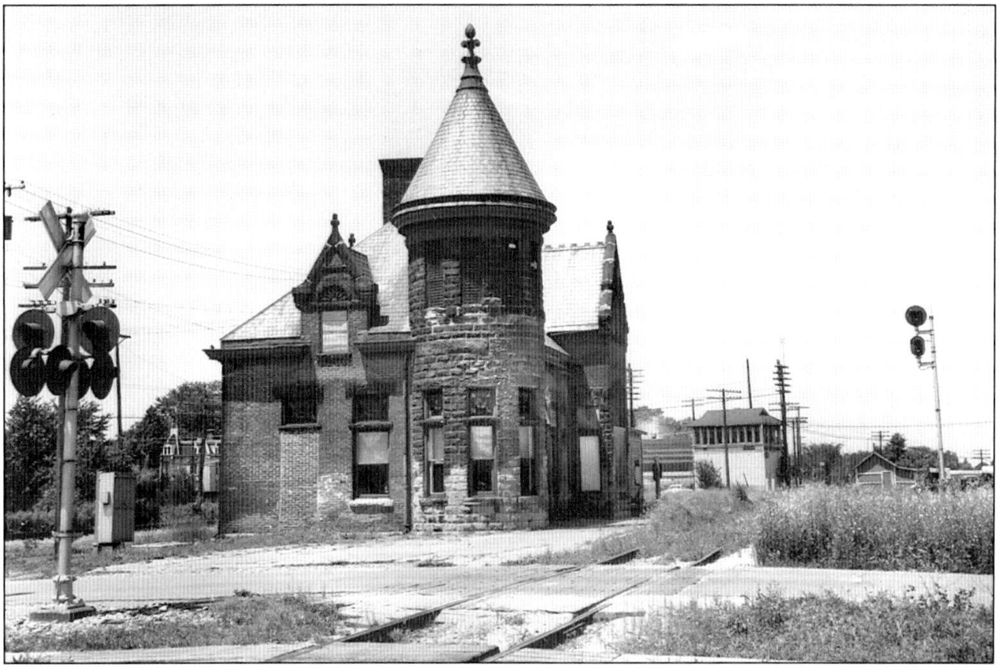

By 1970, the division office building, adjacent to the depot, was torn down. North of the depot was Colsan tower at the crossing of the PRR. South of the depot was a T&OC brick freight house. The Bucyrus Station Association is restoring the depot for community use. The shop complex also remains.

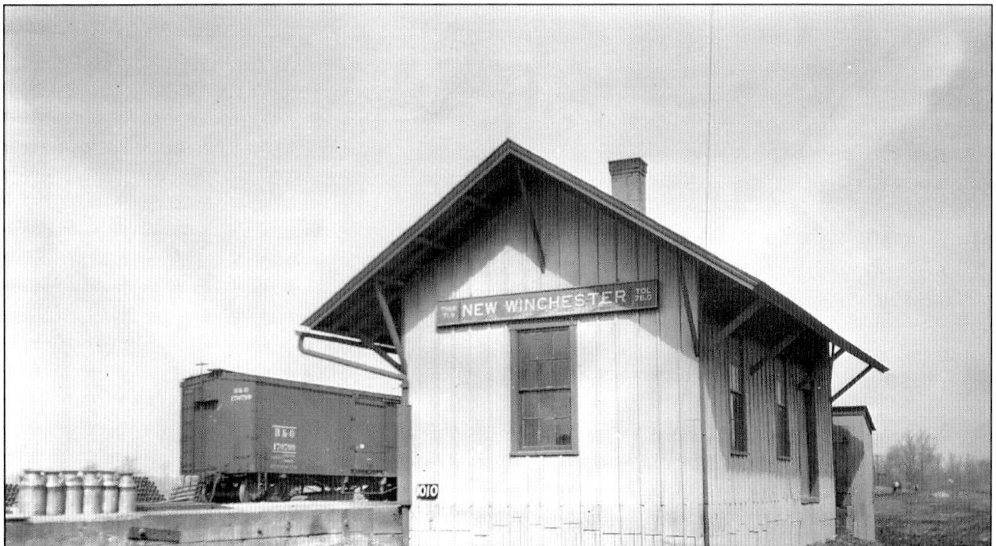

Milk cans sit on the platform at New Winchester's T&OC depot, built to the same plan as Deunquat, Lemert, and Spore. Across the track are piles of field tile, another local product. The depot still exists as a house, relocated a few miles from its original site. (T&OC 1919 photograph, Allen County [Ohio] Historical Society collection.)

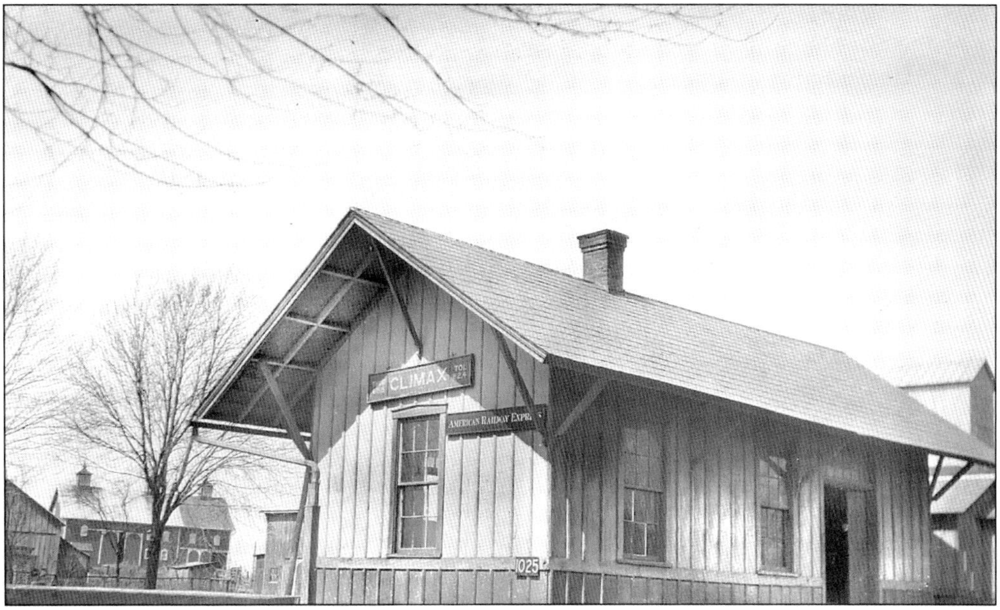

Once again, the Deunquat-style depot was used at Climax. Climax was where the north and south constructions of the Ohio Central joined. The depot disappeared before the 1960s. (T&OC 1919 photograph, Allen County [Ohio] Historical Society collection.)

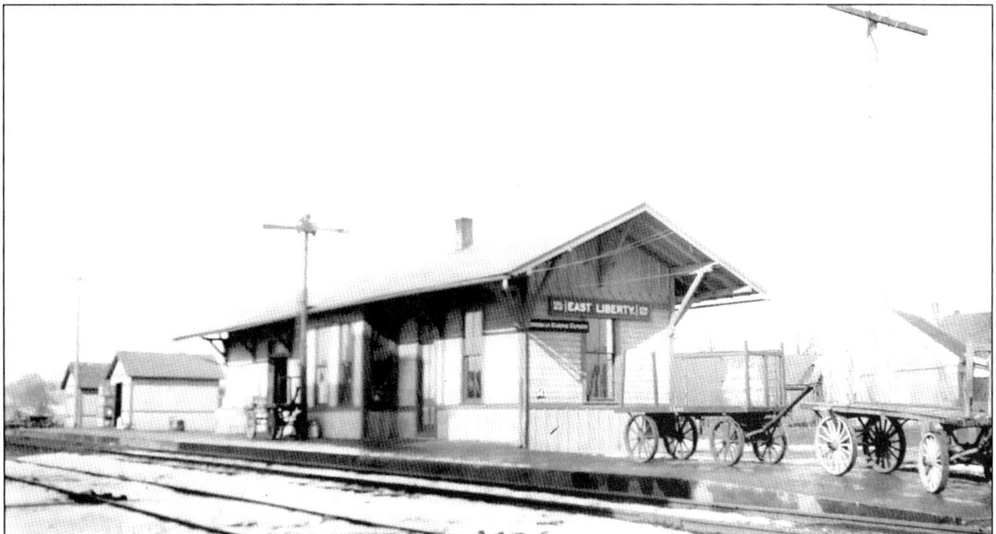

A number of the T&OC's St. Marys branch depots appear to have been built during D&LN ownership around 1898. The East Liberty depot is a good example of the general plan. The scalloped siding in the eaves is characteristic. After abandonment in 1935, the depot was used for storage by the grain elevator across the track. Today it and the grain elevator sit abandoned and derelict. (T&OC 1919 photograph, Allen County [Ohio] Historical Society collection.)

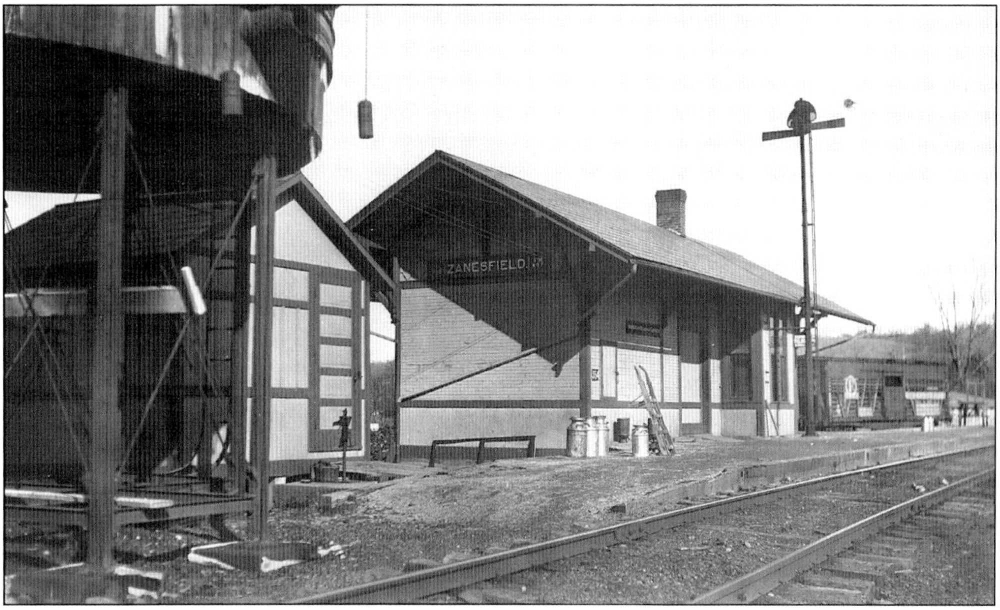

Zanesfield was a water station on the St. Marys branch. This D&LN-designed depot was moved to become a clubhouse, only to burn to the ground. (T&OC 1919 photograph, Allen County [Ohio] Historical Society collection.)

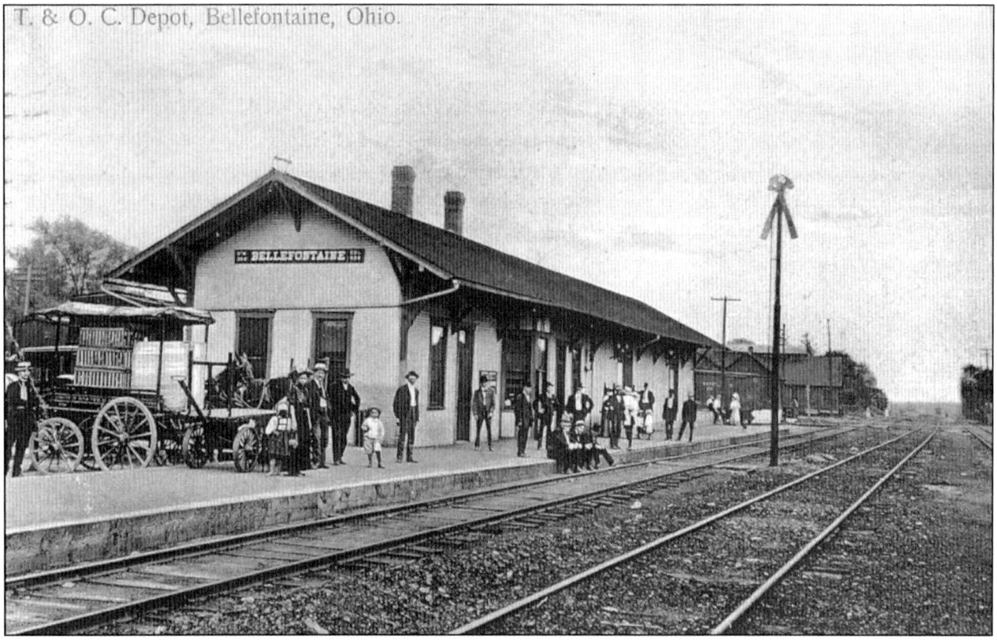

The D&LN used this depot along Water Street in Bellefontaine. The first T&OC train arrived in town March 1, 1901. At the peak of service, two daily passenger trains stopped at the depot running to either St. Marys or Columbus. It was used until around 1918 when the T&OC began to run its trains into the Big Four depot. A large freight house at this site burned down in March 1999. (Mark J. Camp collection.)

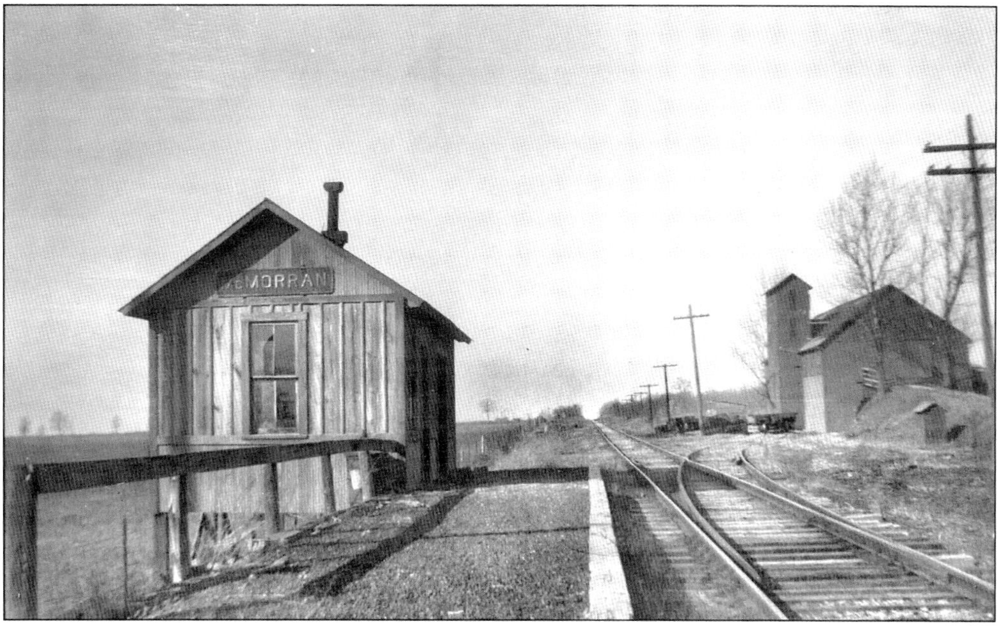

Passengers at McMorran had to literally flag down trains, thus the term "flag stop." Even though the depot was small, the potbelly stove kept it cozy on cold days. The stop was known as Hazleton until around 1910. (Clyde Helms photograph; Mark J. Camp collection.)

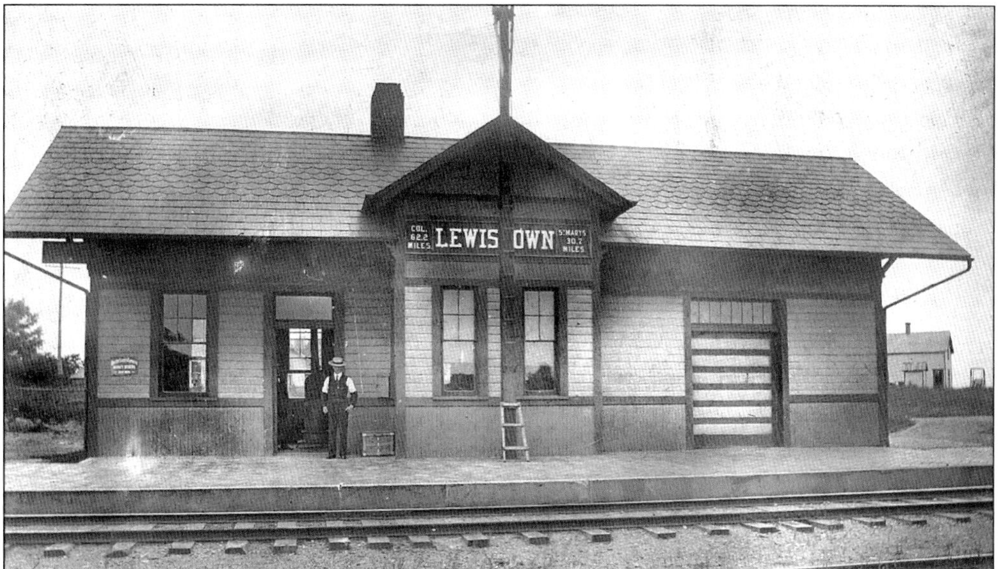

This is the second depot at Lewistown, pretty much a copy of the original that was struck by lightning in June 1902 and burned to the ground. The depot closed around 1958 and later was torn down. (Mark J. Camp collection.)

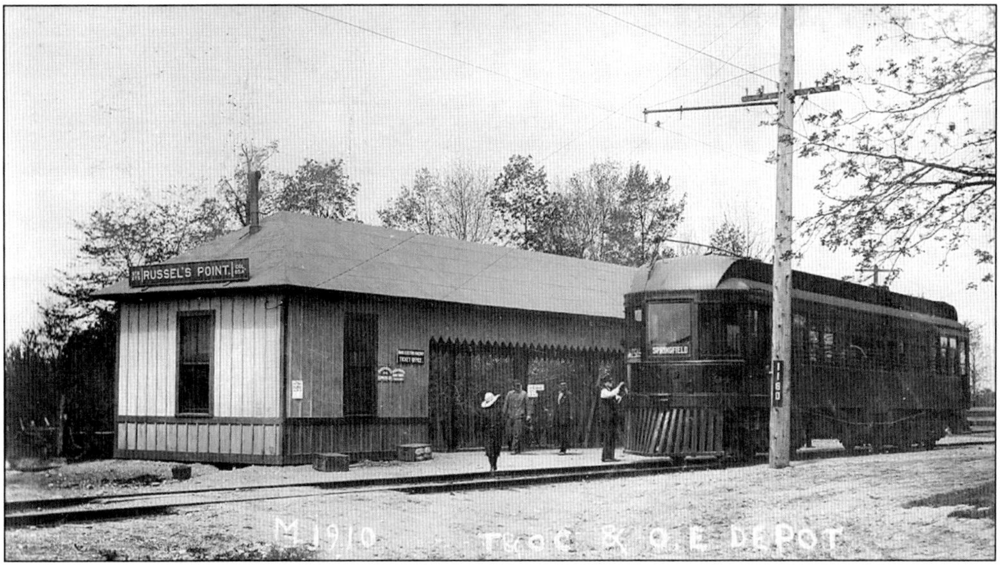

Russells Point depot was a busy spot during the summer around 1900 as people flocked to Lewistown Reservoir, later Indian Lake. This depot, with its outdoor waiting area, was also a ticket office for the Ohio Electric. The local to Springfield is seen here ready to leave. The depot closed in 1958. (Mark J. Camp collection.)

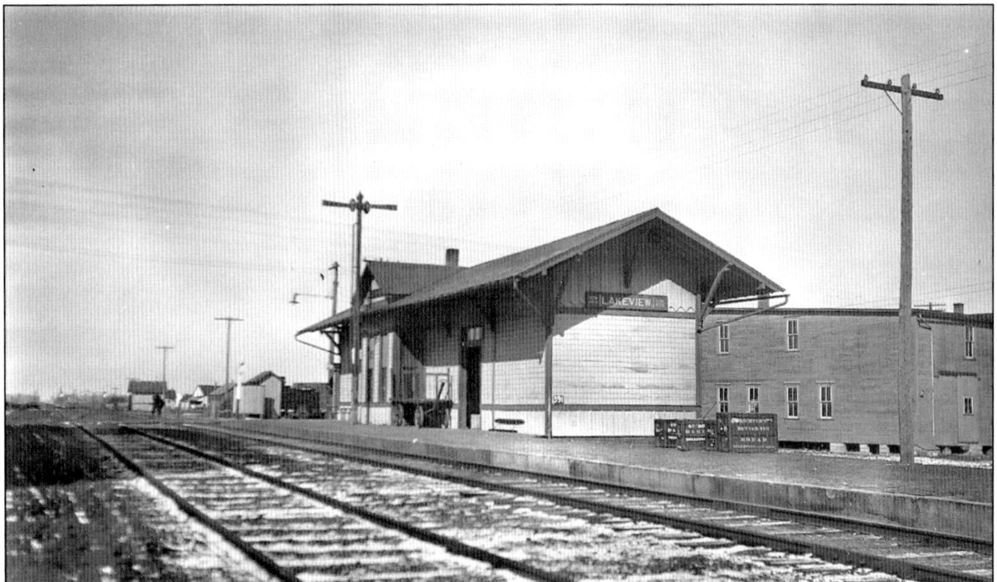

Also on Lewistown Reservoir was Lakeview. Bread hampers from a Bellefontaine bakery wait to be returned on the next local. The depot was torn down in the late 1960s. (T&OC 1919 photograph, Allen County [Ohio] Historical Society collection.)

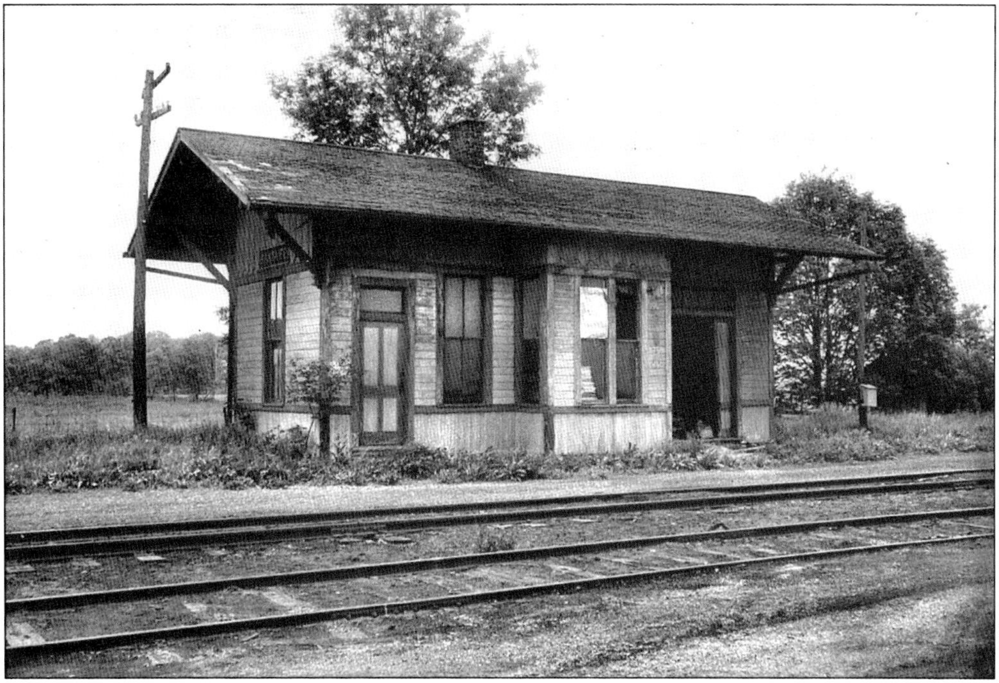

This D&LN-designed combination depot sits abandoned in 1968 at Santa Fe, a town founded when the Columbus and Northwestern was surveyed through the area. It has since been demolished. (Charles Garvin photograph; Mark J. Camp collection.)

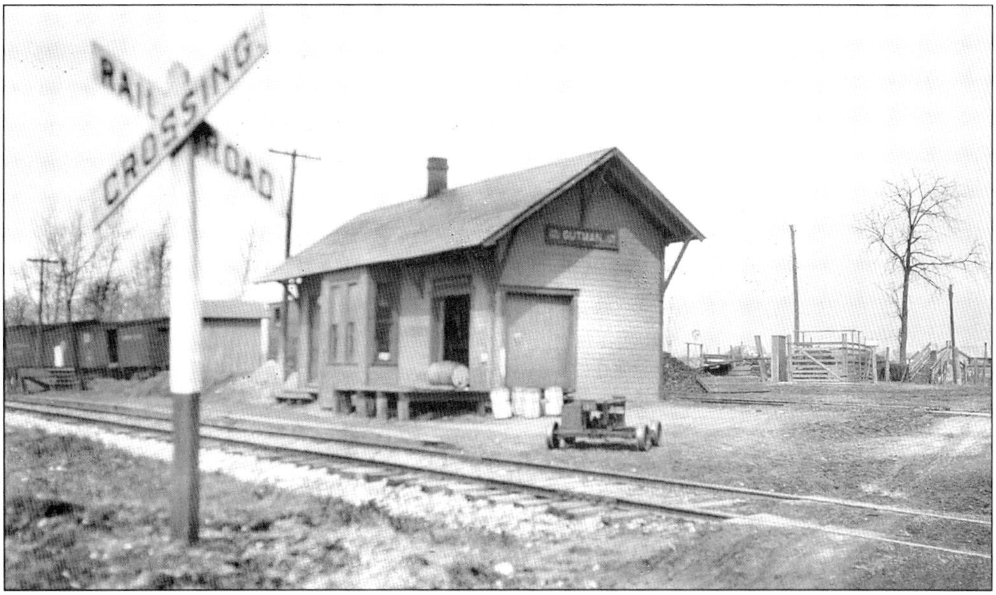

The Gutman combination depot was located just east of Slater at the old wye with the Ohio Southern. There were three depots within just a few miles; one wonders if there was ever enough business. (T&OC 1919 photograph, Allen County [Ohio] Historical Society collection.)

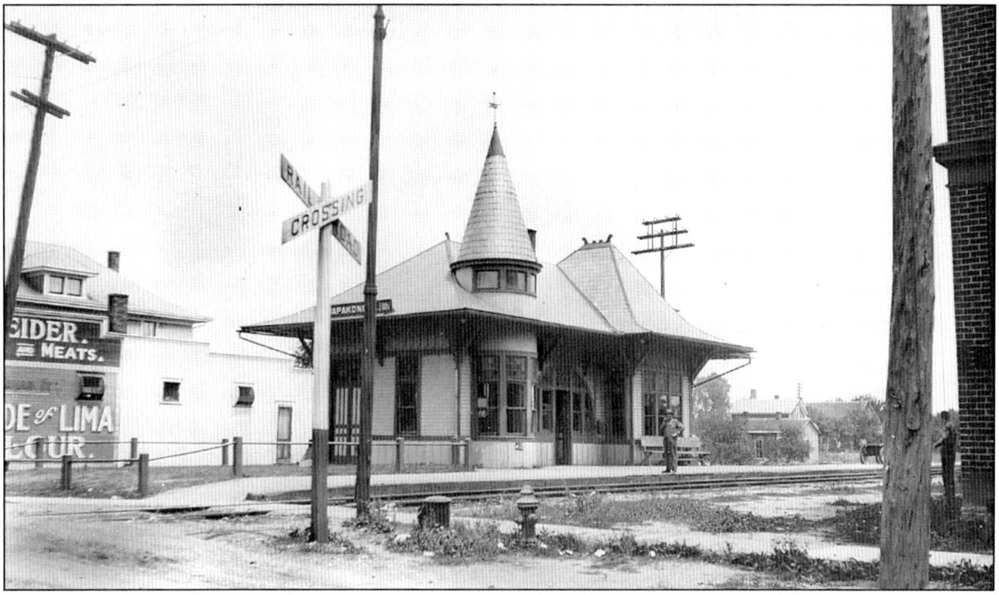

The T&OC passenger depot in Wapakoneta was an attractive structure. Nearby was a frame freight house. By the 1960s, the passenger depot was gone, and the freight house had received cast-iron town boards. The freight house now resides at the Auglaize County fairgrounds. A frame depot at Moulton lasted until Palm Sunday, March 28, 1920, when a tornado roared through town and ripped off the roof as well as destroying much of the town. It is not clear if it was rebuilt. If so, it did not survive the 1940s. (T&OC 1919 photograph, Allen County [Ohio] Historical Society collection.)

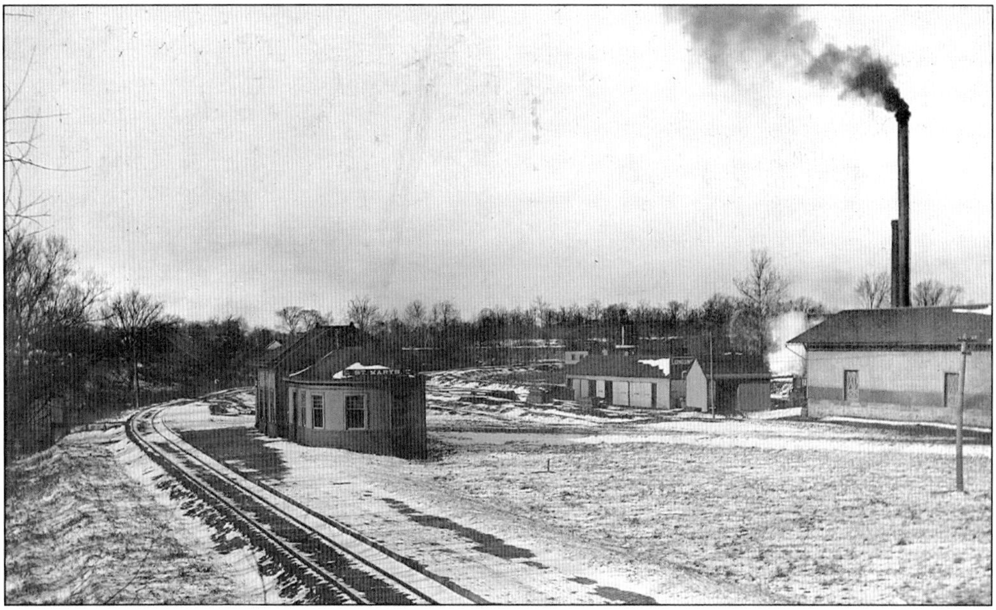

The destination of passenger trains on the St. Marys branch was this 1910 passenger depot in the river valley at St. Marys. The depot was periodically inundated with floodwaters. Nearby was a large frame freight house, which outlived the passenger depot by many years. The earlier depot reportedly is a residence in town. (Mark J. Camp collection.)

Four

Nickel Plate Lines

The New York, Chicago and St. Louis Railroad (NYC&StL), commonly known as the Nickel Plate, opened between Buffalo and Chicago in 1882. By 1964, when it was taken over by the Norfolk and Western Railway, the line had acquired the Lake Erie and Western (LE&W), Toledo, St. Louis and Western (TStL&W), and Wheeling and Lake Erie Railroads, providing connections to Peoria, St. Louis, and the southeastern Ohio coalfields. The Lake Erie and Western and Toledo, St. Louis and Western served the west central Ohio area.

September 1872 marked the opening of the Lake Erie and Louisville Railroad between Findlay and Rawson. This was an extension of the original Fremont and Indiana Railroad that linked Findlay and Fremont in 1860. The line reached Bluffton in late September, Lima in November 1872, and St. Marys in September 1873. The original plans called for the line to terminate at Union (City), but the line was only completed through New Bremen and Minster before it was decided to continue the line west from St. Marys to Peoria, Illinois. Celina, Coldwater, and Fort Recovery were reached in 1879. (The New Bremen–Minster stretch was retained as a branch.) After a consolidation with an Indiana line, it became the Lake Erie and Western Railway in August 1879. In 1922, the line was absorbed by the Nickel Plate.

The Toledo, Cincinnati and St. Louis Railroad emerged from the 1881 consolidation of a number of narrow-gauge (three-foot) lines across Ohio, Indiana, and Illinois dating back to 1874. Grandiose plans to link a series of narrow-gauge lines from coast to coast continued but were doomed to failure. In Ohio, the activity centered on Delphos, where several lines met. Financial problems plagued the line from the offset, and it was reorganized as the Toledo, St. Louis and Kansas City Railroad in June 1886. At this time, it became known as the Clover Leaf and connected Toledo with Frankfort, Indiana. In 1887, the line was changed to standard gauge, and by 1889, connections were finalized with East St. Louis, Illinois. Another reorganization in 1900 produced the Toledo, St. Louis and Western Railroad. The NYC&StL took over the Clover Leaf in December 1922.

Both the LE&W and Clover Leaf used standardized depot plans and favored frame construction for all except the largest communities. LE&W depots remain in west central Ohio from Bluffton, Buckland, Fort Recovery, New Bremen, Rawson, and St. Marys. The relocated Clover Leaf depot from Fort Jennings was still standing, but in derelict condition, in 2004.

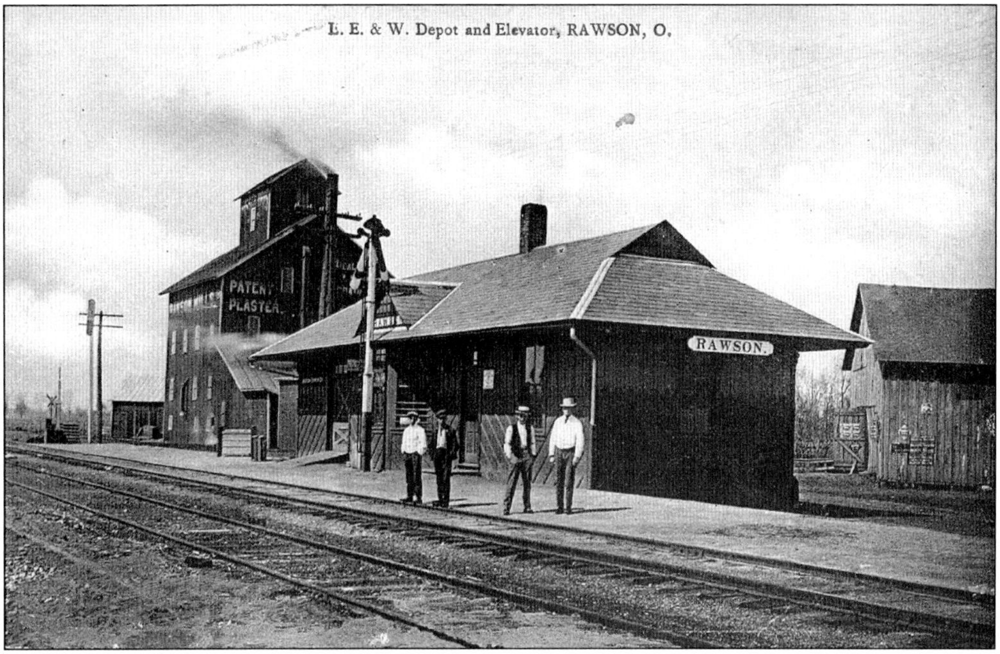

The LE&W built many depots like this along its lines across Ohio, Indiana, and Illinois. The first rails reached town in September 1872. The 1874 Rawson depot now resides in the town park. (Mark J. Camp collection.)

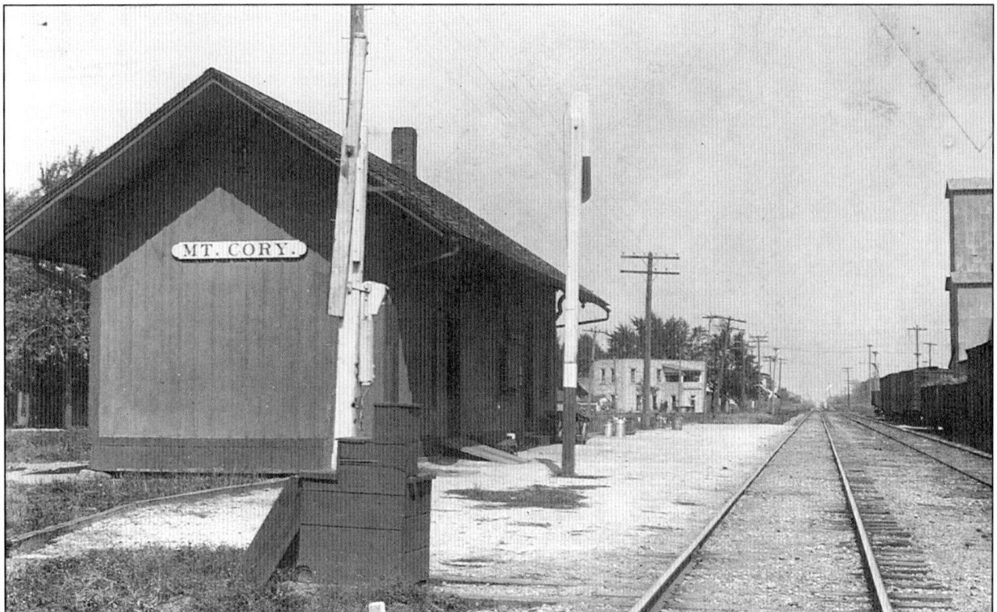

Mount Cory's combination depot follows another plan used by the LE&W. The building dates to 1874, shortly after the town was platted with the surveying of the Lake Erie & Louisville. The depot was gone by the 1960s. (Mark J. Camp collection.)

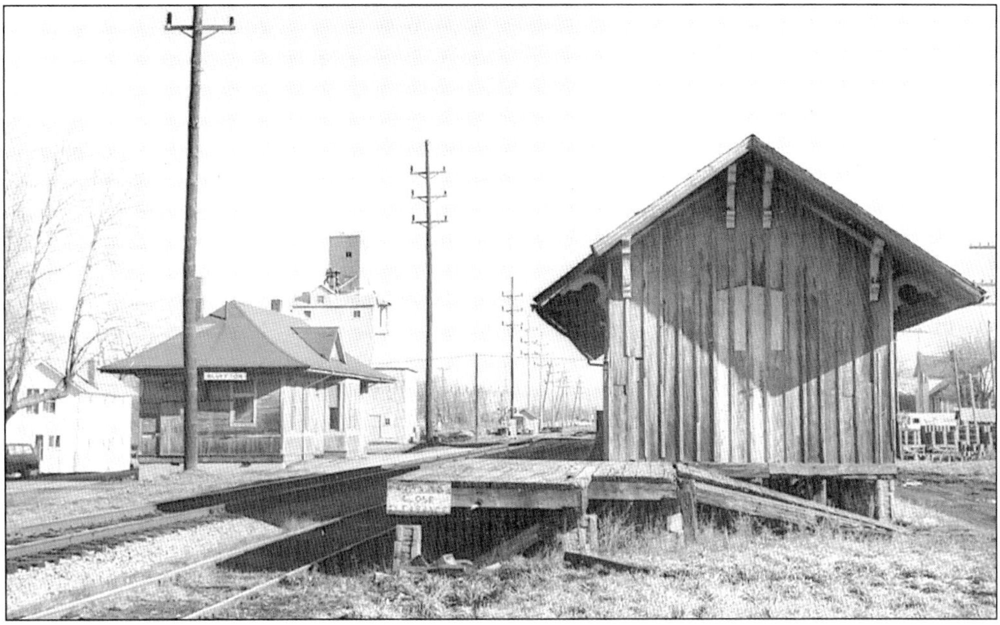

Bluffton in 1876 was served by a combination depot, probably the freight house seen in this 1971 view. It was rebuilt and enlarged in 1896. With the opening of Bluffton College in 1899, passenger business greatly increased, necessitating the new depot across the tracks. The new depot has since been moved downtown and converted to community use.

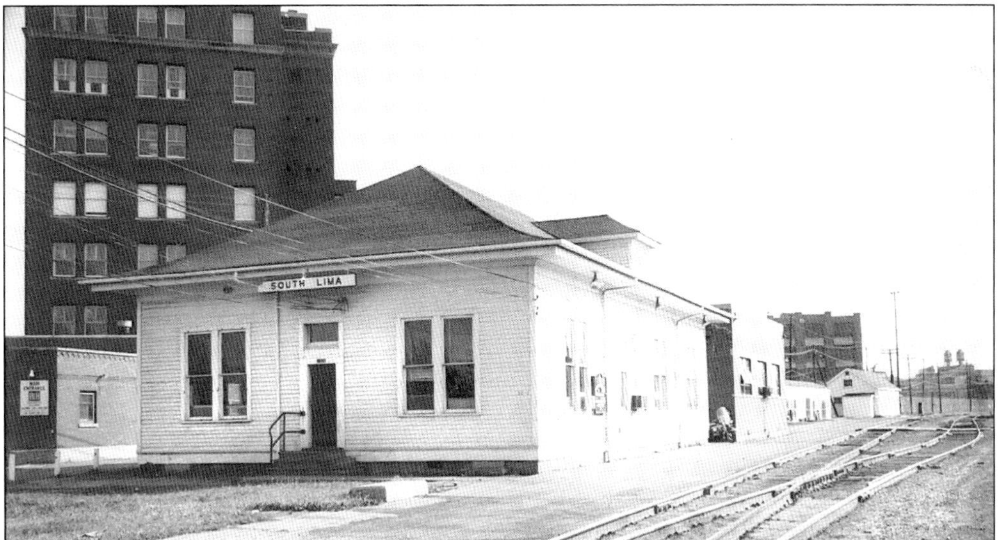

LE&W tracks reached Lima in November 1872. After the demolition of the French House, a railroad hotel in which its ticket office was located, the LE&W reportedly used the baggage building at the CH&D passenger depot across the tracks as its passenger depot. In South Lima, in the shadows of the Lima Locomotive Works, was this office building, which provided passenger service at one time. Note the platform along the tracks. Across the tracks was a roundhouse and other locomotive service facilities. Over the last decade, most of these buildings have disappeared. (Charles Garvin 1969 photograph; Mark J. Camp collection.)

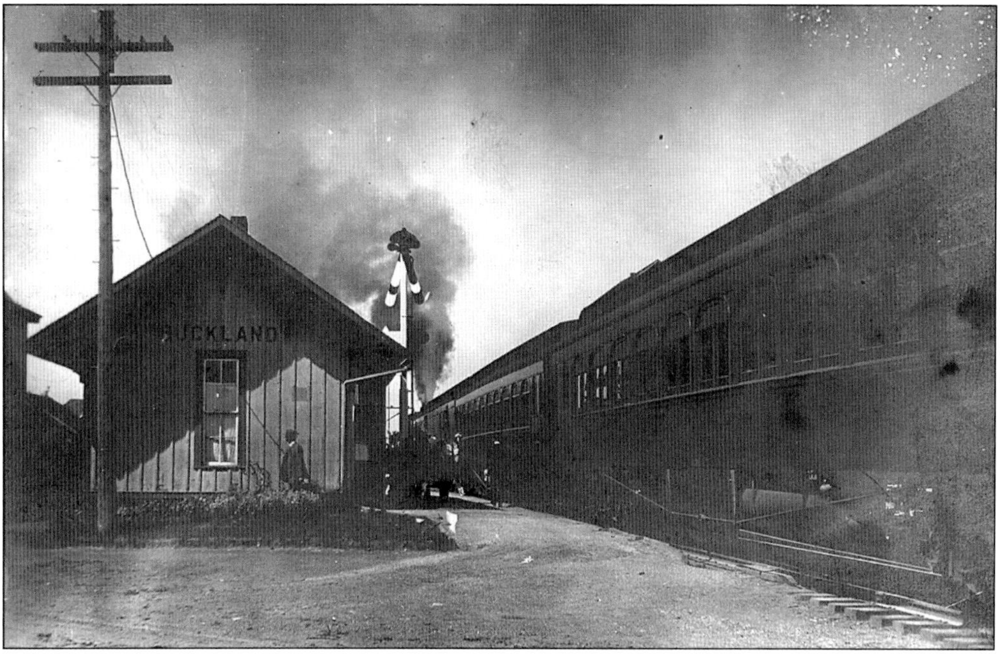

Passengers come and go in this 1908 scene in Buckland. The 1887 depot later was moved off-site and at least partially restored. (Mark J. Camp collection.)

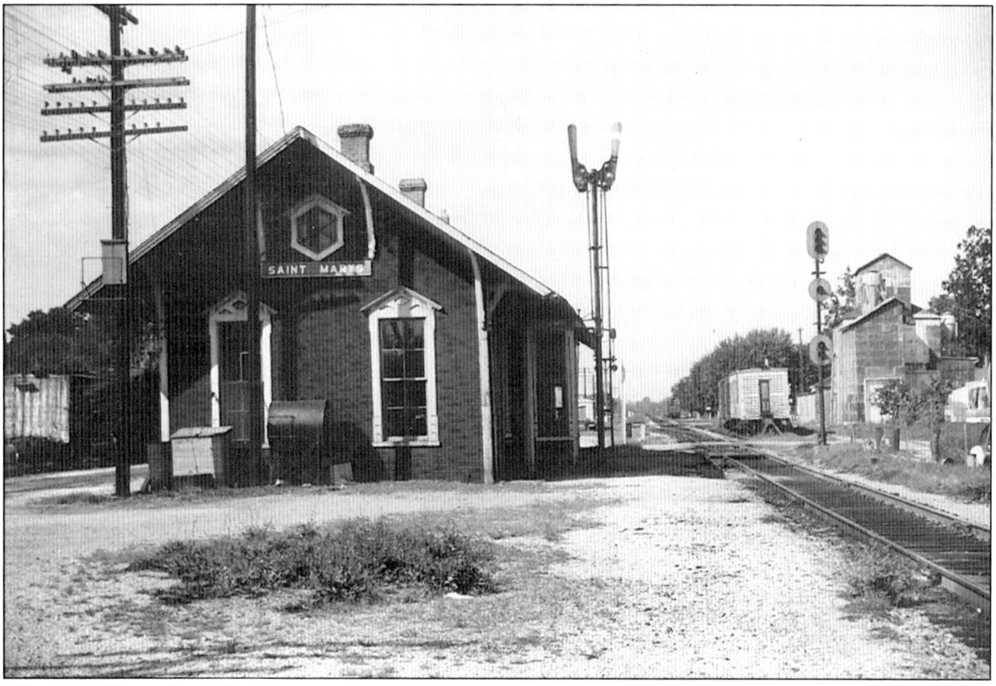

The LE&W reached St. Marys in late 1873. The depot dates to 1878. In the mid-1900s, the line covered many of its depots with brick shingle siding in a depot modernization plan. The depot was allowed to deteriorate in recent years. Its fate is undetermined at the time of this writing. (Charles Garvin 1967 photograph; Mark J. Camp collection.)

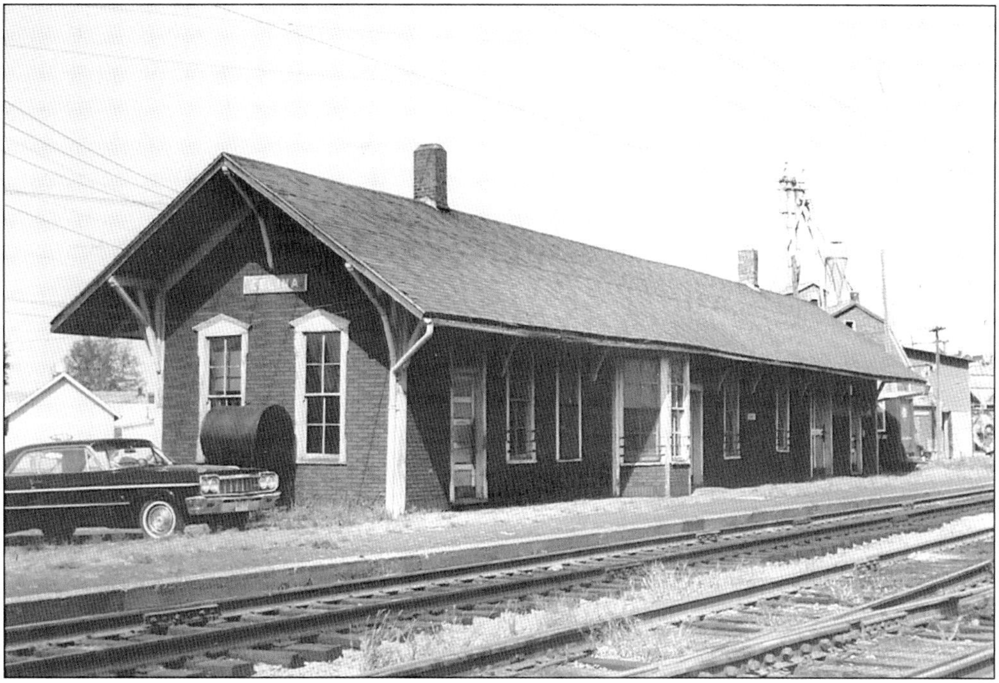

Note the similarity of Celina's now gone depot with that of St. Marys. The depot dates to 1880. It also was originally a frame depot. (Charles Garvin 1966 photograph; Mark J. Camp collection.)

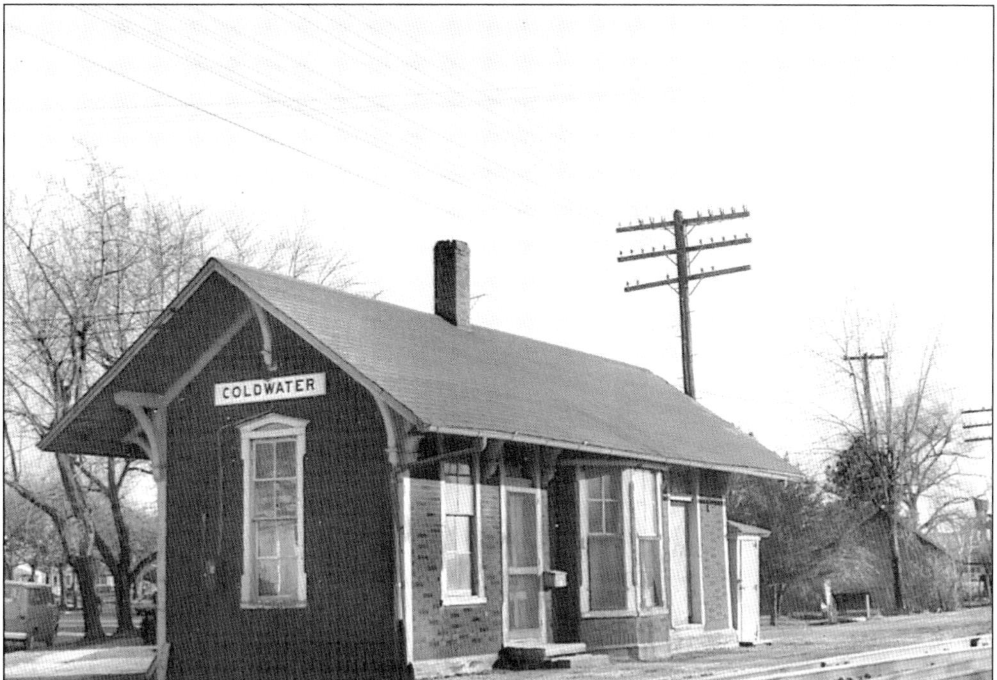

Coldwater, shown here in 1968, is yet another modification of the St. Marys plan. Coldwater was erected in 1880. Nearby was a small frame freight house. Both are now gone.

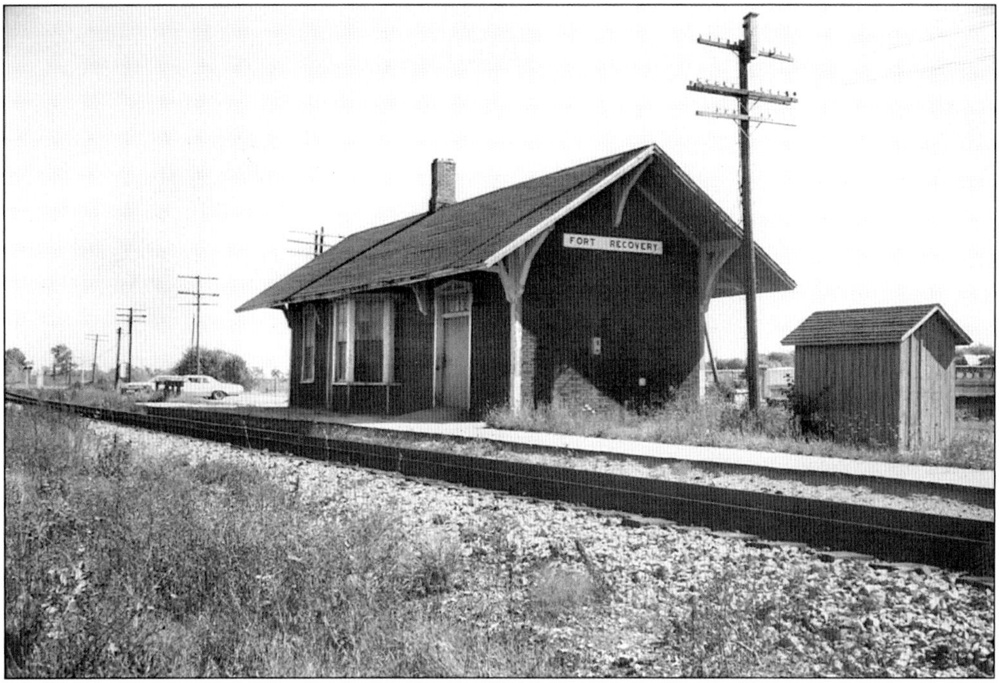

The westernmost LE&W depot in Ohio is this St. Marys variant at Fort Recovery. The 1879 depot was purchased by the town in 1973, relocated to a nearby park, and now serves as a railroad museum. (Charles Garvin 1969 photograph; Mark J. Camp collection.)

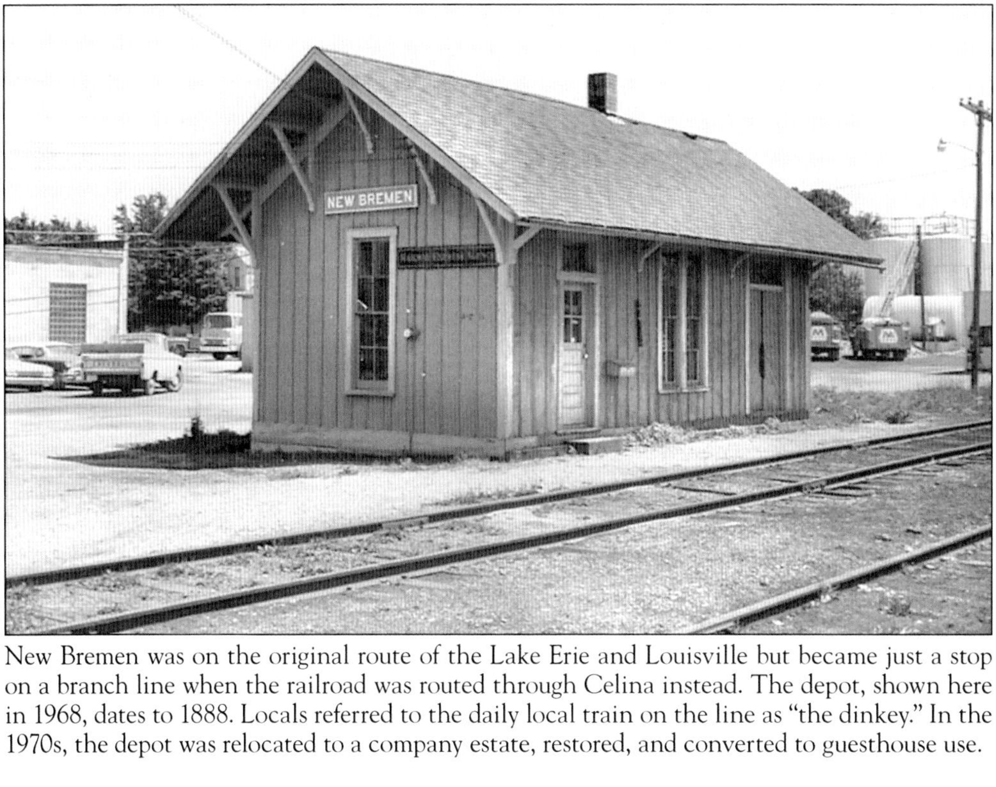

New Bremen was on the original route of the Lake Erie and Louisville but became just a stop on a branch line when the railroad was routed through Celina instead. The depot, shown here in 1968, dates to 1888. Locals referred to the daily local train on the line as "the dinkey." In the 1970s, the depot was relocated to a company estate, restored, and converted to guesthouse use.

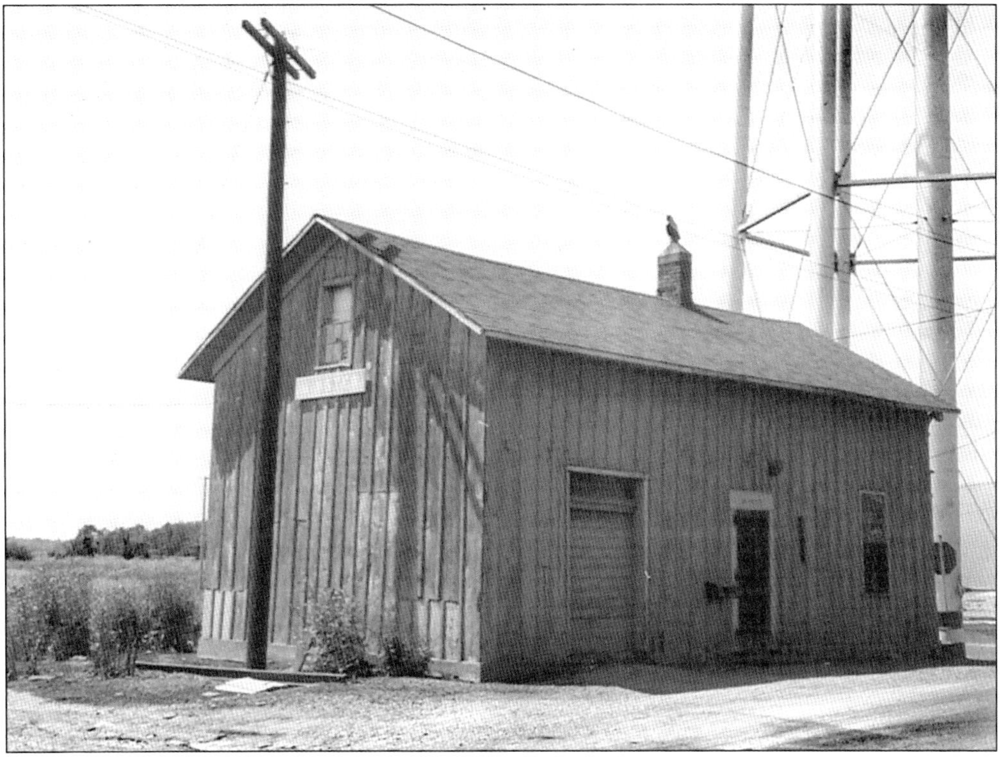

Minster became the terminus of the Minster branch, and this depot was built in 1876. This view of the rather atypical Minster depot was taken shortly before it was torn down in 1968.

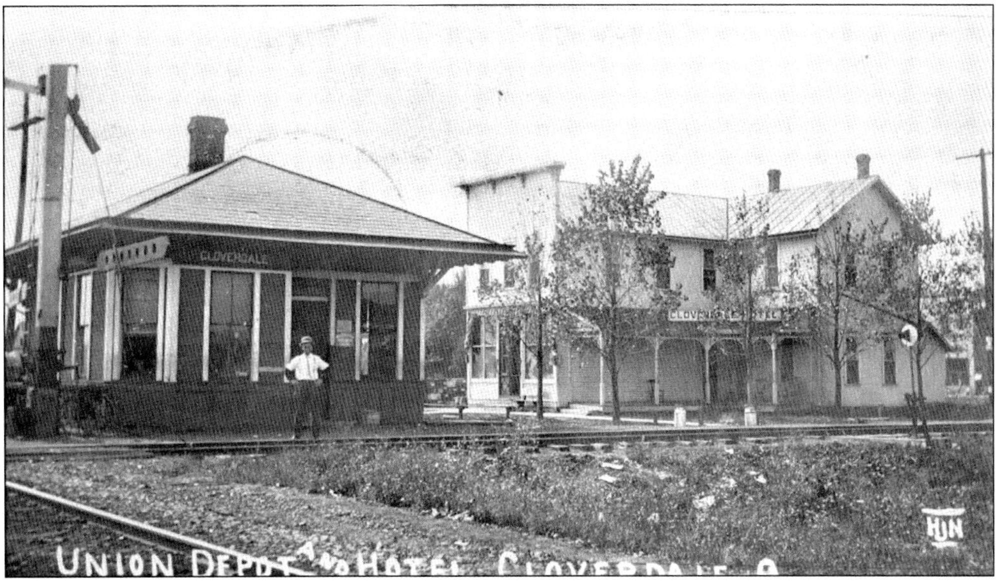

The Clover Leaf crosses the Findlay, Fort Wayne and Western in Cloverdale. The joint depot at this site, painted in CH&D colors, was built around 1891. Smash boards are in use in this 1907 view. (Mark J. Camp collection.)

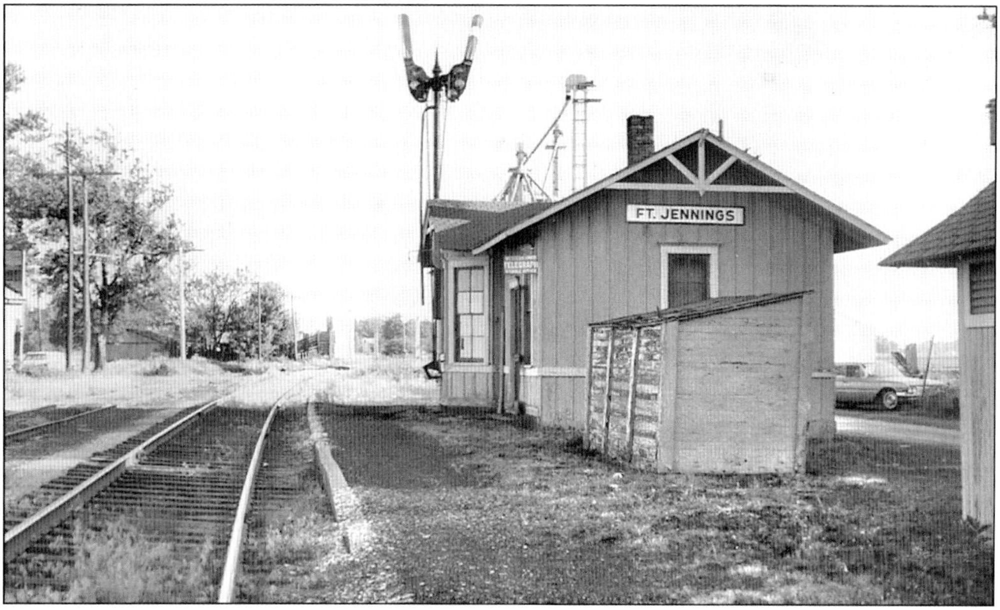

The TStL&W combination depot in Fort Jennings is still an open agency in this 1966 view and typical of small-town Clover Leaf depot architecture. Around 1973, the depot was moved into the country near Cloverdale. It was used as a residence for a while but now sits abandoned. (Charles Garvin photograph; Mark J. Camp collection.)

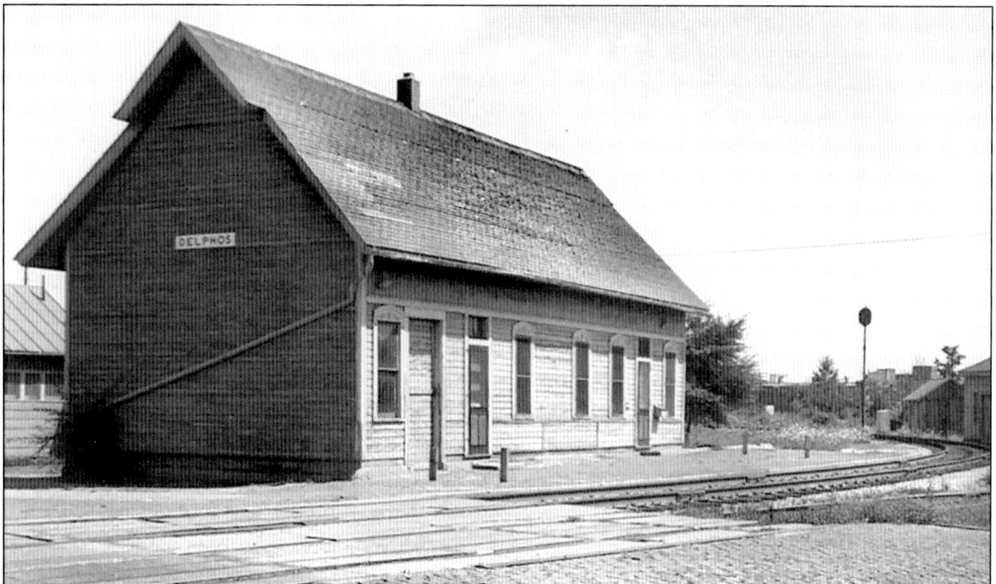

The Clover Leaf passenger and freight depots were located on this sweeping curve in Delphos just south of the PRR depot by 1883. The high peaked roof of this depot was uncharacteristic of TStL&W depots. The freight house is just to the right in this 1967 view. The old Toledo, Delphos and Burlington shops were located on the north edge of town. Originally the Toledo, St. Louis and Kansas City depot was located diagonally across from the PRR depot. Nothing remains in Delphos except for a newer concrete block building near the former interchange with the Akron, Canton and Youngstown.

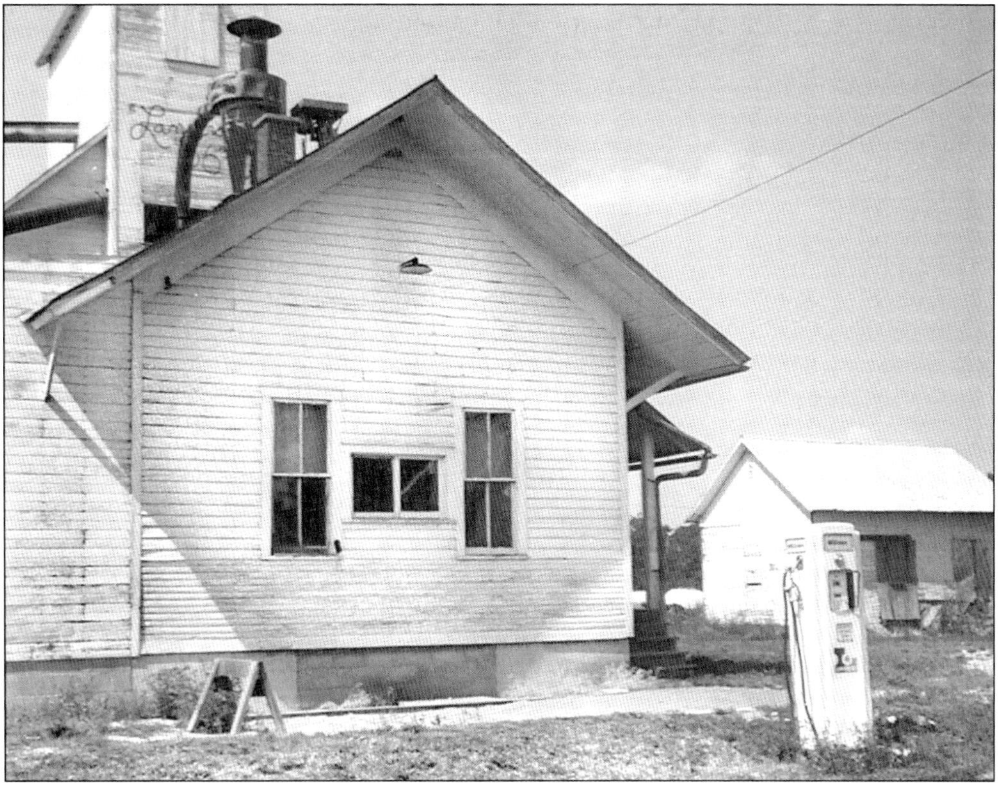

Venedocia's TStL&W depot was relocated and, in 1967, was part of this grain facility. It has since been torn down.

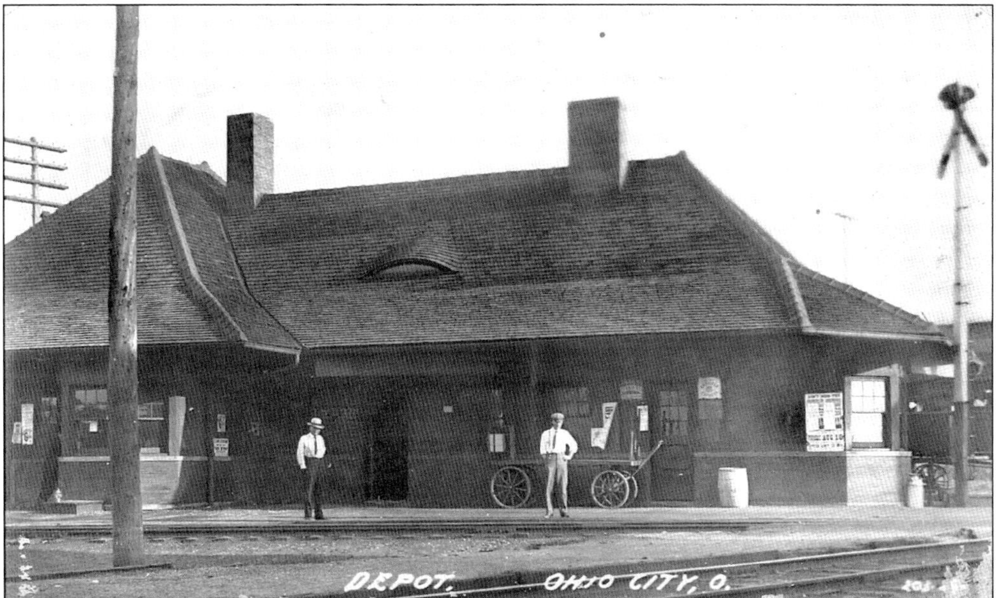

Ohio City's union depot also served the Clover Leaf. Here is still another view on the TStL&W side of the building. Track in the foreground belongs to the CN. (Mark J. Camp collection.)

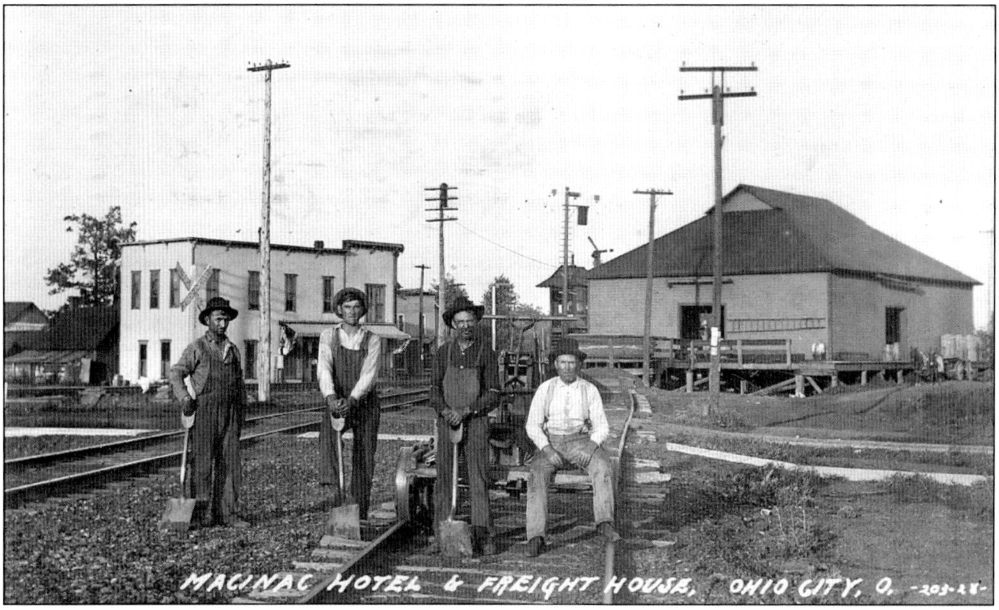

Union depot in Ohio City is hidden behind this freight house. Gandy dancers pose with their handcar, taking a break from a hard day's work with the ballast. (Mark J. Camp collection.)

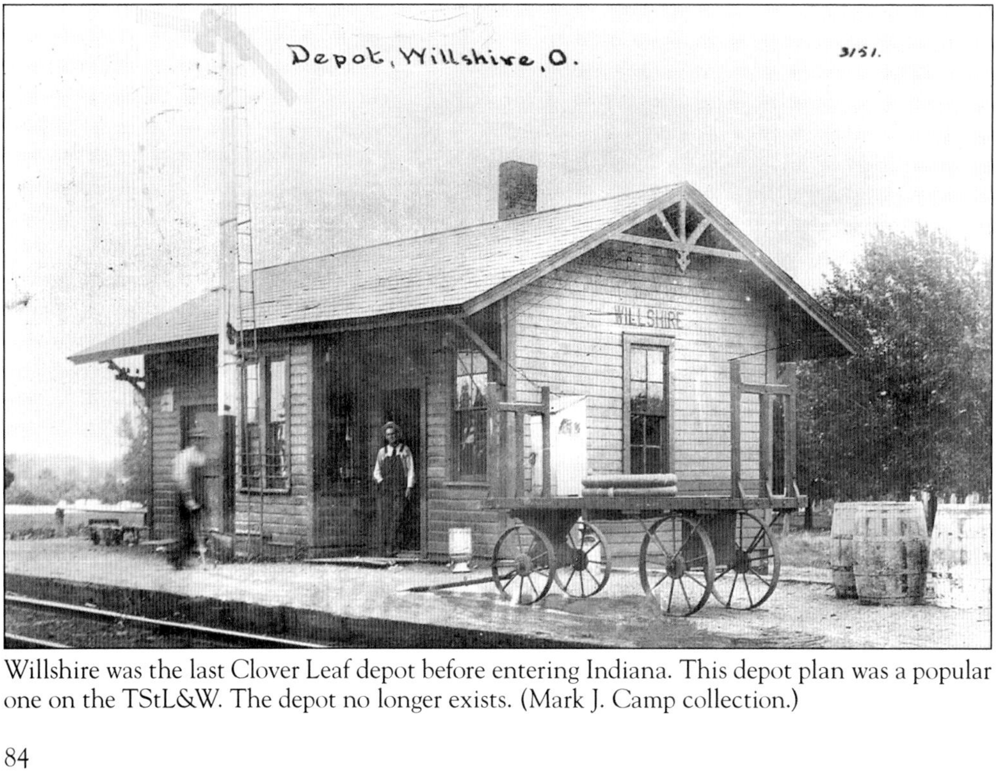

Willshire was the last Clover Leaf depot before entering Indiana. This depot plan was a popular one on the TStL&W. The depot no longer exists. (Mark J. Camp collection.)

Five

THE PENNSYLVANNIA RAILROAD

The year 1848 marks the chartering of the Ohio and Pennsylvania Railroad, a line projected west from the Ohio River across Ohio. As early as 1851, this corporation drew the attention of the Pennsylvania Railroad as it continued its western push. By 1852, the Ohio and Indiana Railroad formed to extend the Ohio and Pennsylvania line from Crestline to Fort Wayne and beyond. By 1855, both lines had been completed from near Pittsburgh to Fort Wayne. Financial problems arose by 1856, and the two lines along with the Fort Wayne and Chicago Railroad, the under construction connection to Chicago, consolidated to become the Pittsburgh, Fort Wayne and Chicago Rail Road (PFtW&C) in July 1856. Continued problems resulted in another reorganization in 1861 when it became the Pittsburgh, Fort Wayne and Chicago Railway. The PRR formally leased the Fort Wayne line in July 1869.

The Pennsylvania Railroad's connection to Toledo and Detroit involved four lines. The first of these was the Mansfield, Coldwater and Lake Michigan Railway projected to extend from a point near Mansfield northwest to Allegan, Michigan. The stretch from Toledo Junction on the Fort Wayne line to Tiffin was put in operation in May 1873. The grade was essentially completed to Allegan, but only certain sections ever saw any track. Track between Tiffin and Weston was pulled up around 1874, and the PRR sought other connections to Toledo—the Toledo, Tiffin and Eastern and Toledo and Woodville Railroads. The PRR formally leased this route, then known as the Northwestern Ohio Railway, in 1879. The Pennsylvania Railroad also took over the Columbus, Sandusky and Hocking Railroad (built in 1895) from Sandusky to Columbus by way of Bucyrus and Marion in west central Ohio in 1902. This line later was sold to the Norfolk and Western.

On the west side of Ohio, the Pennsylvania's interest began with the Columbus, Chicago and Indiana Central Railway (CC&IC) formed in 1868. This line had trackage from Columbus to Union City but was building on to Logansport. It completed a line extending off this earlier line from Bradford to New Paris and on to Indianapolis in 1863. In 1869, the CC&IC merged with the Pittsburgh, Cincinnati and St. Louis Railway, known commonly as the Panhandle, to become the Pittsburgh, Cincinnati, Chicago and St. Louis Railway. In 1916, after more consolidations, the line became the Pittsburgh, Cincinnati, Chicago and St. Louis Railroad, also familiarly referred to as the Panhandle. The Panhandle was formally leased to the PRR in January 1921.

The Pennsylvania Railroad had a series of standard depot plans over the years. Those still existing follow early-1900s plans. Unfortunately, depots at Ada, Covington, Lima, Union City, and Urbana are the only ones still extant in this part of Ohio.

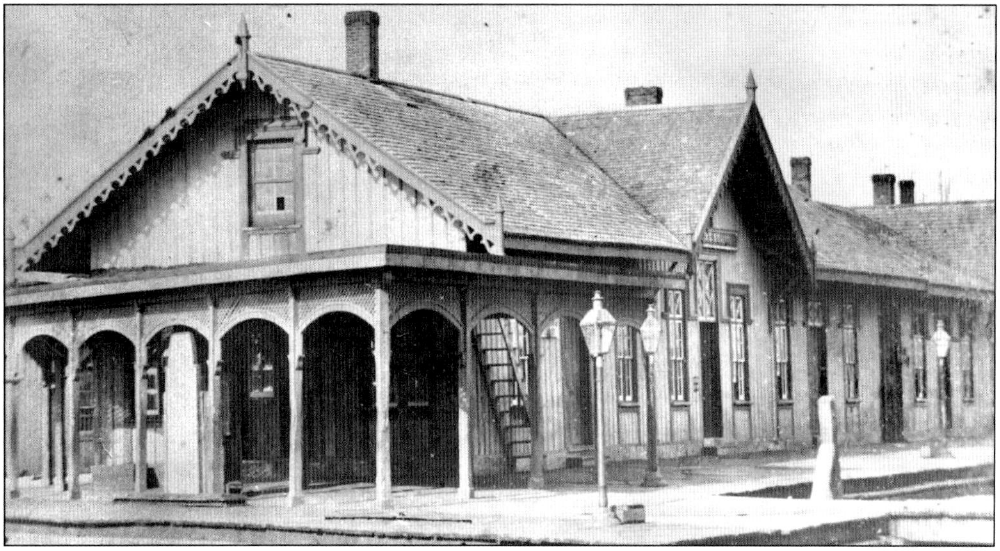

The above depot was completed in Crestline in June 1853 and shared by the Ohio and Indiana, Ohio and Pennsylvania, and Cleveland, Columbus and Cincinnati railroads. This important railroad junction was platted just three years earlier, originally as Livingston. In 1864, this structure was replaced by the three-story, wedge-shaped brick depot-hotel, below, serving the PFtW&C and Bellefontaine or Bee lines. By 1896, the building contained three waiting rooms located at the narrow end of the building with an adjoining ticket office, a lunch room, dining hall, kitchen, and store room on the Big Four side of the building, and a hotel office, reading room, bar, lunch room, and baggage room on the PRR side. The upper floors contained hotel rooms, railroad offices, and crew rooms. Across and down the tracks were an interlocking tower and other hotels, lunchrooms, bars, barbershops, and businesses. By the 1960s, the depot had been reduced to a single-story depot. The New York Central closed its offices in the depot around 1959, while the PRR closed its agency around 1963. The depot was demolished around 1970. (Above, Bob Lorenz collection; below, Mark J. Camp collection.)

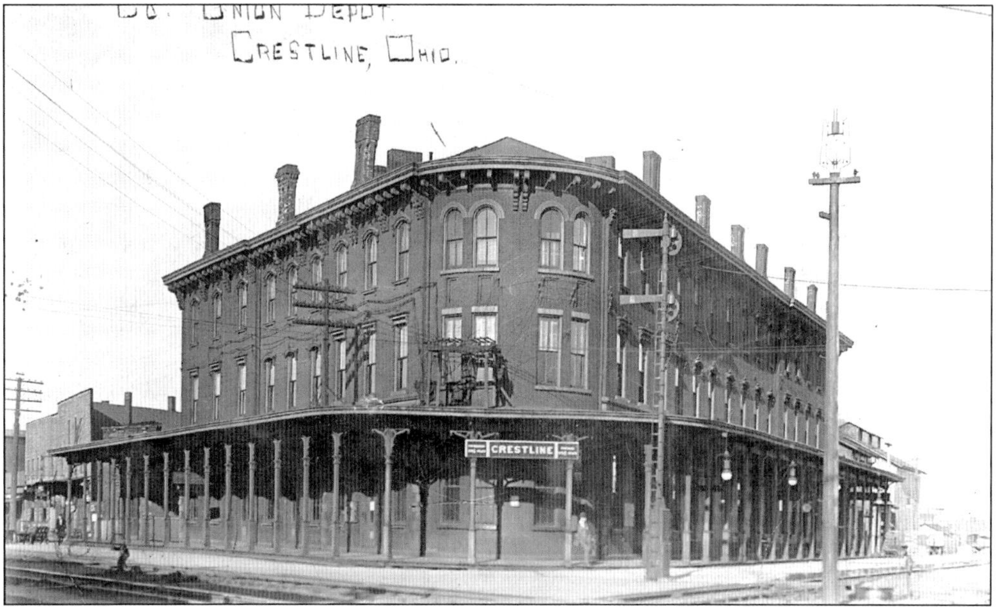

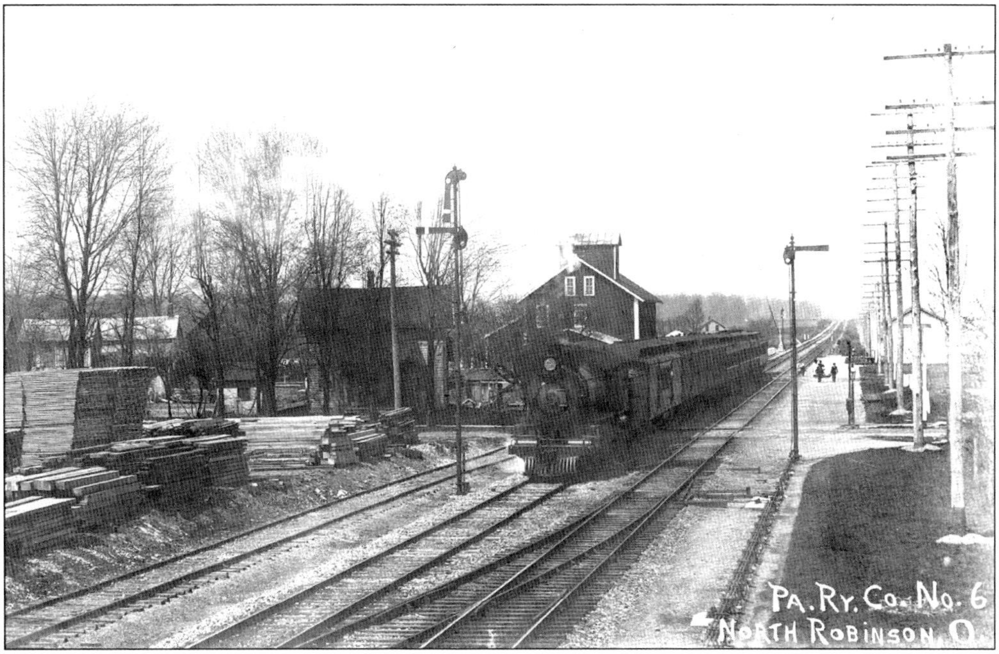

Passengers head home after detraining at the North Robinson depot around 1908. This photograph was probably taken from the stairs of the PRR interlocking tower just out of view in the foreground. Both structures have been gone for some time. (Mark J. Camp collection.)

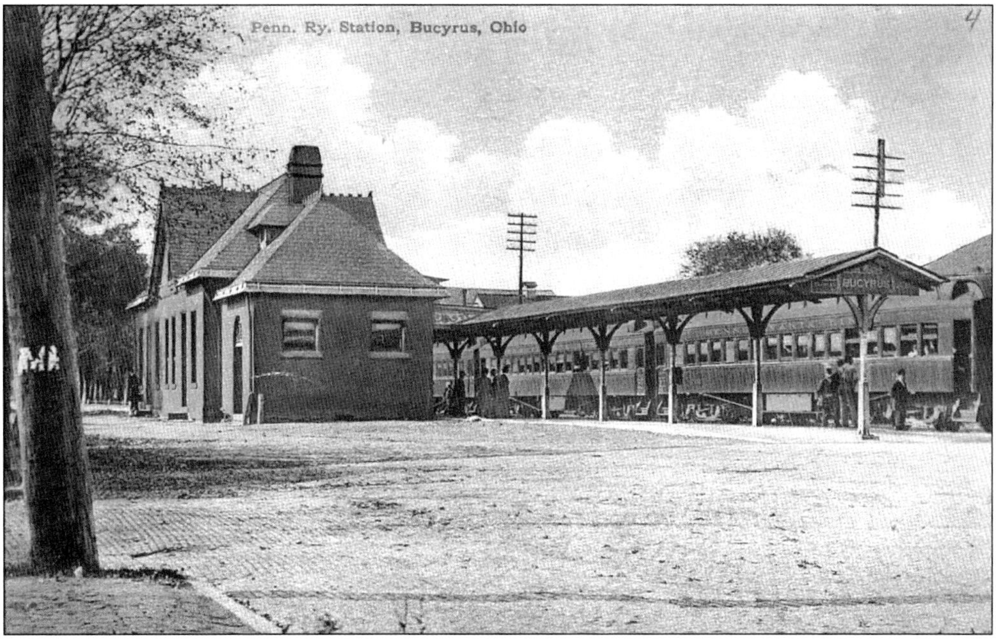

This is Pennsy's main line passenger depot in Bucyrus around 1909. Hidden by the coaches is the freight house, the only structure that still stood by 1967. (Mark J. Camp collection.)

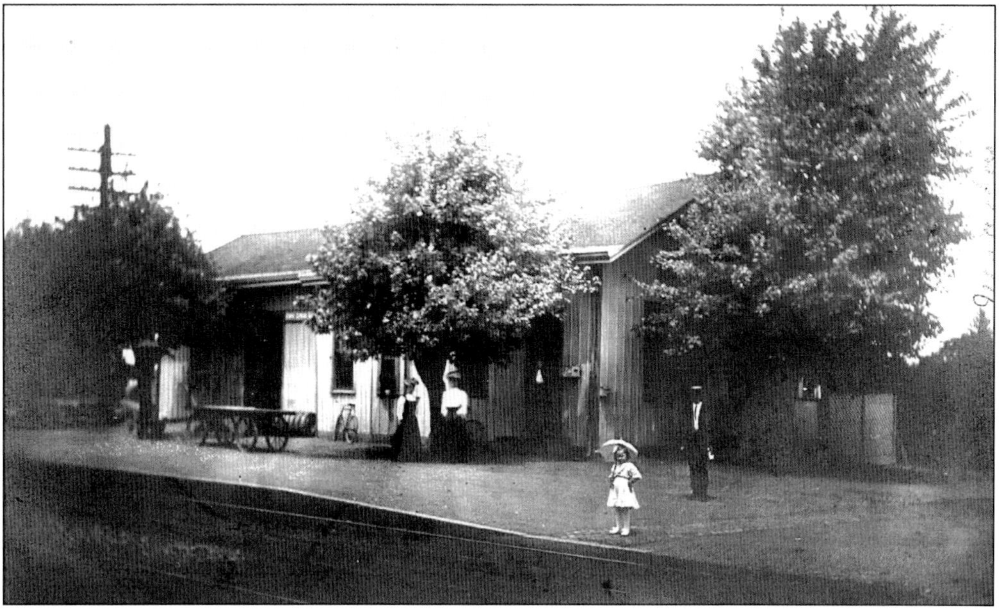

This young lady and her father await the arrival of the next train on the platform of Nevada's PRR depot. The depot probably dates to the 1870s. It was gone by the 1960s. (Mark J. Camp collection.)

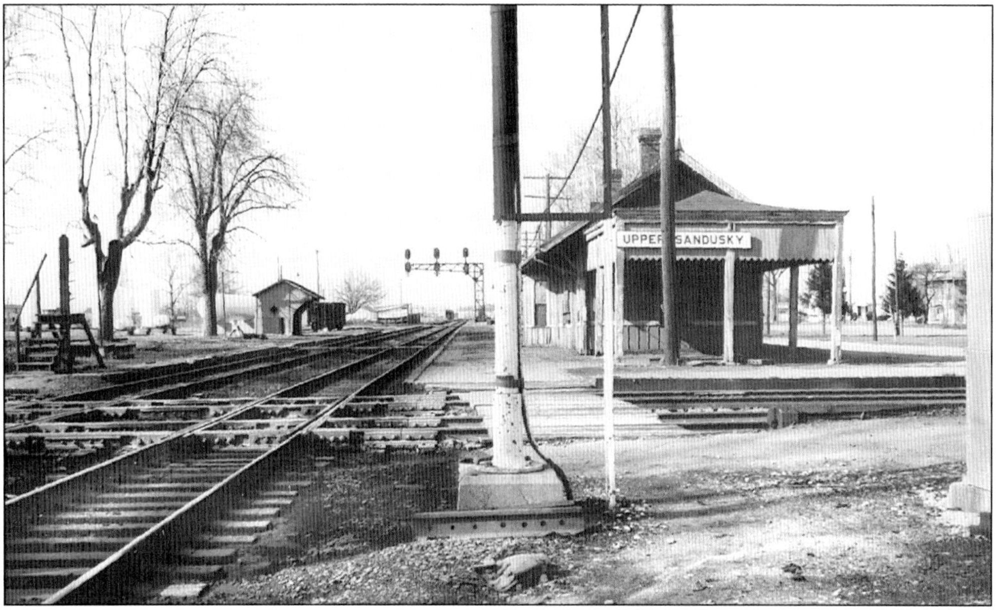

The first Fort Wayne and Chicago train to reach Upper Sandusky was on January 1, 1854. Later passenger and freight depots were built; the brick freight house was still standing in the 1960s. In October 1901, the PRR switched its passenger facility to the Hocking Valley depot, shown above, on the west side of town. A PRR interlocking tower guarded the crossing just out of view to the left. Three water tanks and a pump house along the Sandusky River on the east side of town were also once part of the scene. The tanks were torn down in 1954 for their lumber. Most of the Upper Sandusky structures were removed in the late 1970s. (Charles Garvin 1969 photograph; Mark J. Camp collection.)

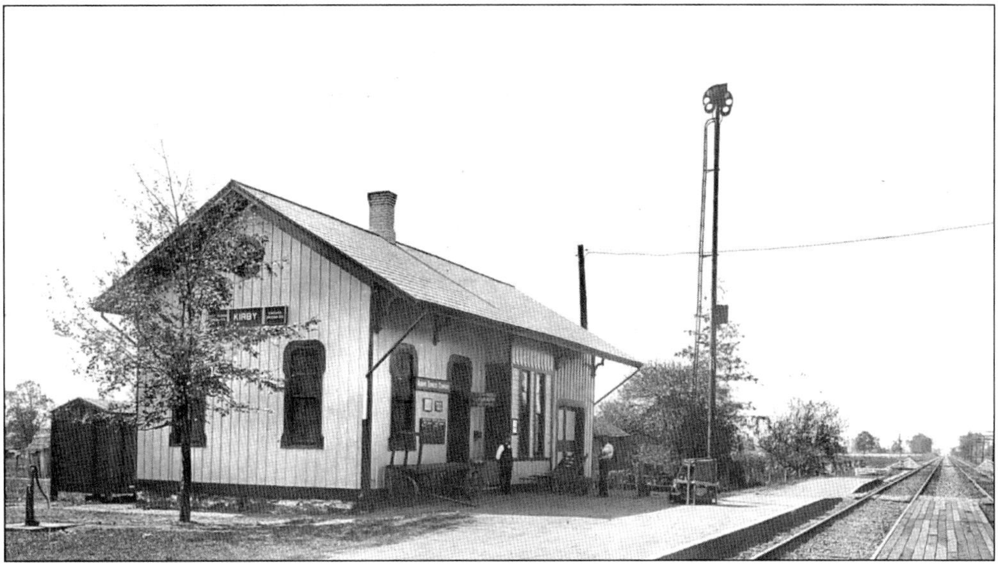

The PRR was double tracked to Fort Wayne by 1904. Here is a typical view of the PRR main at Kirby. Note the neatly manicured depot grounds and roadbed. It looks like the depot is getting a new order board. The Kirby combination depot is a design repeated many times along the Pennsy. (Mark J. Camp collection.)

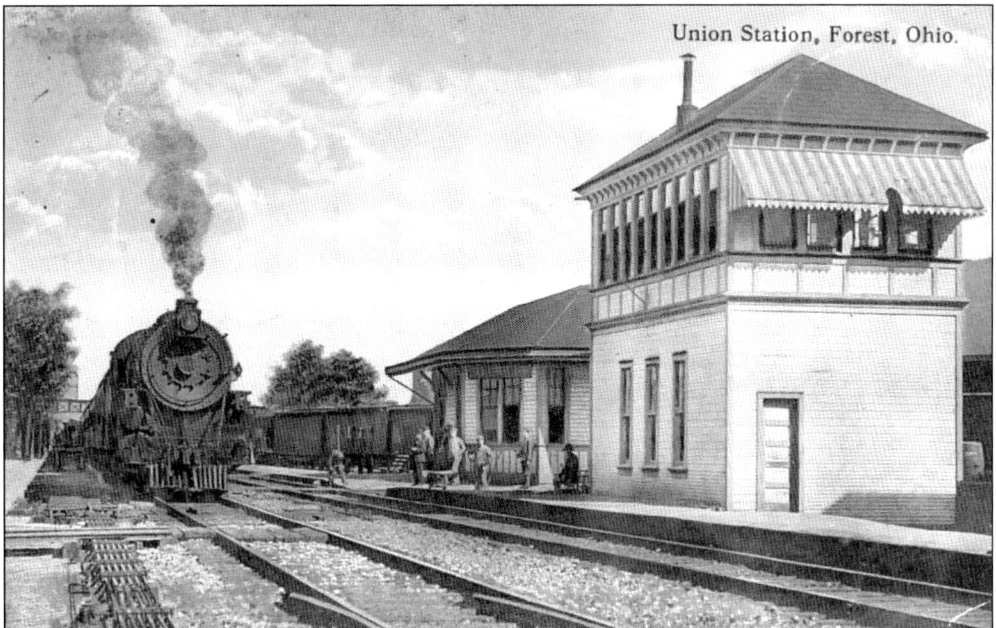

The Big Four crosses the PRR at this union depot and interlocking tower at Forest. Forest was laid out in 1855 with the arrival of the railroad. After a 1927 fire destroyed the union depot, a portion of the joint brick freight house was converted to handle passengers. This building later became a restaurant and now houses Forest-Jackson Public Library. (Mark J. Camp collection.)

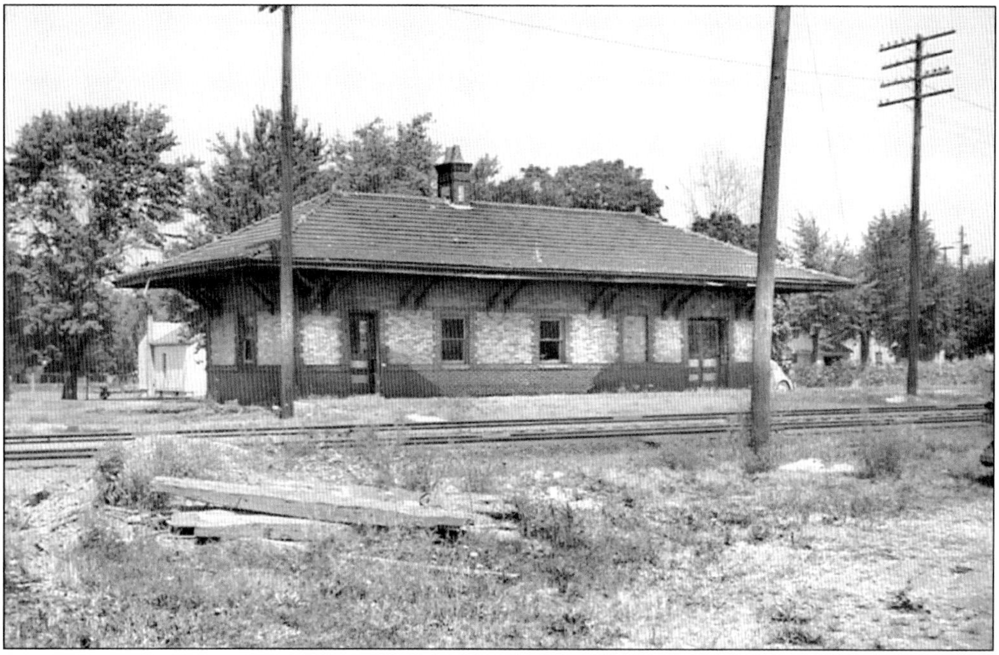

Dunkirk was born with the surveying of the Ohio and Indiana Railroad around 1852. This depot, shown in 1967, dates to around 1904, a replacement for an earlier frame depot. It was located near the diamond with the T&OC. The depot agency closed around 1956; the building was used by railroad maintenance crews into the 1970s. A brick interlocking tower remains diagonally across the diamond.

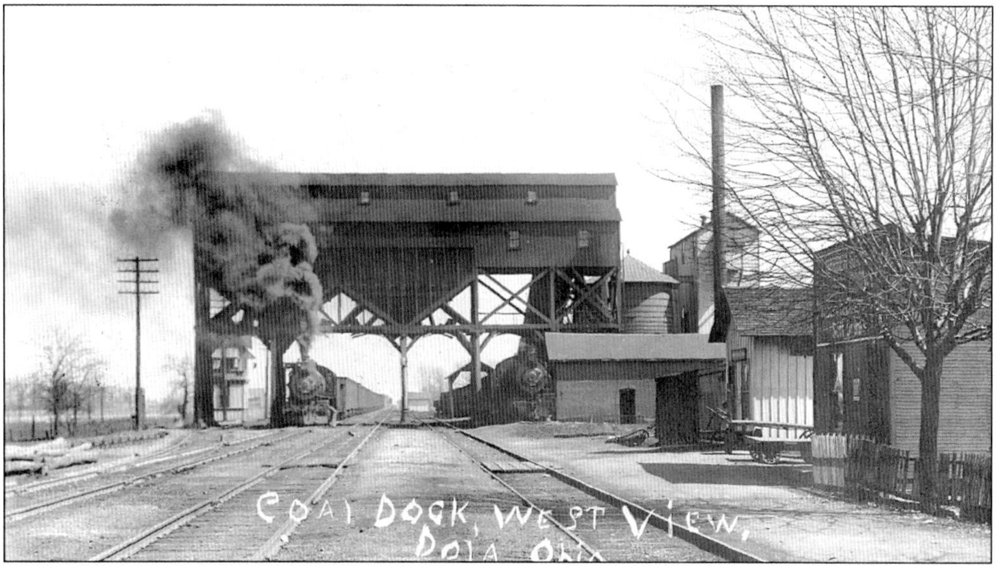

Dola is another child of the Ohio and Indiana—a necessary water station. The site was laid out in 1852. Later facilities included this coaling tower, water tank, and telegraph tower. To the right, next to the barbershop/store, is one of the smaller depot styles used on the PRR. Note the switcher on the coaling tower siding. Coal was dumped from hoppers into the pit under the shelter and then taken by conveyor belt to the bins above the tracks. The present village of Dola gives little indication of its former importance to the railroad. (Mark J. Camp collection.)

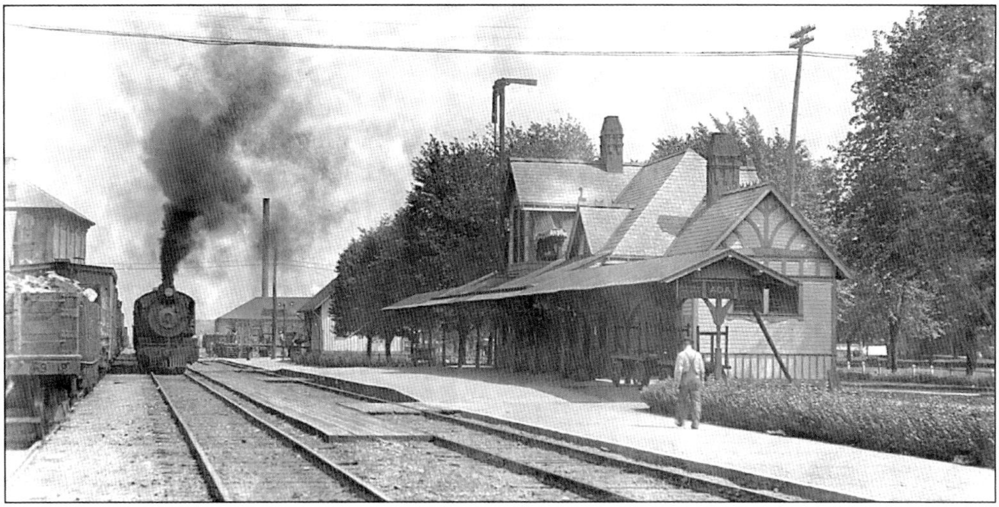

December 1887 marked the opening of Ada's new PRR depot. It replaced a frame combination depot that also served as a hotel. This was then relegated to freight use. The rapid growth of Ohio Normal University, now Ohio Northern University, in the 1880s was certainly instrumental in convincing the railroad new facilities were needed. The above view shows the passenger depot and freight house around 1910. The dormer room housed the telegraph operator in the early 1900s. After a number of crossing accidents, pneumatic gates and a gate-crossing tower were installed in 1904–1905 near the depot. The gate tower was removed in 1960. With the impending abandonment of the depot by the railroad, the Ada village council took steps to preserve the depot. The restored depot and surrounding depot park are now on the National Register of Historic Places. The older depot was torn down around 1950. (Mark J. Camp collection.)

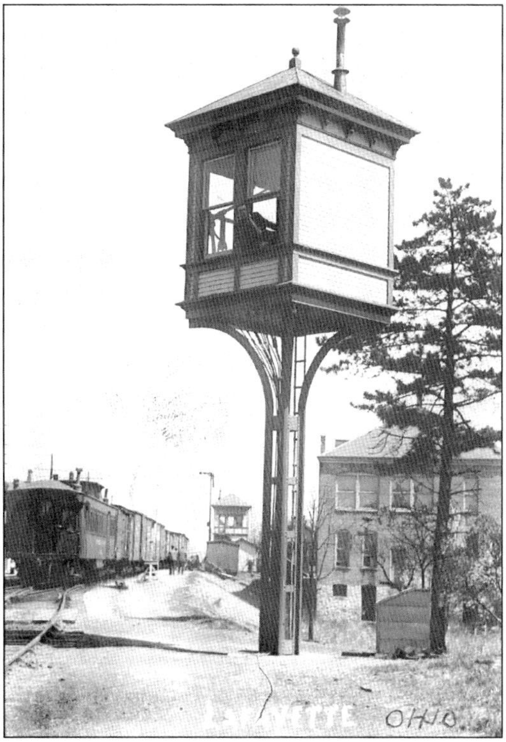

Although the depot is hidden behind the train, this Lafayette view from around 1907 shows a gate-crossing tower identical to the one constructed at Ada. Many of this design were built and lasted into the 1960s in many towns. A typical PRR signal tower is in the background. All are now gone. (Mark J. Camp collection.)

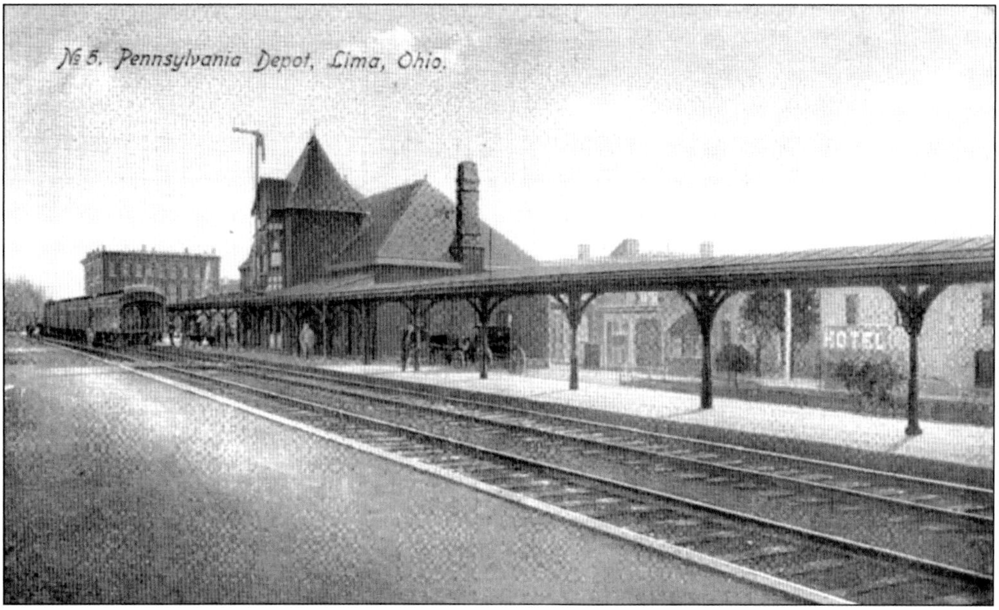

The PRR built this depot west of the crossing of the CH&D and LE&W in downtown Lima in the late 1800s, replacing an earlier frame structure. The telegraph operator occupied the second-story dormer in the early days. At the end of the platform shelter in the foreground was a brick freight house. Beyond the depot in the *c.* 1907 scene above is the French House, one of a number of railroad hotels stretching along the CH&D and LE&W tracks to the south. Out of view behind the depot is the CH&D passenger depot. By the 1970s view below, the platform shelter had been removed and depot maintenance curtailed. Note the passenger shelter across the tracks and the edge of the freight house just beyond the depot. An interlocking tower guarded the B&O and PRR crossing behind the photographer. After an interval of Amtrak service, the depot was closed. The French House and CH&D depot are gone. Only the PRR depot remains at this once important junction. (Mark J. Camp collection.)

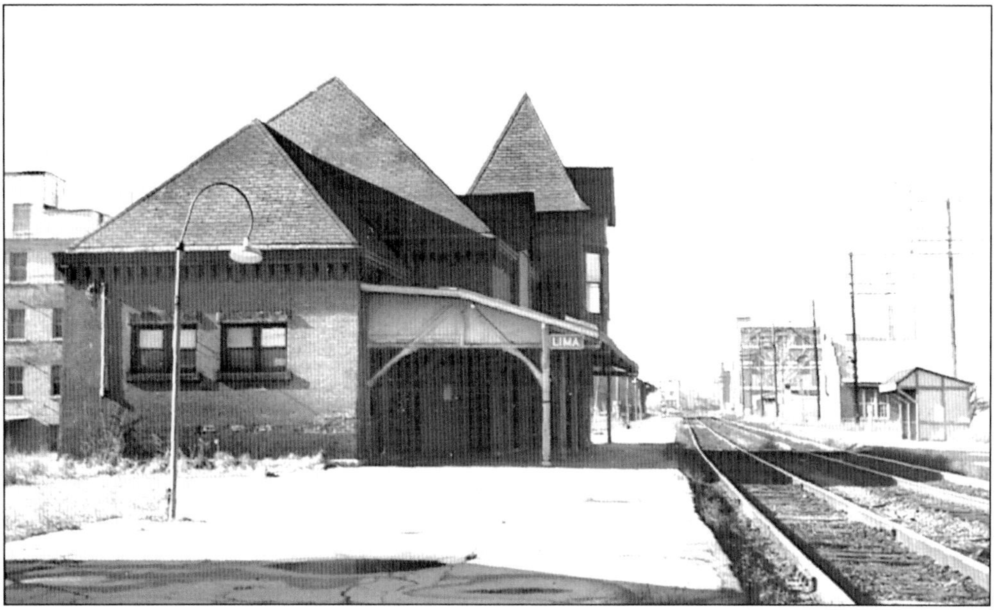

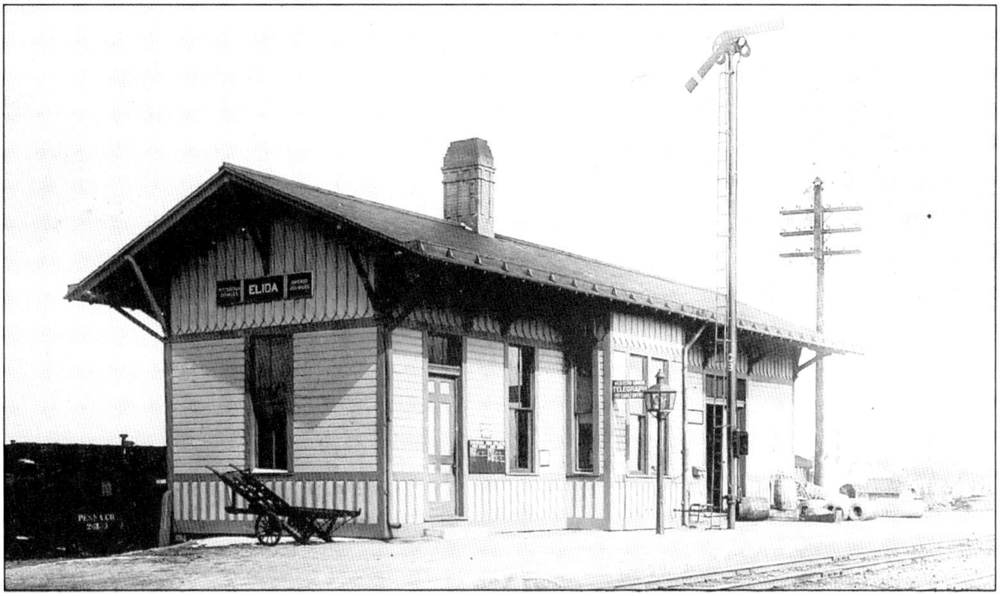

Elida's depot is an excellent example of a standard plan, small-town depot on the PRR of the late 1800s. Between AY tower, three miles east, and this depot, the PRR's Pennsylvania Special set a speed record of 127.1 miles per hour in June 1905. The record stood until 1966. Elida's depot was gone by that date. (Mark J. Camp collection.)

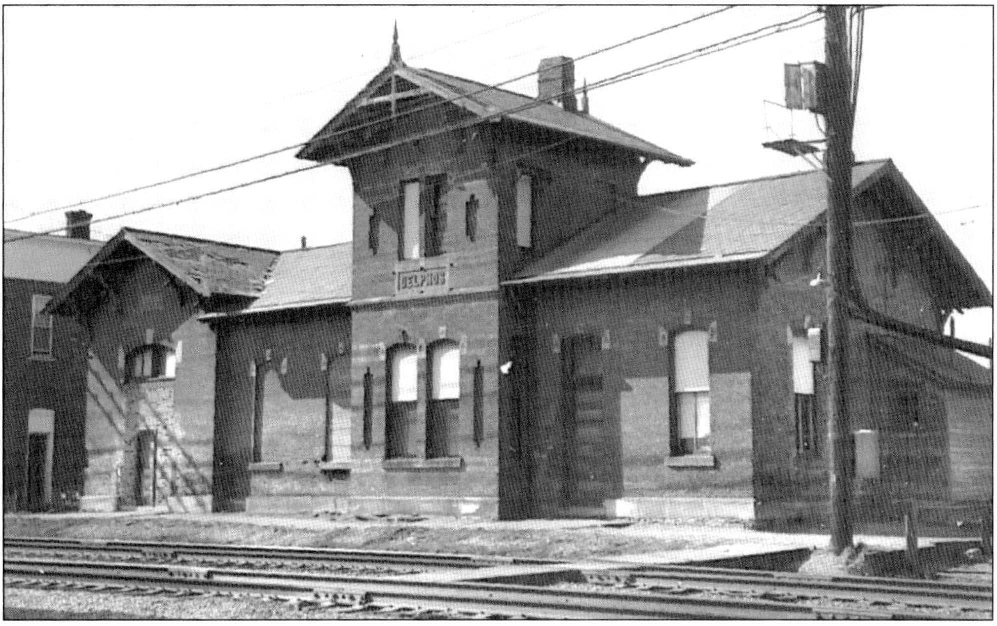

The PRR passenger depot in Delphos was erected in 1879; the date is embossed above the door on the left in this 1975 view. This early design, like Ada and Lima, included second-floor space for a telegraph office. This design was used at only a couple of locations in Ohio. Like in Crestline, rooming houses, lunchrooms, and other businesses fronted on the tracks next to the depot. To the right was an interlocking tower at the Clover Leaf crossing. Across the diamond was the former Cleveland, Delphos and St. Louis (later CH&D) depot and the former Toledo St. Louis and Kansas City depot. Nothing remains today.

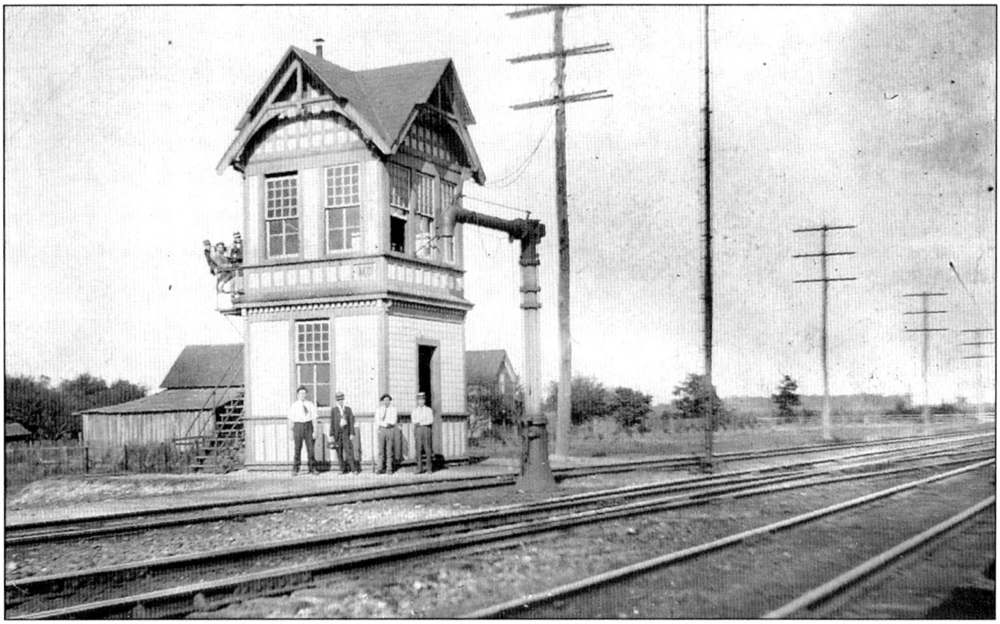

Middle Point began as a water station on the railroad in the early 1850s. This telegraph tower was built to a 1870s standard plan out of the PRR's engineering office. In the early 1900s, this style was replaced by a less ornate one. Besides the tower, Middle Point facilities included a water tank (note the water plug in above view) and the combination depot shown below in 1967. PRR closed its agency in Middle Point around 1962. All have since been removed from trackside. (Mark J. Camp collection.)

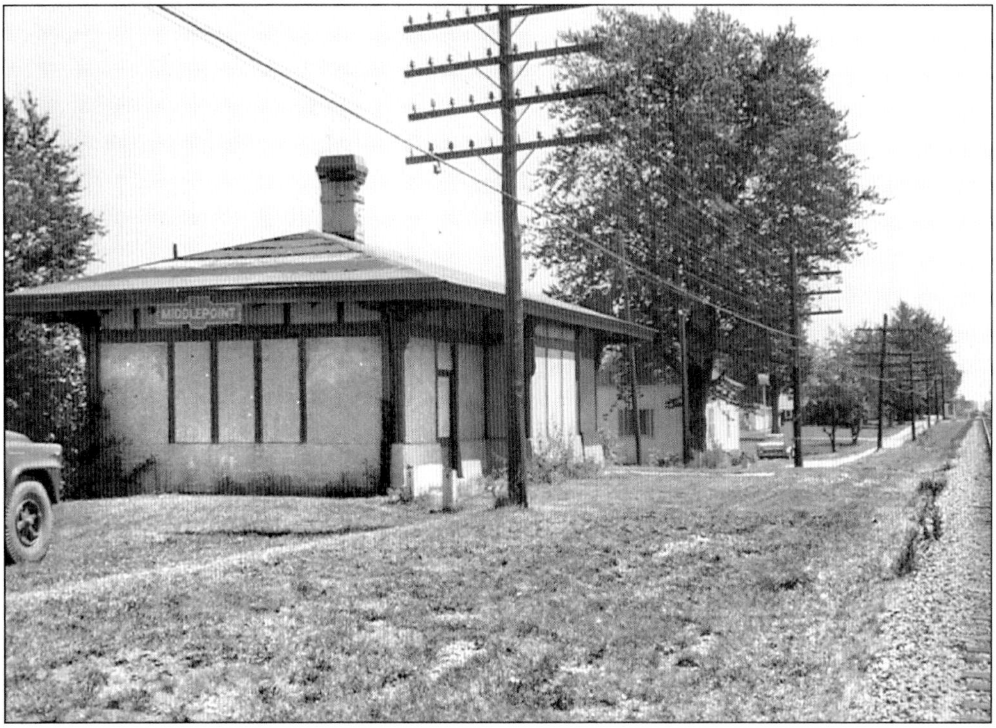

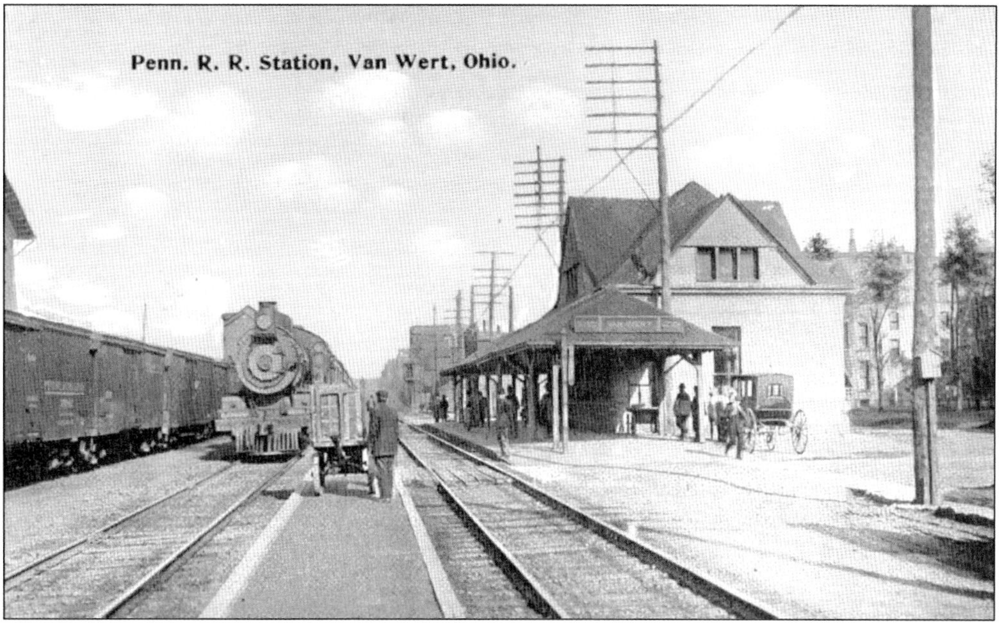

The PRR had separate passenger and freight depots at the Van Wert county seat, shown here around 1907 and in 1967. The Van Wert depots appear to date to the late 1870s through the early 1880s. Note that passengers await a train in both views, just about 60 years apart. PRR crossing-gate towers were located both east and west of the depot. The passenger depot was demolished in 1984. (Mark J. Camp collection.)

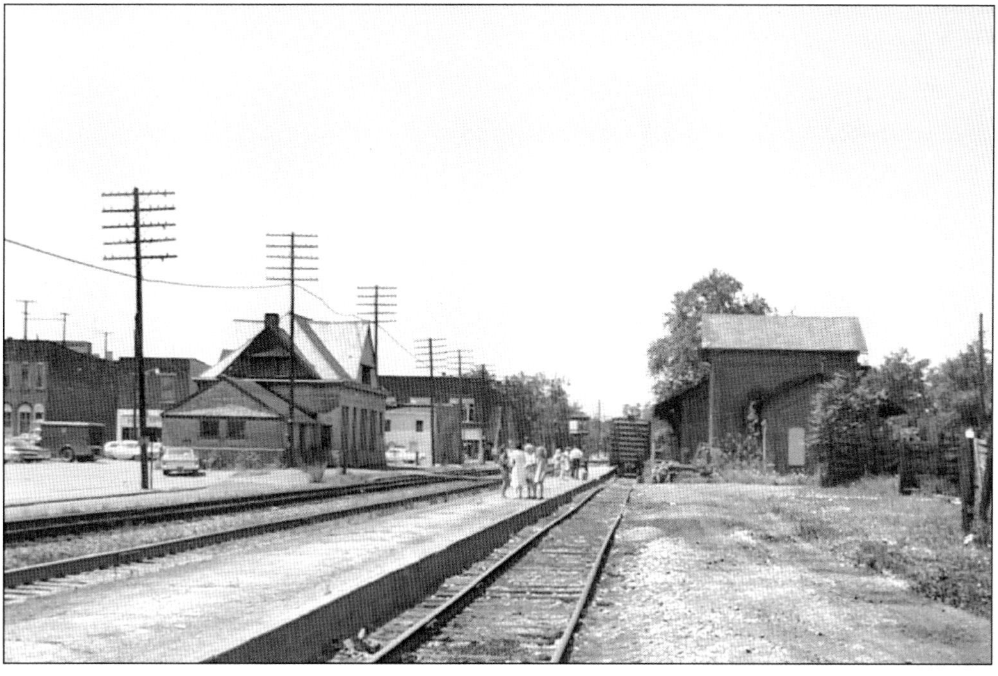

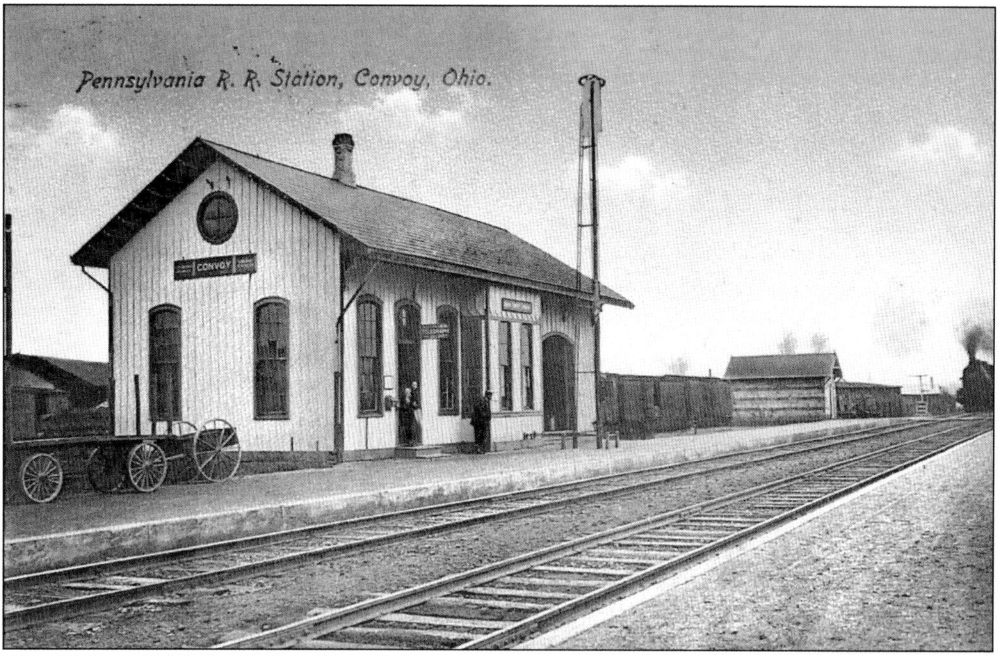

The PRR probably built the above depot at Convoy in the 1870s. It follows the same plan as the Kirby depot. The circular window and arched window frames and freight door made this an attractive design. By the 1960s, the depot had been replaced by this small structure, which handled mainly freight business. It is not clear if it was built on-site or moved in from another location. It has since been removed. (Mark J. Camp collection.)

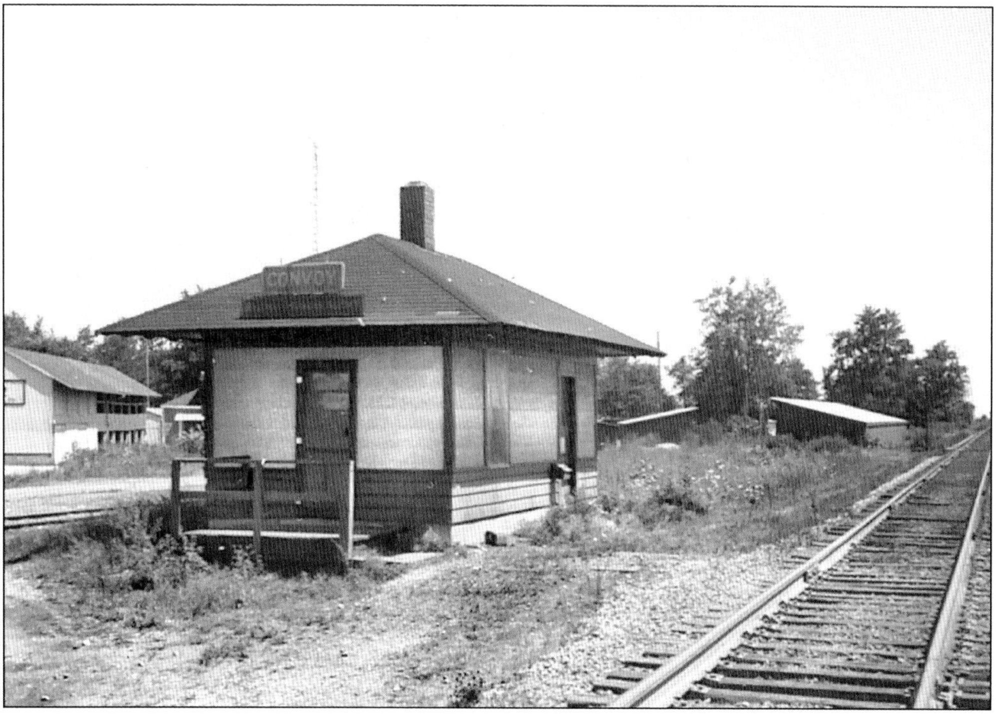

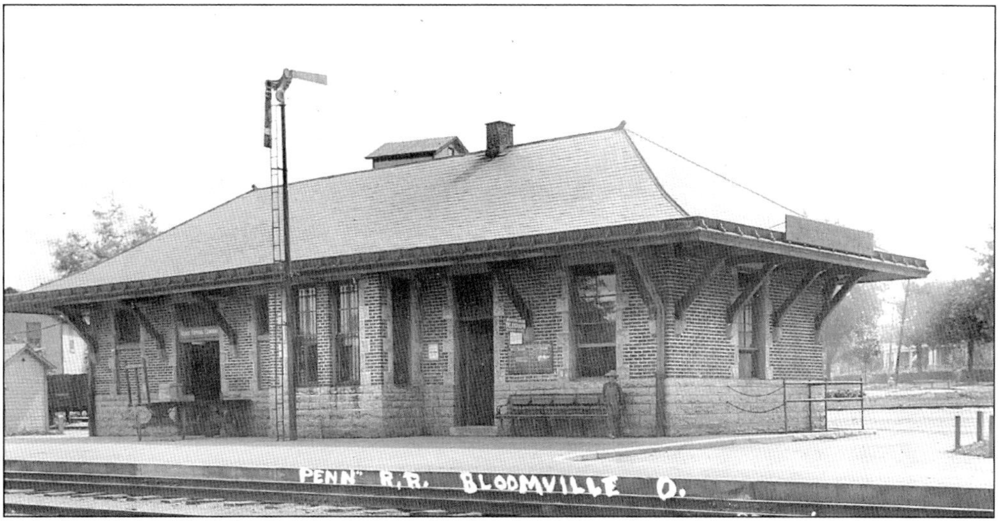

This attractive brick and stone depot was probably erected at Bloomville in the 1880s, when the quarries opened and began supplying crushed stone to the Northwestern Ohio Railway for fill and ballast. Bloomville became an important site on the new railroad and gave rise to the France Stone Company that would eventually open quarries throughout the northwestern counties of the state. Certainly the foundation and trim stone came from the local quarry, which produced excellent building stone as well. The agency closed around 1962. Unfortunately, the depot no longer exists. (Drake photograph; Mark J. Camp collection.)

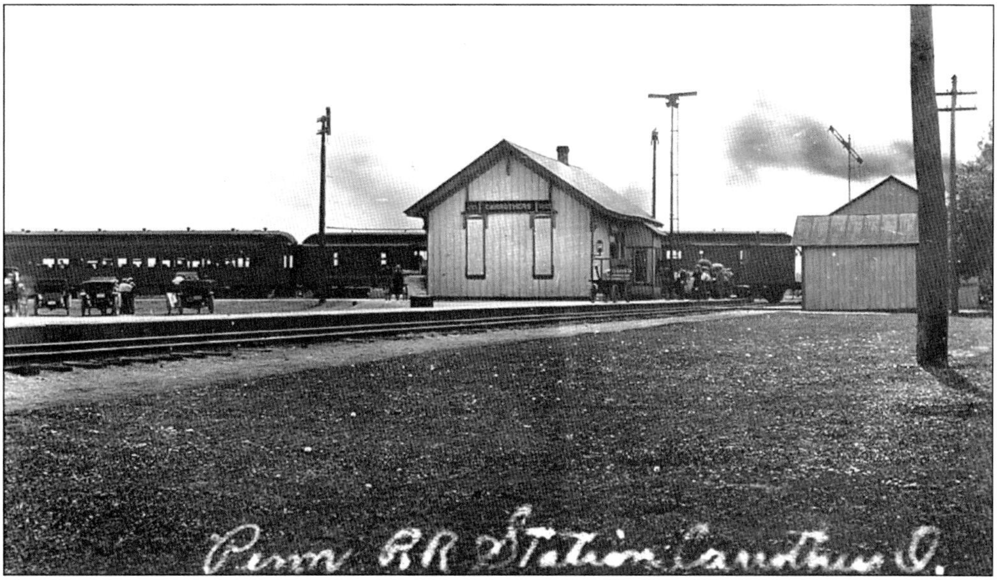

The depot at Carrothers probably dates to the 1870s and the time of the Northwestern Ohio Railway, which stretched from Tiffin to Toledo Junction between Crestline and Mansfield. This plan was used at many towns along the line, including the former Toledo, Tiffin and Eastern Rail Road between Tiffin and Woodville. The passenger train blocking the diamond is on Pennsy's Sandusky branch, the former Columbus, Sandusky and Hocking Railroad. A harbinger of railroad passenger service is the presence of early automobiles at the depot. By the 1960s, the agency had closed, and the depot was more or less converted to a tower. It has since been torn down. (Mark J. Camp collection.)

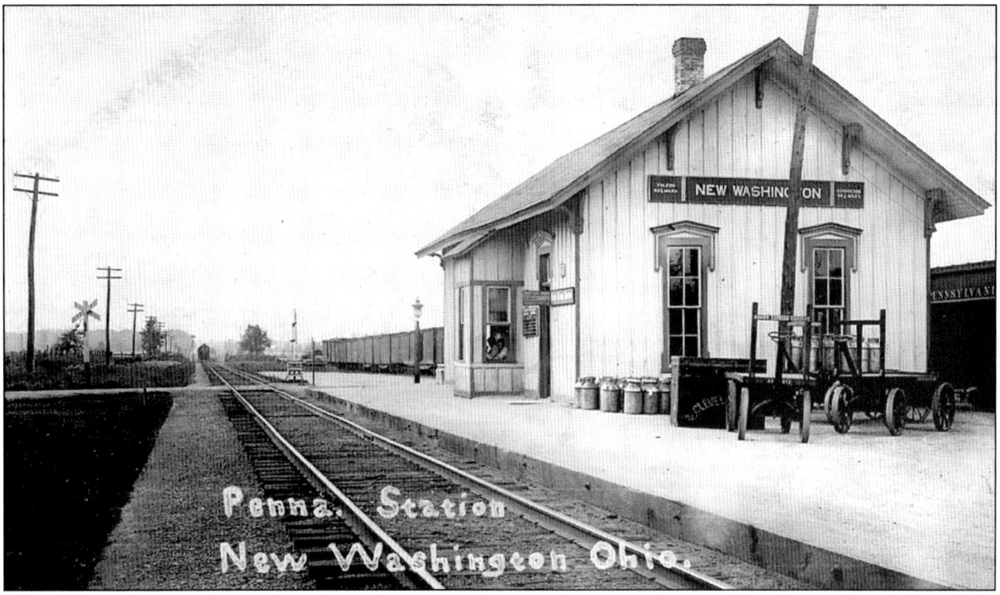

The New Washington depot was built to the same plans as the Carrothers depot, probably in the 1870s. Around 1908, the staff waits in the office as a train approaches. This was an important milk and poultry shipping point. Behind the photographer is PRR's Stack tower and the crossing of the Northern Ohio, later the Akron, Canton and Youngstown. A 1951 freight train derailment sent cars crashing into the depot. Carpentry crews rebuilt the depot, and it remained an agency until around 1961. The depot lasted until 1966; Stack tower was gone by 1974. (Mark J. Camp collection.)

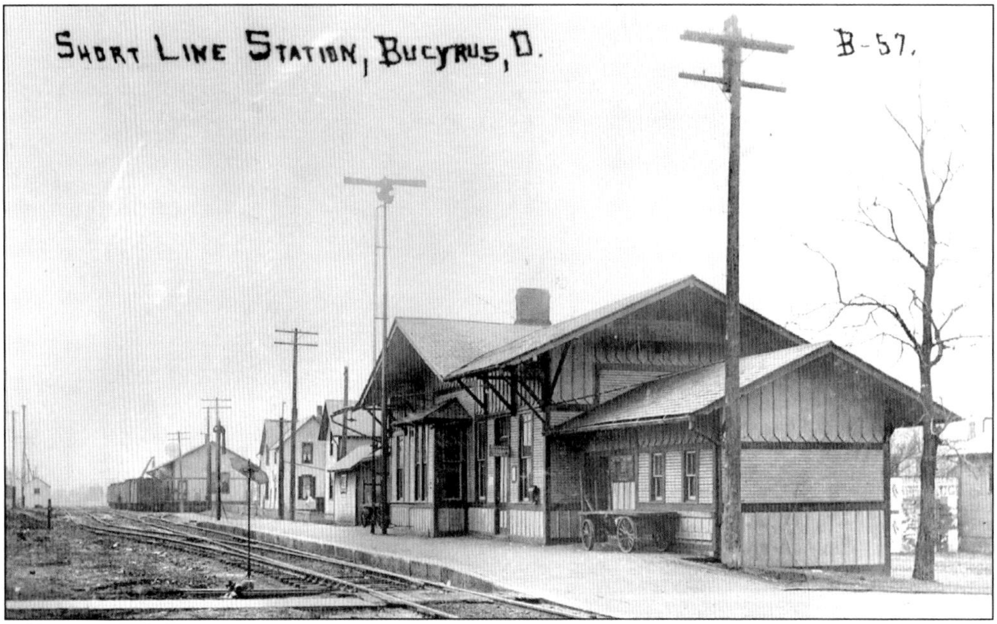

The PRR built this depot at Bucyrus after taking over the Columbus, Sandusky and Hocking Rail Road in 1902. This attractive design was one of the later designs to come out of the PRR offices and was repeated across the system. Down the track is the freight house. Both have been gone for some time. (Bob Lorenz collection.)

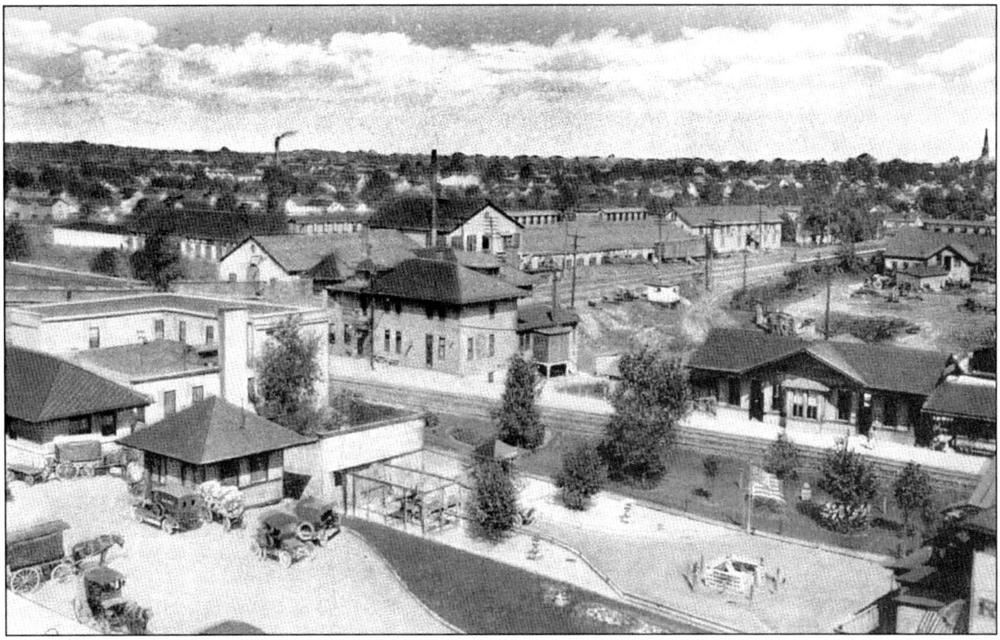

The PRR repeated the Bucyrus design at Marion. This aerial view also shows the railroad hotels and lunchrooms located at the junction with the Big Four and Erie. Just an edge of Marion Union Station shows in the lower left of this 1920s postcard. The PRR depot disappeared by the 1960s. (Mark J. Camp collection.)

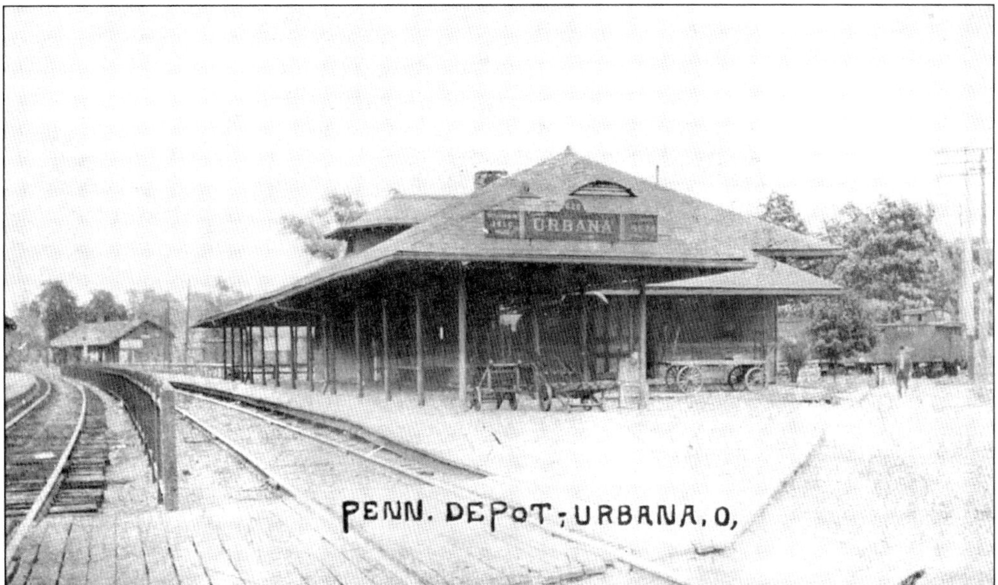

The PRR originally used the old Big Four depot in Urbana but in the early 1900s constructed the passenger depot seen in this c. 1907 postcard view. In the distance is the Erie passenger depot. The depot has lost its shelter but remains as a business. (Mark J. Camp collection.)

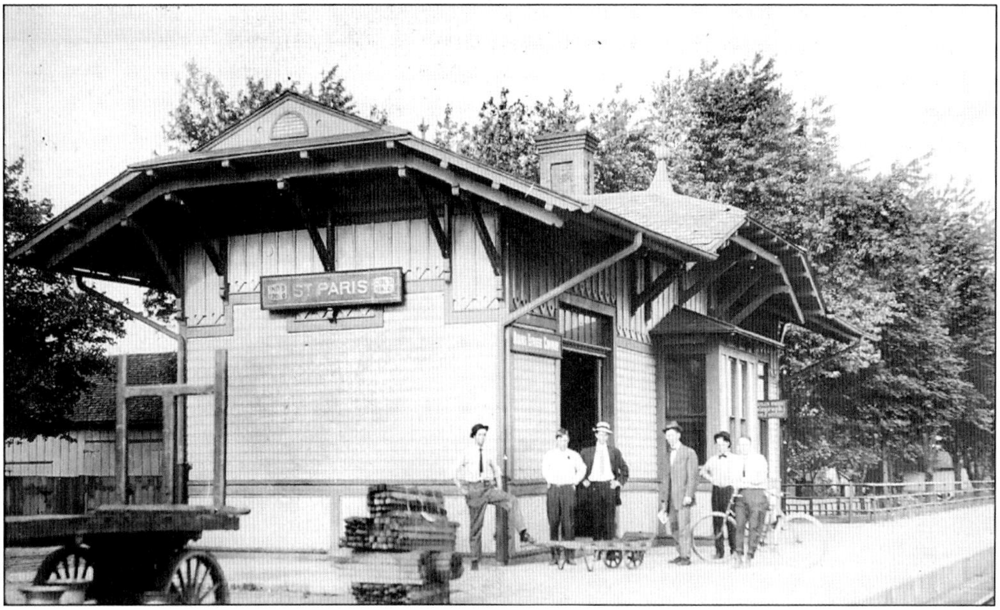

The DT&I crosses the PCC&StL at St. Paris. The PRR built this passenger depot according to the latest engineering office blueprints. The depot crew poses for the photographer in this *c.* 1907 postcard view. The agency closed around 1961, but a frame freight house still remains. (Mark J. Camp collection.)

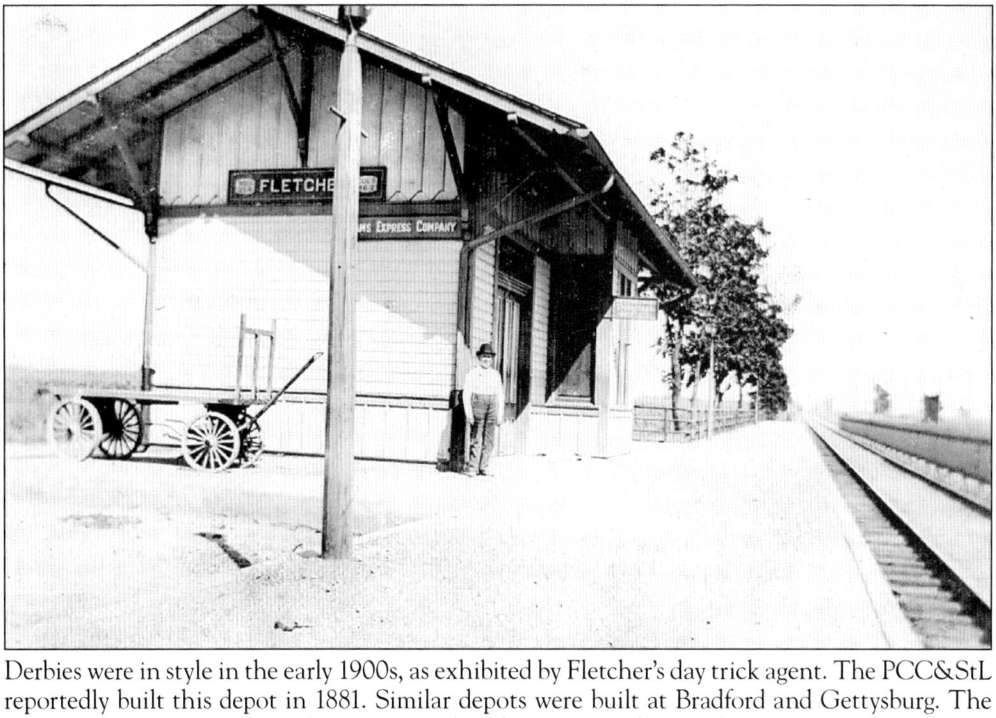

Derbies were in style in the early 1900s, as exhibited by Fletcher's day trick agent. The PCC&StL reportedly built this depot in 1881. Similar depots were built at Bradford and Gettysburg. The Fletcher depot apparently no longer exists. (Mark J. Camp collection.)

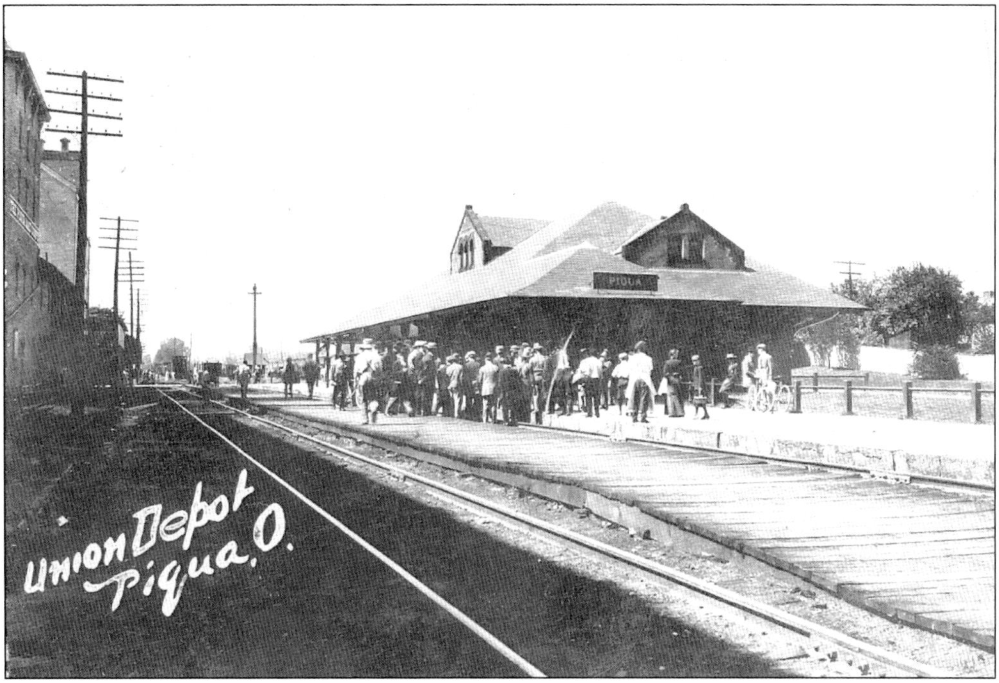

Elevation of the PCC&StL line through Piqua in 1912–1913 necessitated the erection of a new passenger depot. Above is the earlier depot around 1907. This structure was built in 1893. The occasion for the crowd is unknown. Before the reconstruction began, the depot was carted down the line to Union City where it remains today. The new depot, below, dates to 1913. It lasted until 1969. (Mark J. Camp collection.)

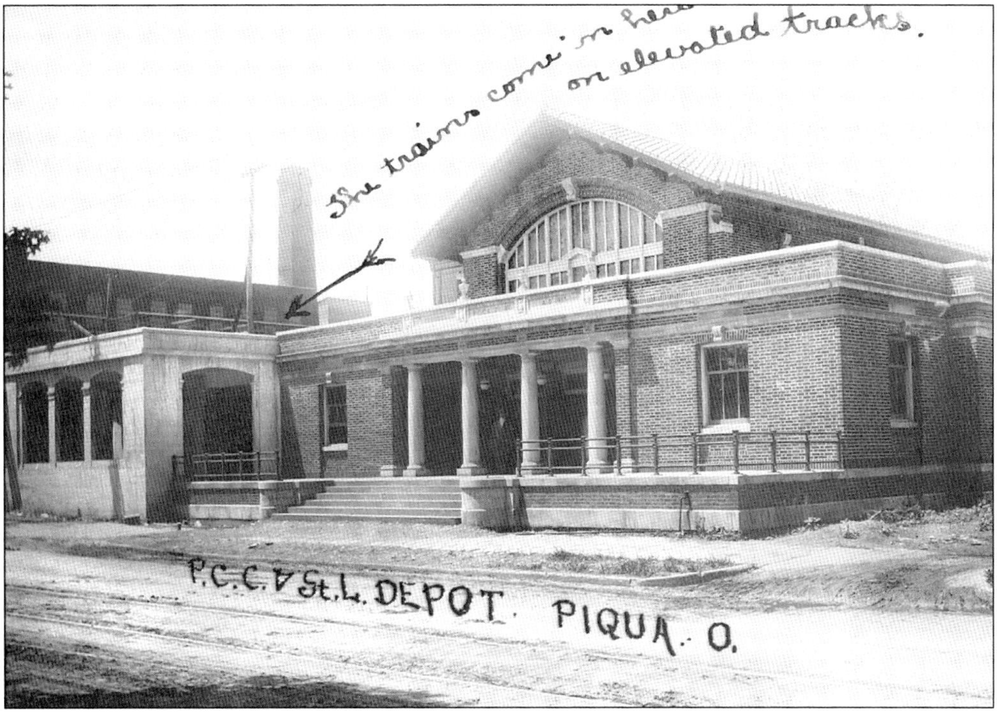

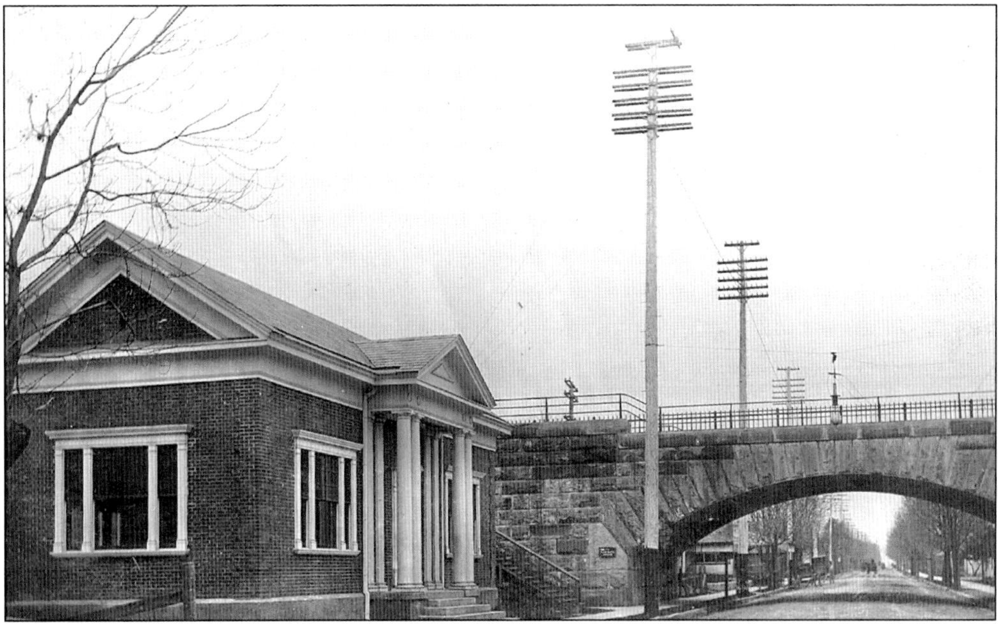

Covington's new PCC&StL passenger depot also dates to the 1912–1913 track elevation project. Steps led to a platform at track level. The older frame depot was relegated to freight use and still exists under private ownership on the opposite side of this stone underpass. (Mark J. Camp collection.)

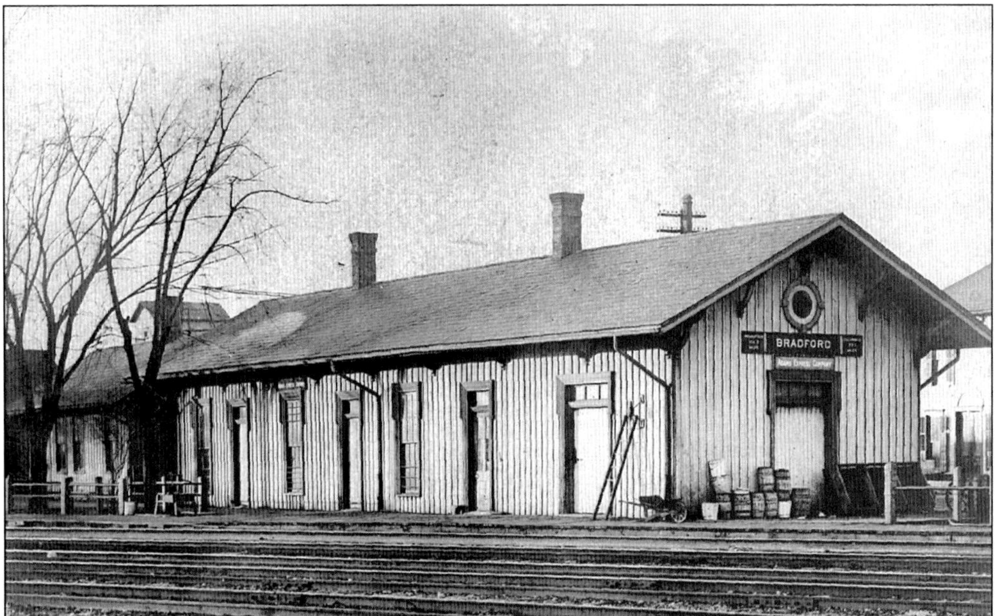

The first depot at Bradford, or Bradford Junction, appears to have been an old boxcar. In 1881, the PCC&StL built a depot to the same plan as Fletcher. In the late 1880s, the depot was lengthened. The depot was shortened and covered with siding by the 1960s. The agency closed around 1963; demolition came in 1977. (Mark J. Camp collection.)

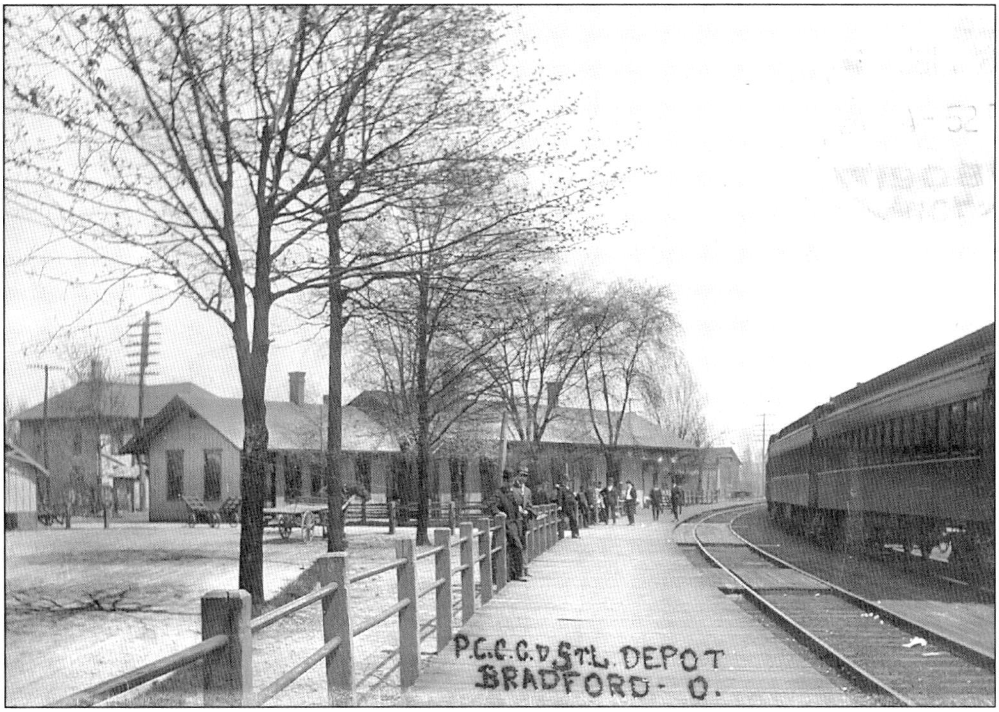

Looking east down the Indianapolis Division (old Richmond and Covington Railroad, later CC&IC) around 1907 shows the Bradford depot area to be a busy place. Behind the depot and to the left or west is the old Columbus, Piqua and Indiana line to Union City. South of here was the roundhouse and other terminal structures; east was BJ tower, the only significant railroad structure remaining in this rail-less town in 2005. (Mark J. Camp collection.)

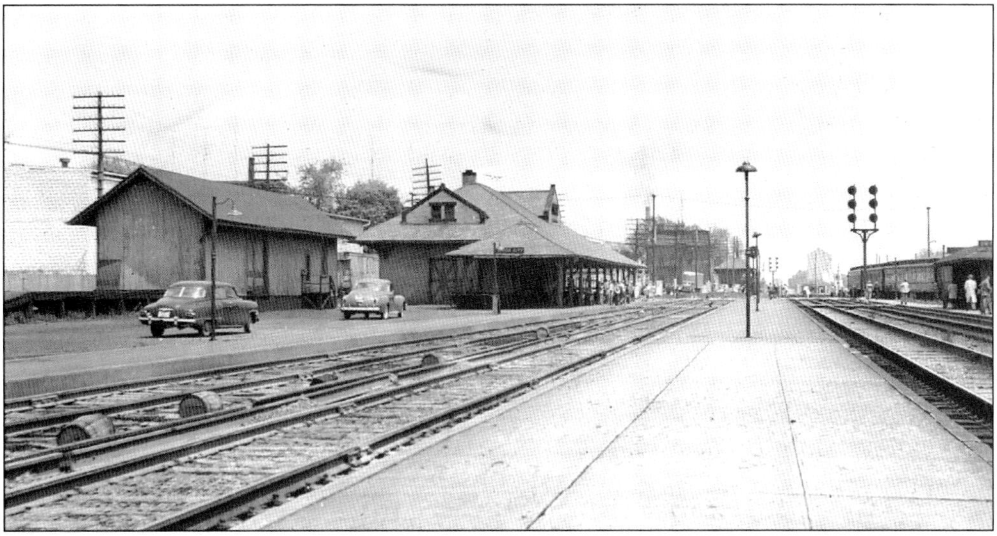

The PRR facilities at Union City are actually in the Indiana side of the city. The passenger depot was built in 1893 in Piqua. When the track was elevated through Piqua in 1912–1913, the depot was moved west down the line to Union City. Once in Union City, brick was added over the original frame siding. A small passenger shelter is to the far right. In the distance is the brick Big Four State Line tower. The depot is now a museum and art gallery. (Mark J. Camp collection.)

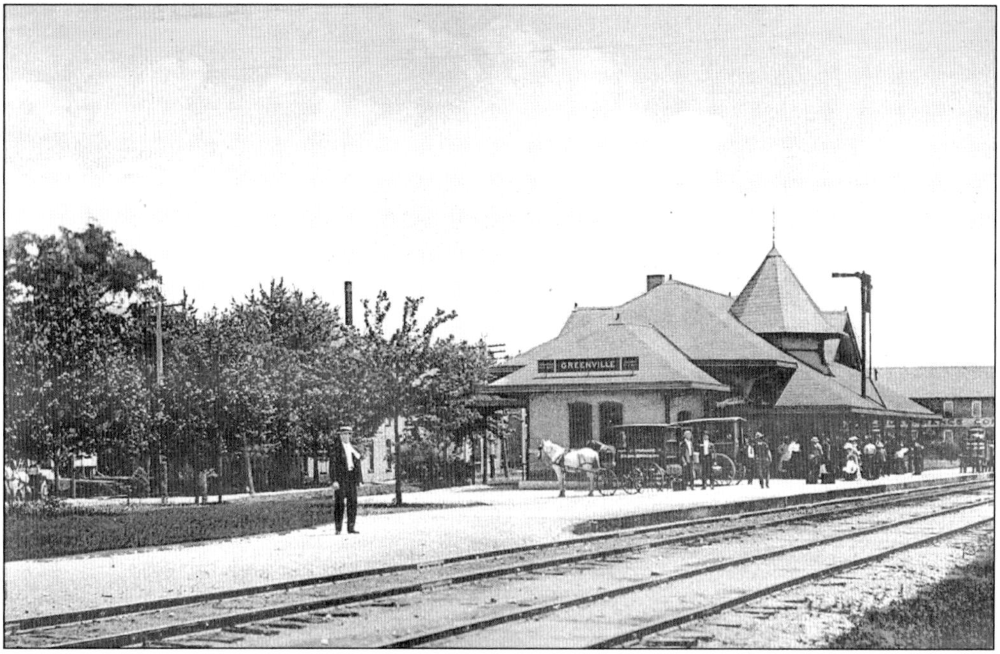

A train is due soon at Greenville's PCC&StL passenger depot around 1907. The PRR ticket office closed in 1961. A fire gutted the interior of the depot January 19, 1985. It was torn down in March 1985. (Mark J. Camp collection.)

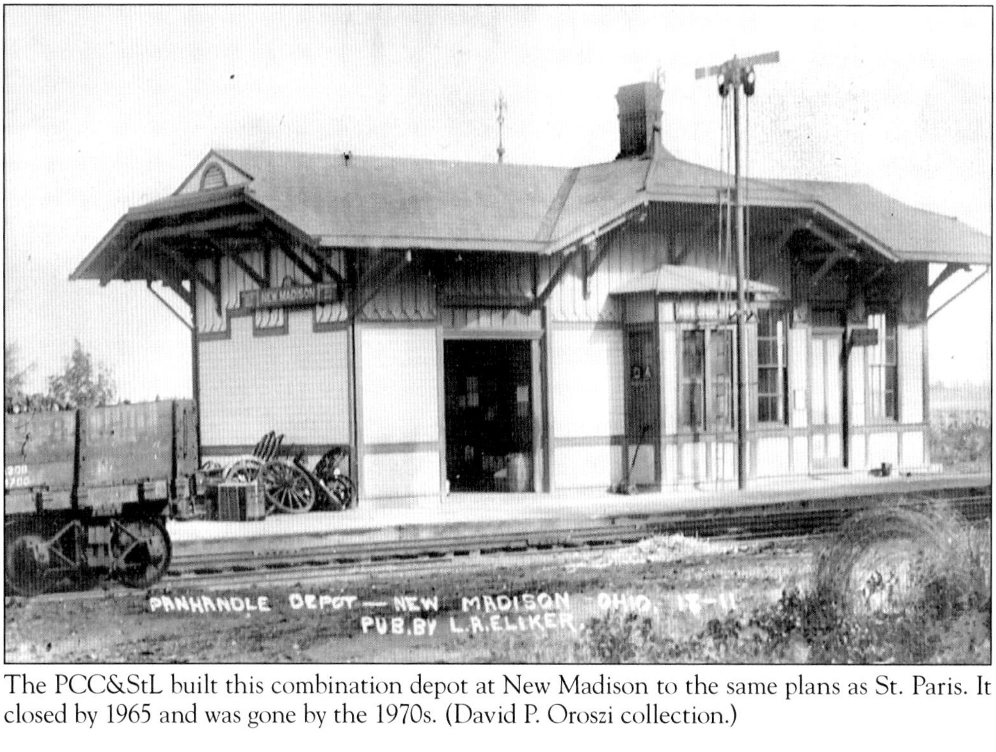

The PCC&StL built this combination depot at New Madison to the same plans as St. Paris. It closed by 1965 and was gone by the 1970s. (David P. Oroszi collection.)

Six

Other Lines

THE AKRON, CANTON AND YOUNGSTOWN RAILROAD

On January 1, 1883, the first narrow-gauge trains of the Cleveland, Delphos and St. Louis Railroad began regular service between Delphos and Mount Blanchard. The line stretched to Carey by the summer of 1883. The late 1880s brought a number of corporate reorganizations and name changes. In 1890, the line was converted to standard gauge and became the Pittsburg, Akron and Western Railroad (PA&W). It was reorganized as the Northern Ohio in 1895 and leased to the Lake Erie and Western. The Akron, Canton and Youngstown (AC&Y), then a shortline connecting Akron and Mogadore, took over the lease of the Northern Ohio in 1920 and merged it into the AC&Y in 1944. The AC&Y merged with the Norfolk and Western in 1964 but operated as a separate unit until 1982. Tracks from Carey to Delphos are gone, but those east continue to see trains of the new Wheeling and Lake Erie. The PA&W engineering office designed a standard frame combination depot that was repeated many times along the line from 1890 through 1895. The only ones remaining in west central Ohio are from Bluffton and New Washington.

DETROIT, TOLEDO AND IRONTON RAILWAY

In September 1893, rails of the Ohio Southern Railroad reached Lima, and with completion of the bridge over the Great Miami River at Quincy, traffic between Springfield and Lima commenced. Building north from Lima in 1895 was the Lima Northern, reaching Malinta in January 1896. This line became the Detroit and Lima Northern Railroad (D&LN) in 1898. The D&LN procured an ill-advised branch in 1898—the Columbus and Northwestern Railroad from Peoria to St. Marys with trackage rights over the Ohio Southern. The line was only owned until 1901, but the D&LN apparently erected depots during this stretch (this trackage became the St. Marys branch of the T&OC). The merger of the Ohio Southern and D&LN in June 1901 produced the Detroit Southern Railroad. The Detroit, Toledo and Ironton Railway (DT&I) was born in spring 1905 and after emerging from financial difficulties in 1914 became the DT&I Railroad. Passenger service north of Springfield ended September 17, 1932. The year 1984 marked the end of the DT&I as it disappeared into the Grand Trunk Western. Today the Indiana and Ohio Railroad operates the line as far south as Washington Court House.

The only D&LN designed depots still extant are at East Liberty and Lima. Ohio Southern depots from Jackson Center, Quincy, Rosewood, St. Johns, and Uniopolis remain.

THE HOCKING VALLEY RAILWAY

The Hocking Valley Railway began with the construction of the Mineral Railroad, later Columbus and Hocking Valley Railroad (C&HV), between Columbus and the coalfields of southeast Ohio. In 1881, the Columbus, Hocking Valley and Toledo Railway (CHV&T) formed when the C&HV merged with the Columbus and Toledo Railroad, opened in 1877, forming a line stretching from Gallipolis to Walbridge. The line became known as the Hocking Valley. The Chesapeake and Ohio (C&O) took over the line in 1920, and today it is CSX. The CHV&T engineering office designed an attractive frame combination depot with characteristic hipped roof that was replicated at most smaller stations along the line. Unfortunately, only Union Station at Marion remains in west central Ohio.

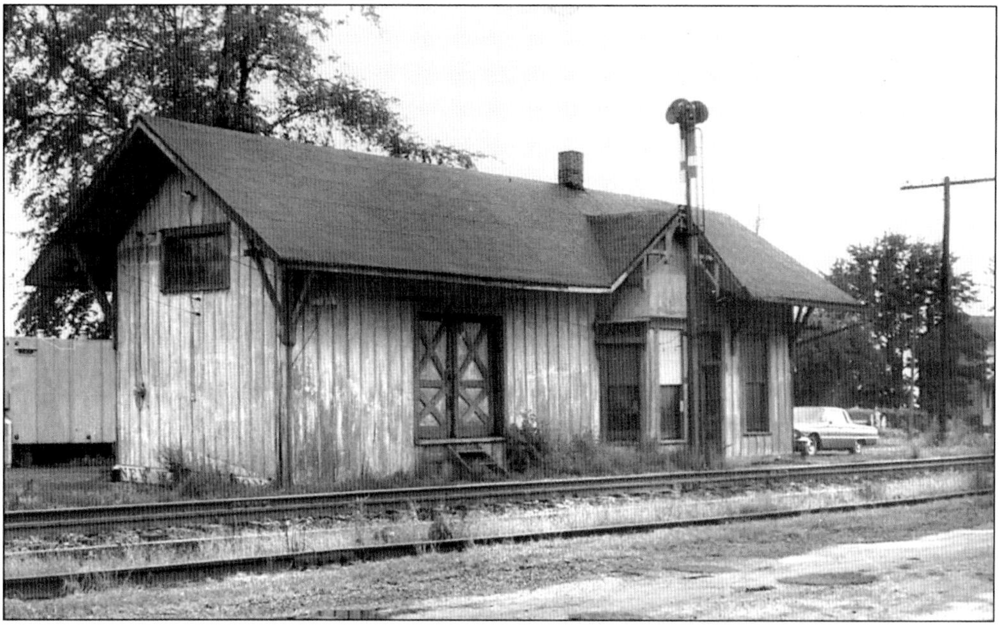

The New Washington depot is an example of the standard plan depot of the PA&W. The last passenger train left the depot in July 1951. The 1890 depot was disassembled and moved to near Norwalk where it has been restored by a rail enthusiast. (Charles Garvin 1966 photograph; Mark J. Camp collection.)

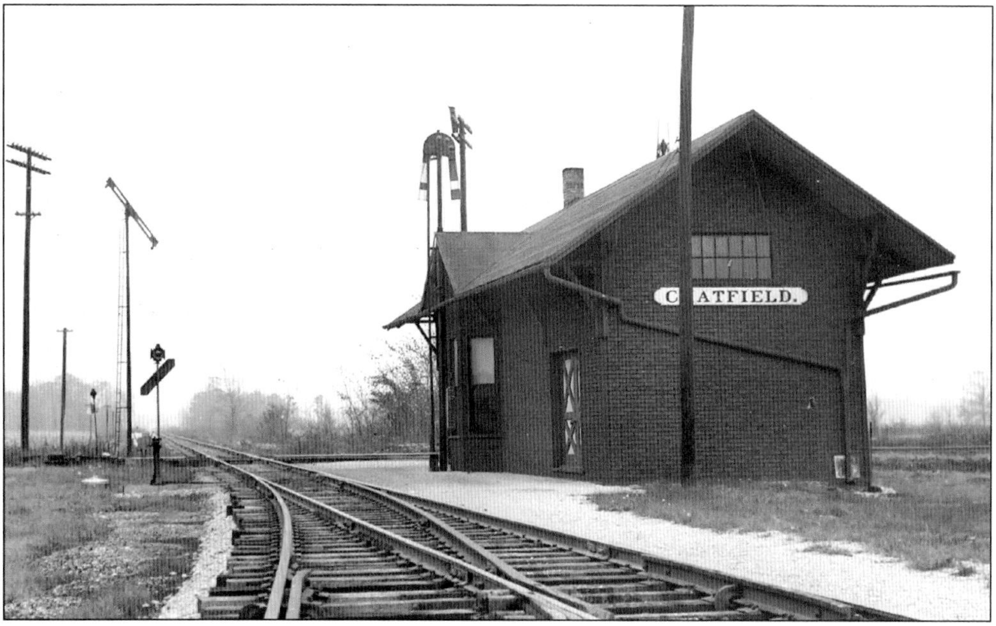

Another example of the PA&W standard 1890 design was at Chatfield, seen here in this photograph from around 1947. The Chatfield structure was a joint facility built at the crossing of the PRR's Sandusky branch. At one point, the AC&Y applied brick shingle siding to a number of its structures, including the Chatfield depot. The Chatfield agency closed around 1962 (the PRR removed its agent around 1961), and the building was torn down in May 1968. (Clyde Helms photograph; Mark J. Camp collection.)

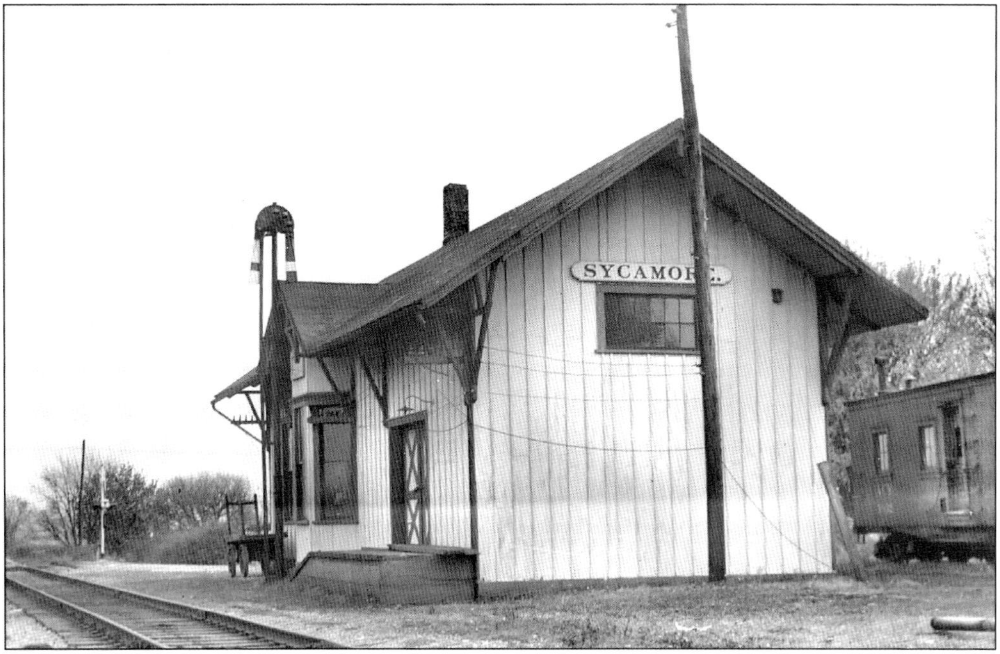

This photograph shows the Sycamore combination depot around 1947. It was built to the same 1890 plans as Chatfield. The depot was gone by the late 1960s. (Clyde Helms photograph; Mark J. Camp collection.)

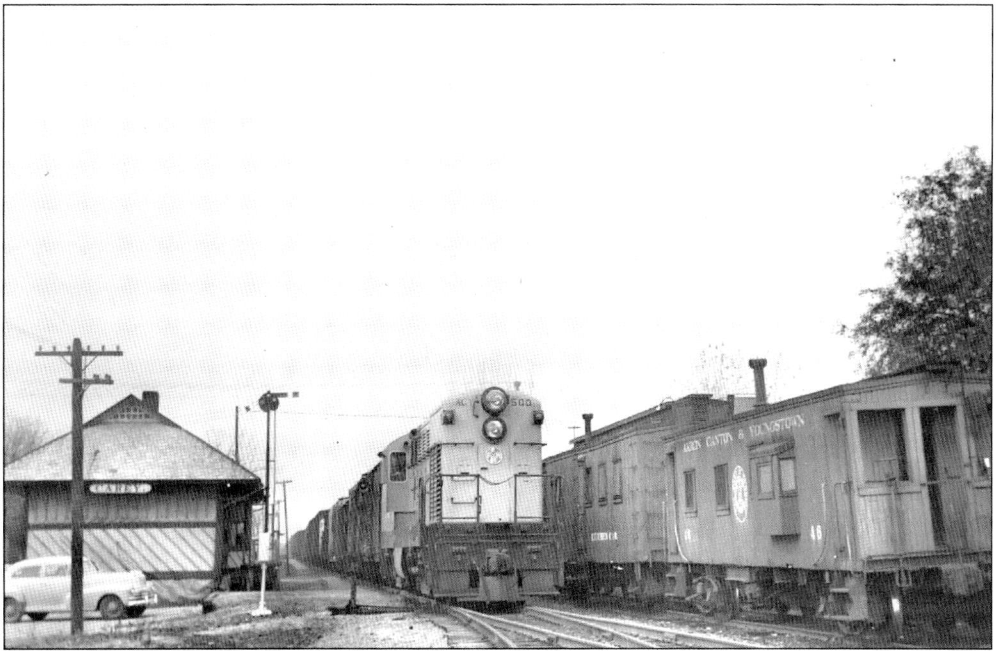

In the early days, the predecessors of the AC&Y used the old Big Four depot in Carey. This depot was erected in 1896. It was a busy place in the late 1940s. Lime and crushed stone were the main shipments from this station. Here a freight passes an AC&Y work train in the siding. The depot has since been removed. (Clyde Helms photograph; Mark J. Camp collection.)

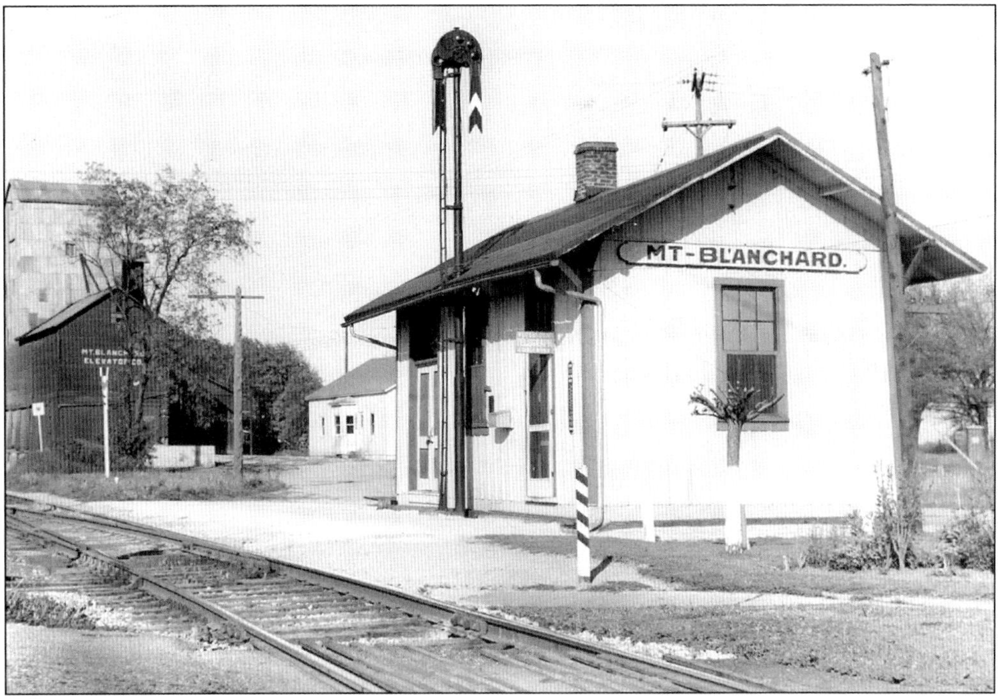

Mount Blanchard's 1898 combination depot lacked a bay window and was typical of another design used along the line. It was still there in the late 1960s, as seen here around 1947, but little trace of the "Pumpkin Vine" remains today. (Clyde Helms photograph; Mark J. Camp collection.)

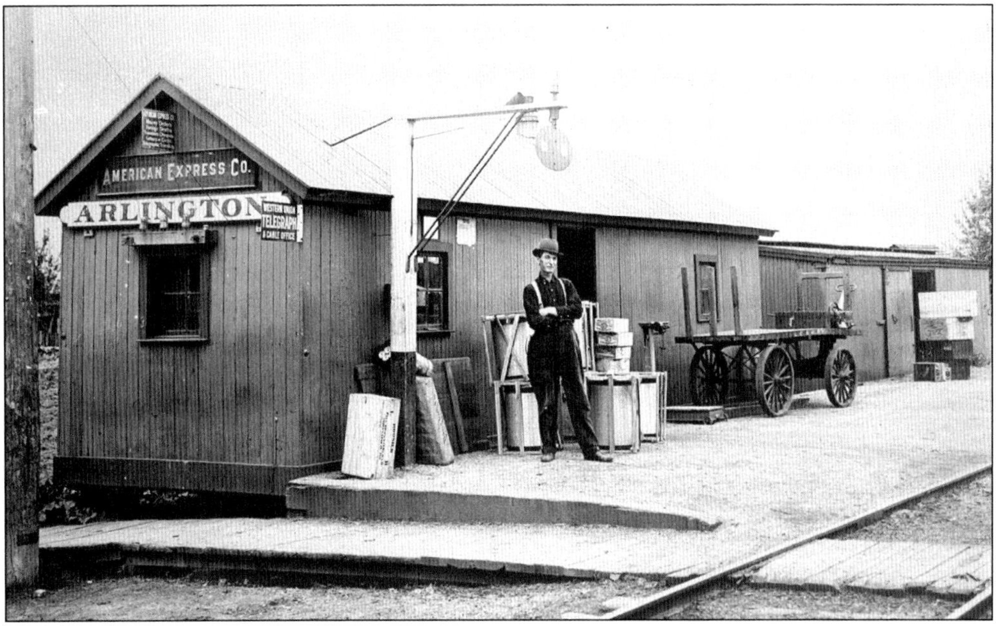

The depots in Arlington, and nearby Jenera, were perhaps the least inspiring design along the line. Even so, the dapper agent is ready to be of service. Separate passenger and freight buildings are present, with the freight shed being an old boxcar. The Arlington agency closed around 1962 and was torn down by 1973. (Mark J. Camp collection.)

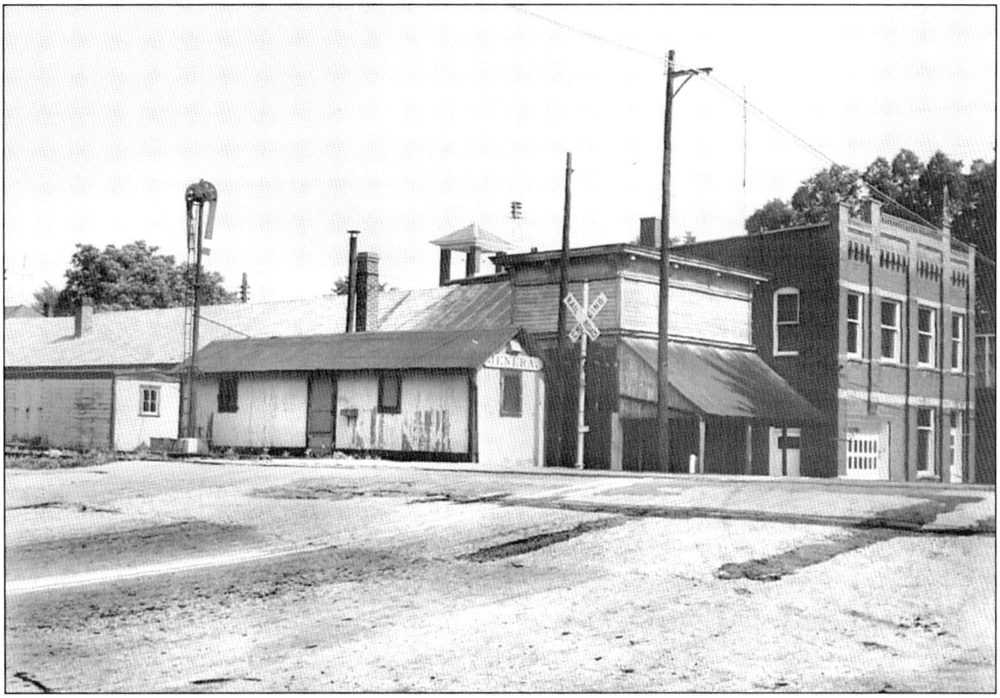

The Jenera facilities were similar to Arlington, but the depot served the community adequately for many years. Note the facilities also include an ex-boxcar freight shed. It lasted until 2000. (Charles Garvin 1965 photograph; Mark J. Camp collection.)

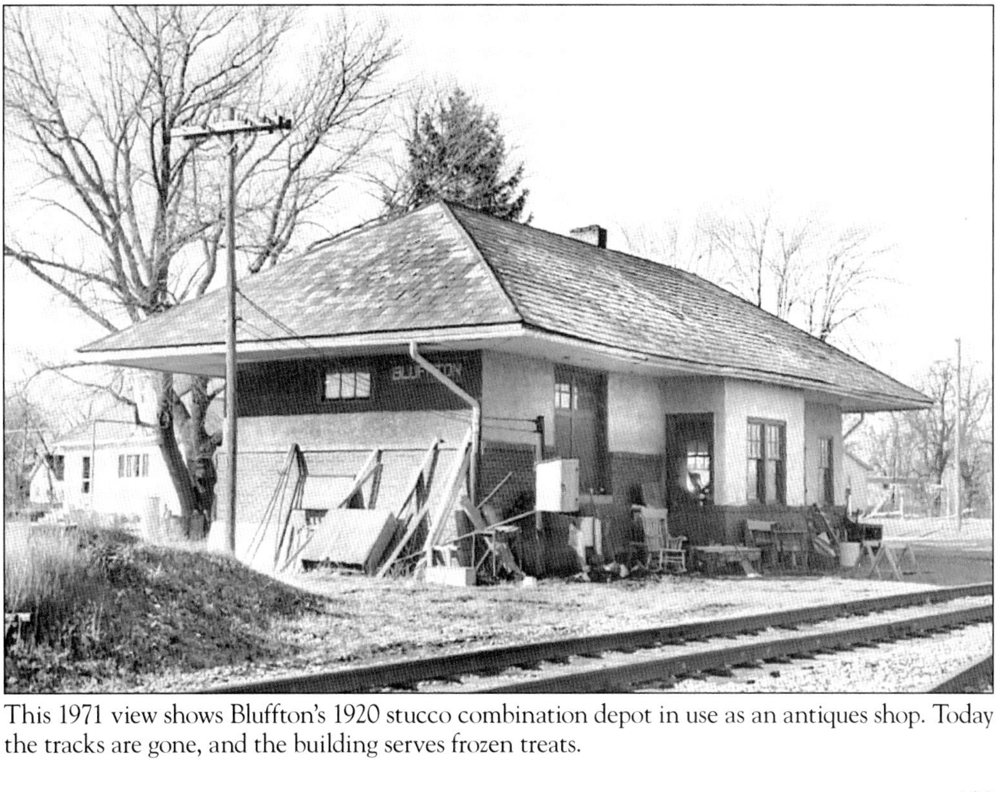

This 1971 view shows Bluffton's 1920 stucco combination depot in use as an antiques shop. Today the tracks are gone, and the building serves frozen treats.

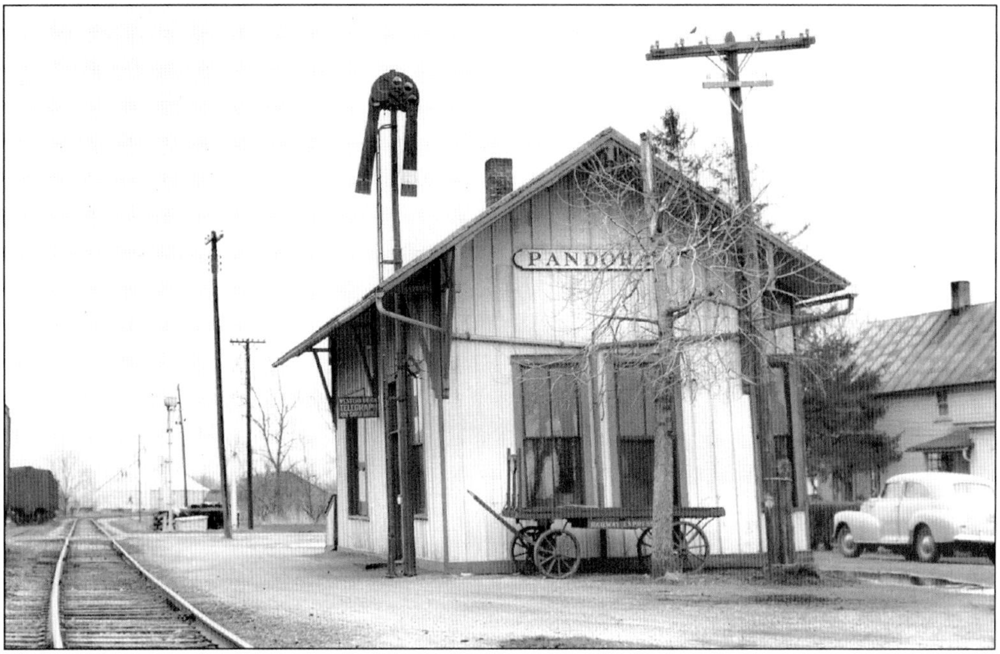

Pandora's depot experienced some modifications during its service. A bay window on the street side of this building suggests a track realignment in past years. The 1891 depot was still standing in the late 1970s but is seen here around 1947. (Clyde Helms photograph; Mark J. Camp collection.)

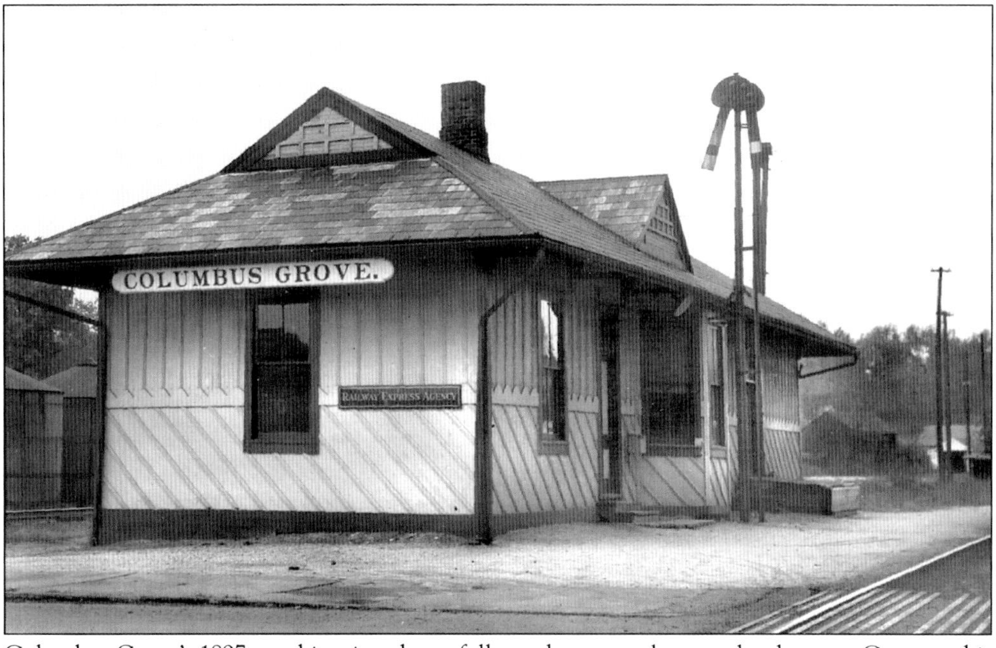

Columbus Grove's 1897 combination depot follows the same plans as the depot at Carey and is seen here around 1947. The offset bay window is a quirk in the architecture. This building was replaced by the late 1960s by a smaller prefab freight office. (Clyde Helms photograph; Mark J. Camp collection.)

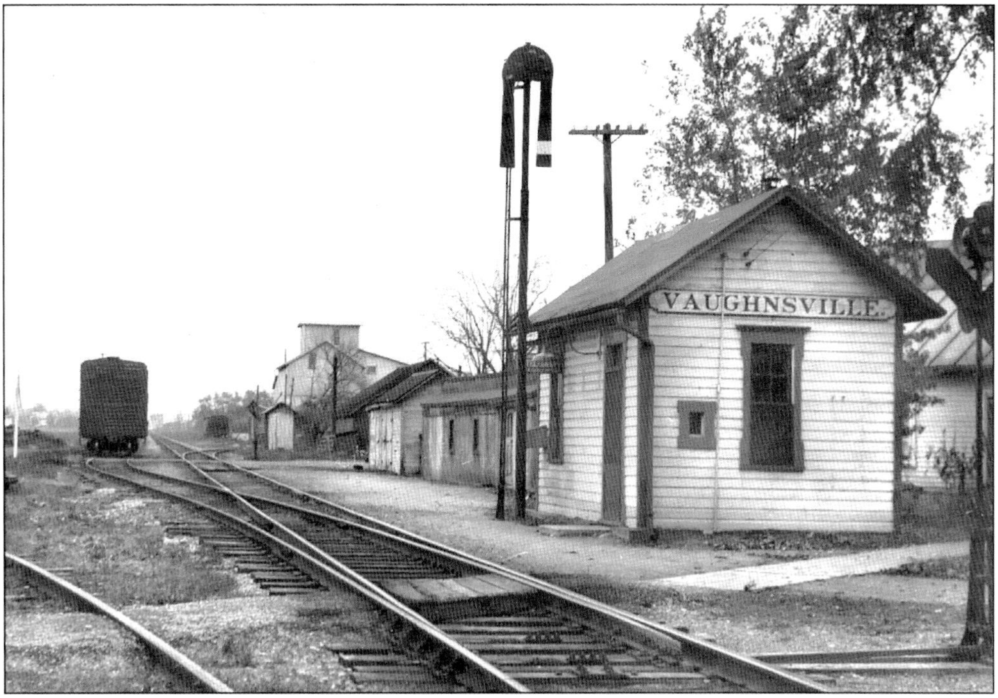

One of the smallest AC&Y depots was located at Vaughnsville. Note the old coach being used as a freight house around 1947. The small depot was still there in the late 1960s. (Clyde Helms photograph; Mark J. Camp collection.)

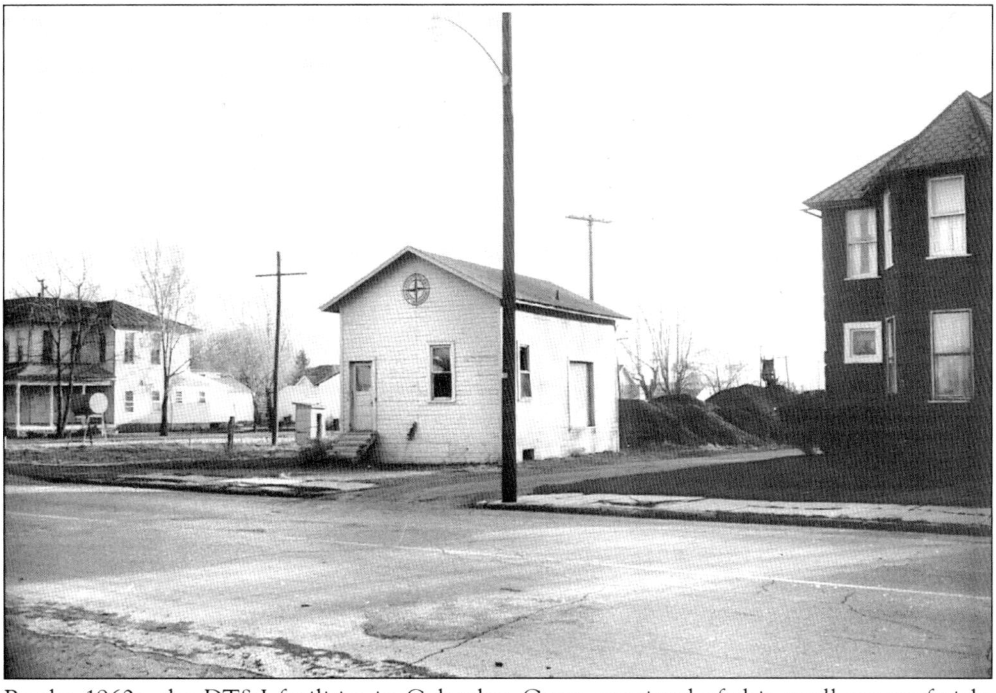

By the 1960s, the DT&I facilities in Columbus Grove consisted of this small vacant freight house. (Charles Garvin 1965 photograph; Mark J. Camp collection.)

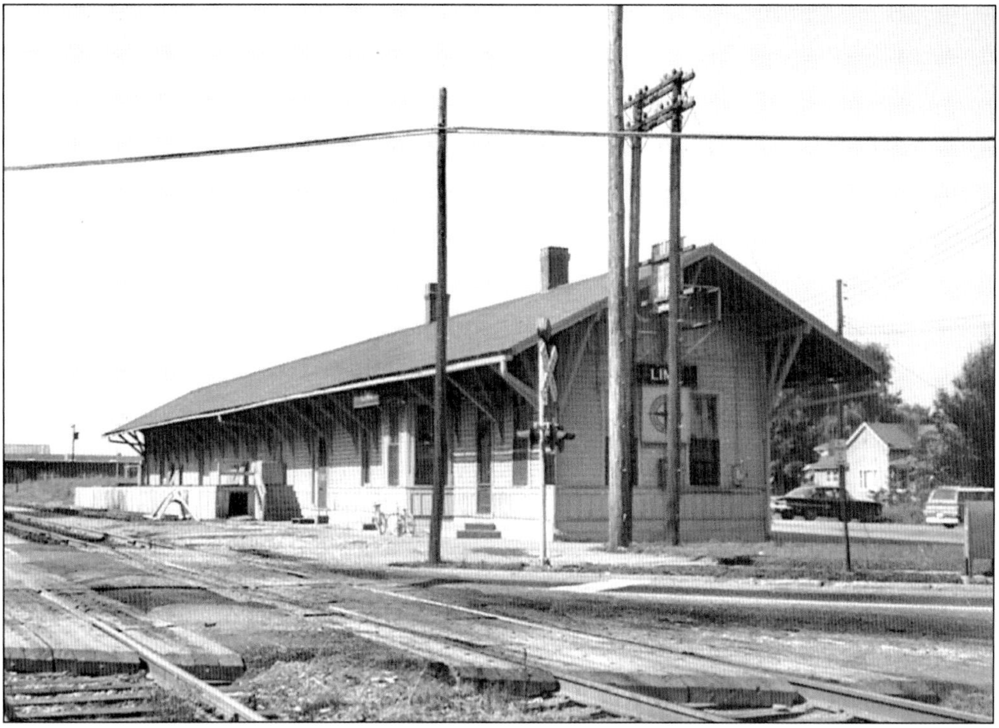

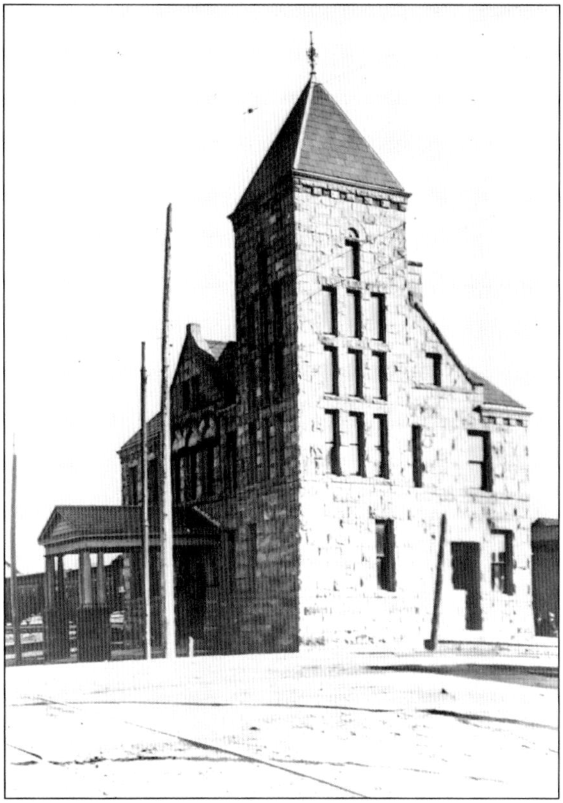

In 1895–1896, the above joint depot was built to D&LN plans at the point where the D&LN and Ohio Southern met on the east side of Lima. In 1923–1924, the building was lengthened with the addition of more freight space. After railroad use ended, the depot has served a number of businesses. The two-story stone depot was erected in downtown Lima by the D&LN around 1898, at the end of a 0.7-mile extension from the main line on the east side of town. It was just southeast of the CH&D depot and was an obvious ploy to siphon passenger traffic from its main competitor—the CH&D. Passenger trains backed in behind the depot. In January 1931, the DT&I abandoned the downtown depot and moved its meager passenger business back to the frame East Lima depot. (Left, Allen County [Ohio] Historical Society collection.)

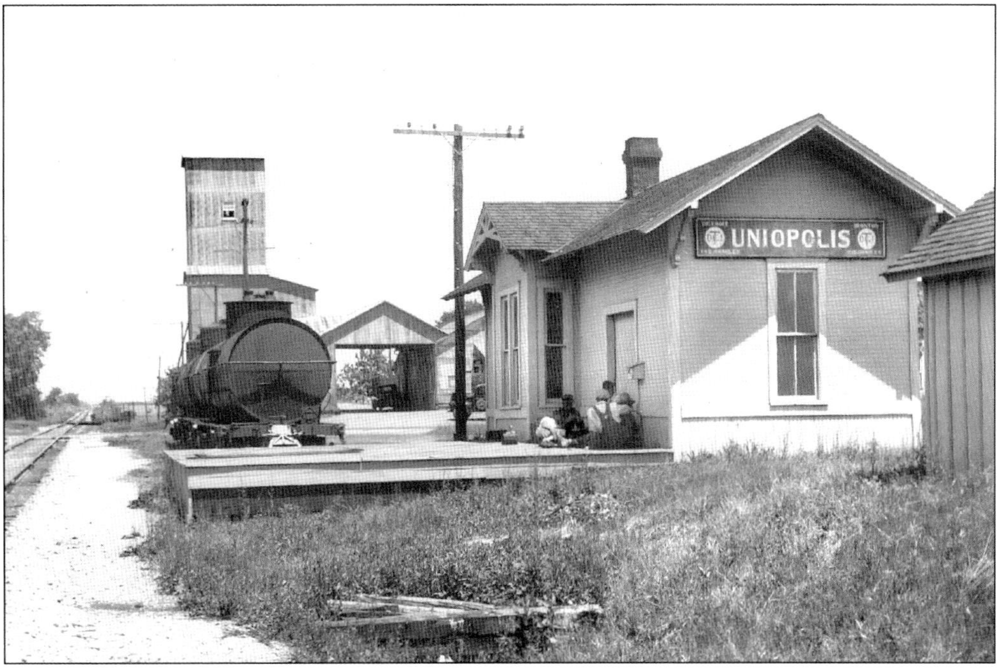

Uniopolis and St. Johns depots follow c. 1893 plans of the Ohio Southern. The difference is that the floor plans were reversed. On a hot and humid day in July 1947, a track crew takes a lunch break in the shade of the Uniopolis depot. The St. Johns depot was also quiet when this view was taken in the 1950s. Both depots survive; Uniopolis was moved to the Lincoln Park railroad exhibit in Lima, where it was restored as a depot museum, and St. Johns was relocated for use by a grain elevator. (Above, Eldon Neff photograph, David P. Oroszi collection; below D. Longsworth photograph, Allen County [Ohio] Historical Society collection.)

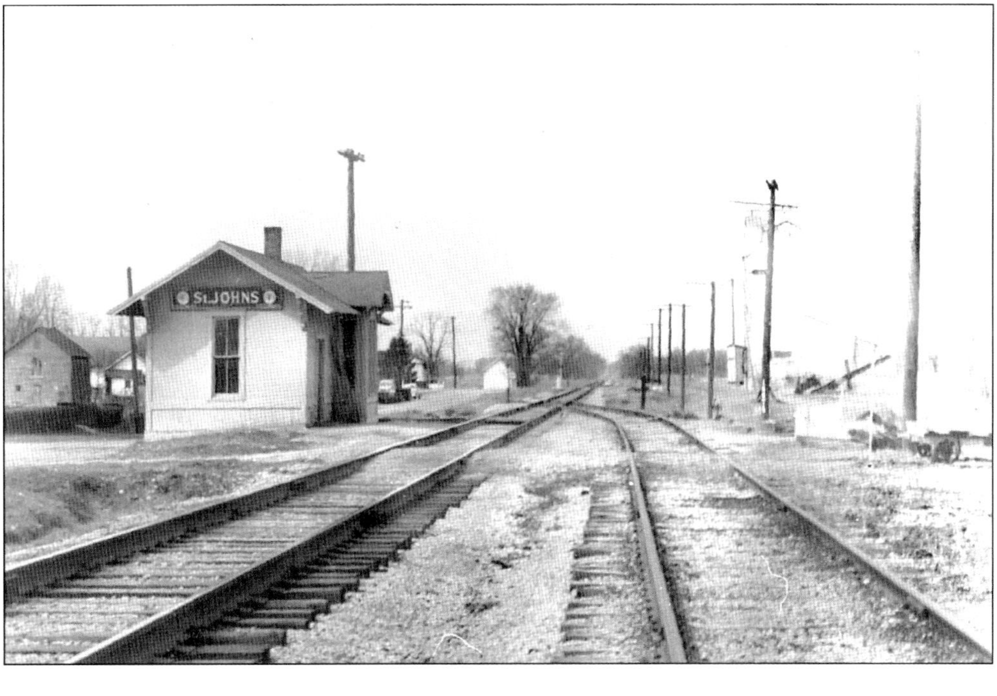

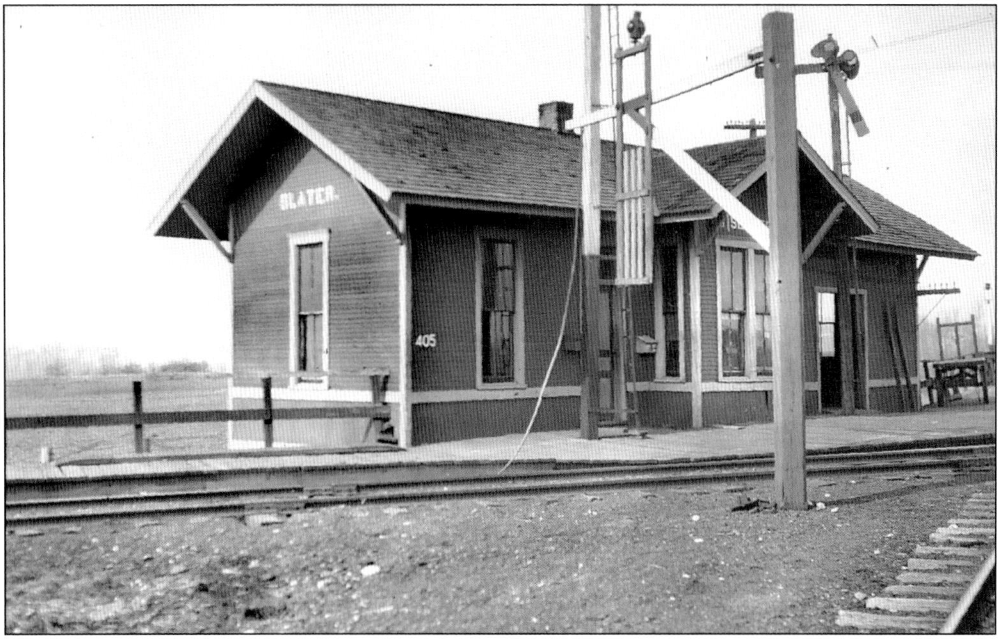

The same Ohio Southern plans were used for the combination depots at Slater and Jackson Center. Slater, at one time called Columbus Junction, was where the Ohio Southern crossed the T&OC St. Marys branch (formerly D&LN). Platforms extend along each line of this joint depot. By the 1960s, this depot was already sitting as a storage shed in a nearby farm field. It has since disappeared. The order board at Jackson Center indicates a passenger train is on its way. A lone traveling salesman has left his bags on the platform. The depot remained on-site until being moved in the 1970s to near Springfield where it was restored. (Above, T&OC 1919 photograph, Allen County [Ohio] Historical Society collection; below, Mark J. Camp collection.)

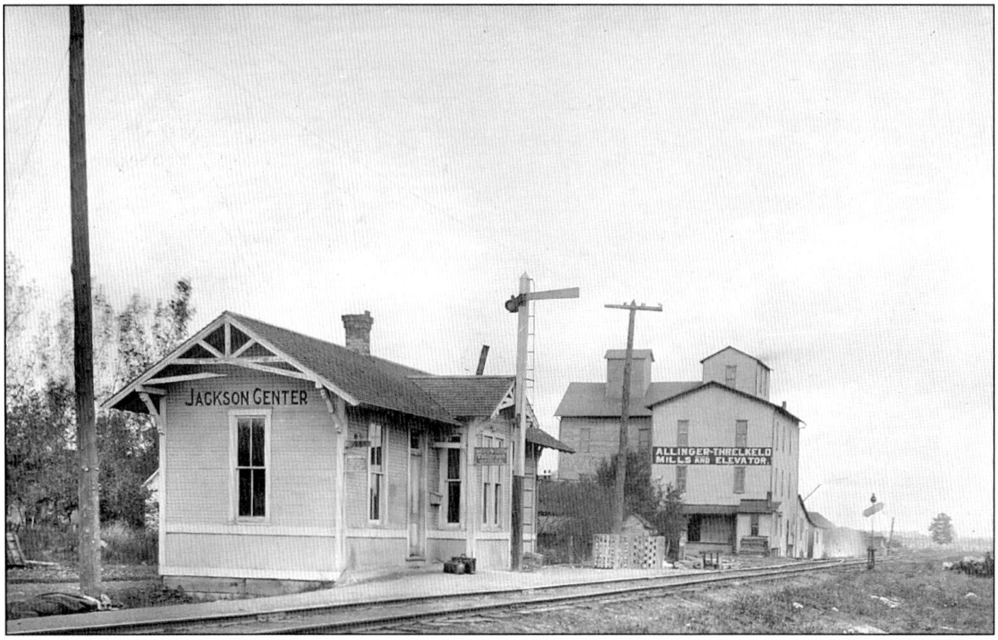

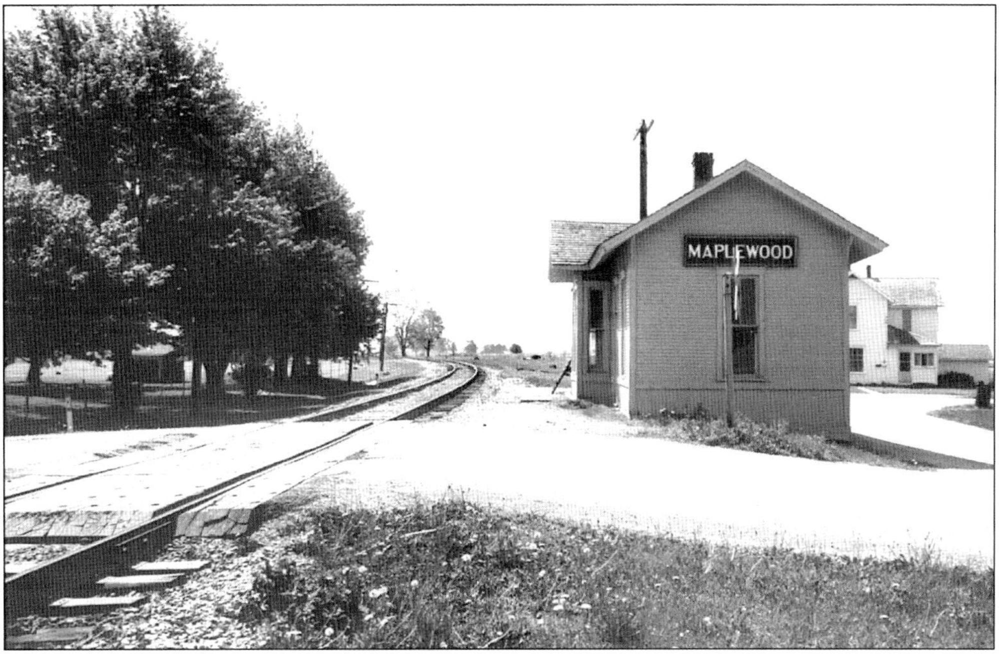

Two more identical *c.* 1893 Ohio Southern combination depots were built at Maplewood and Quincy. In 1932, the Maplewood depot was struck from the list of train order offices along the DT&I. It disappeared in the 1970s. At Quincy, the DT&I interchanged with the Big Four. In the background of this 1968 view is Big Four's Morgan tower, uncharacteristic because the first floor is enclosed. Only the Quincy depot remains, now in private use. (Above, Charles Garvin 1969 photograph; Mark J. Camp collection.)

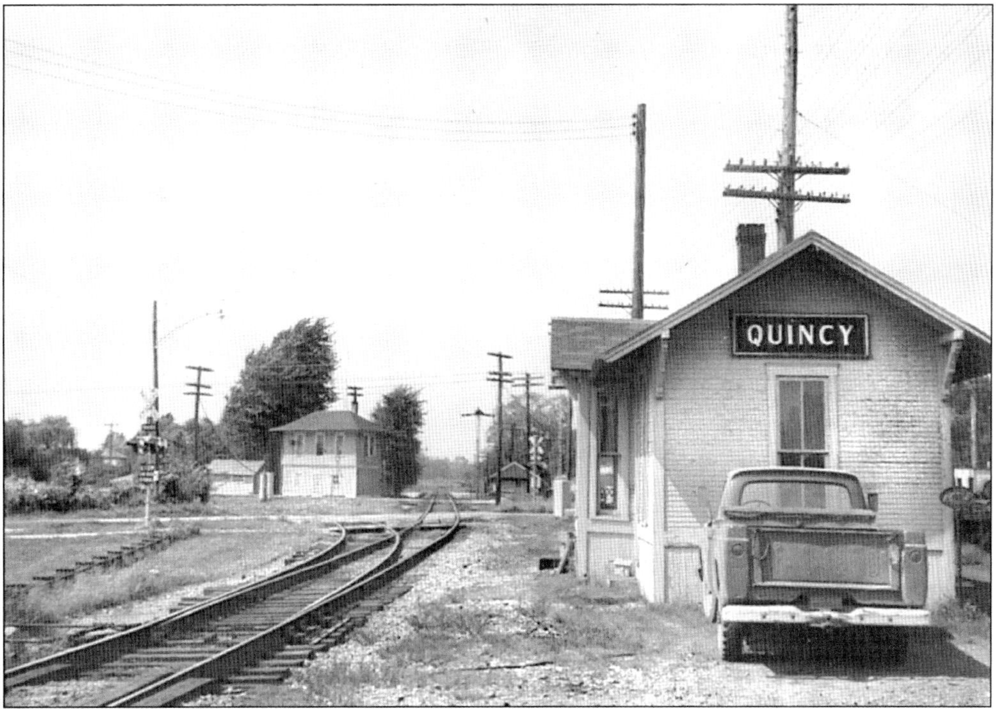

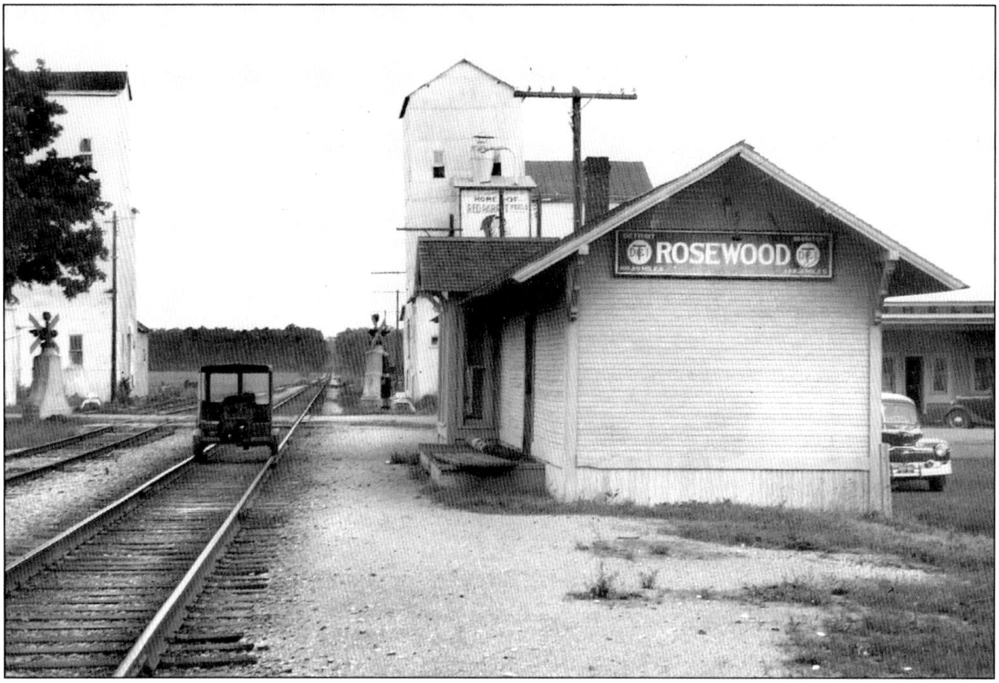

Rosewood and St. Paris depots are further variations on the *c.* 1893 Ohio Southern plan. Rosewood was platted with the coming of the railroad. A speeder sits at the depot in 1947, now in its waning years as a railroad facility. The local elevator now owns the depot and uses it for storage. The DT&I crosses the PCC&StL at St. Paris. This was a slightly wider version of the standard design and still has an order board in this 1968 view. (Above, Eldon Neff photograph; David P. Oroszi collection.)

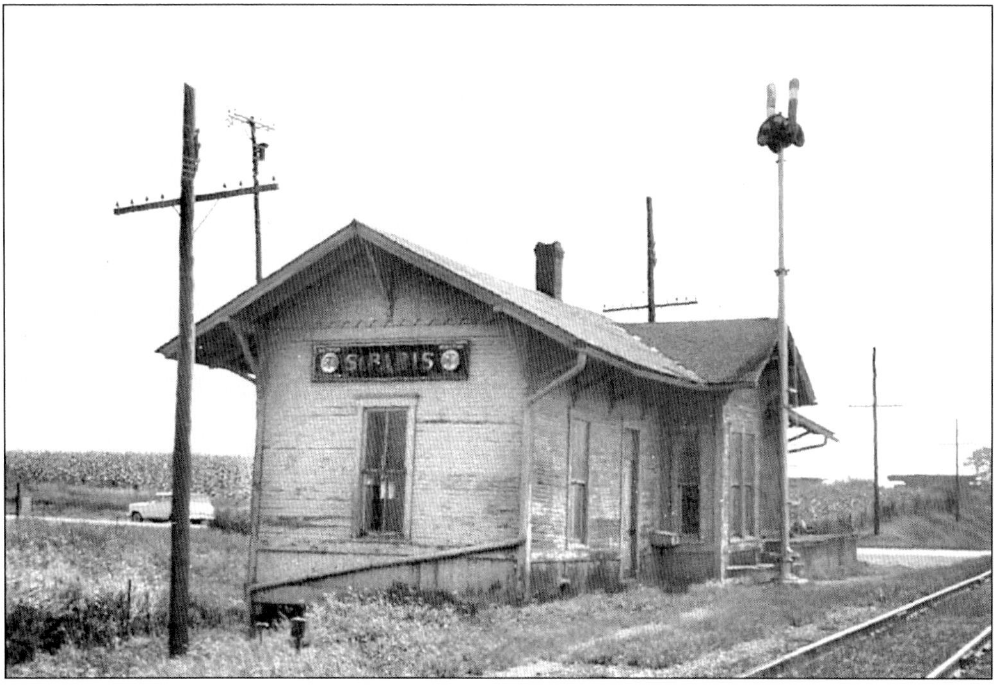

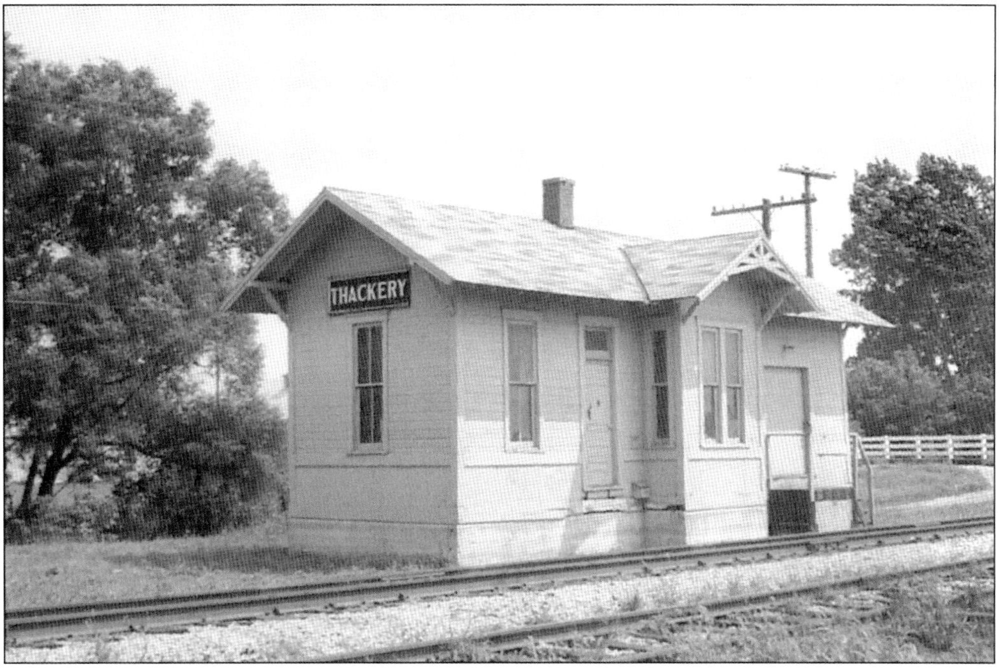

Thackery's *c.* 1893 Ohio Southern (DT&I) combination depot sits on a new foundation in 1968. The depot had been modified for maintenance of the way use. It is no longer present.

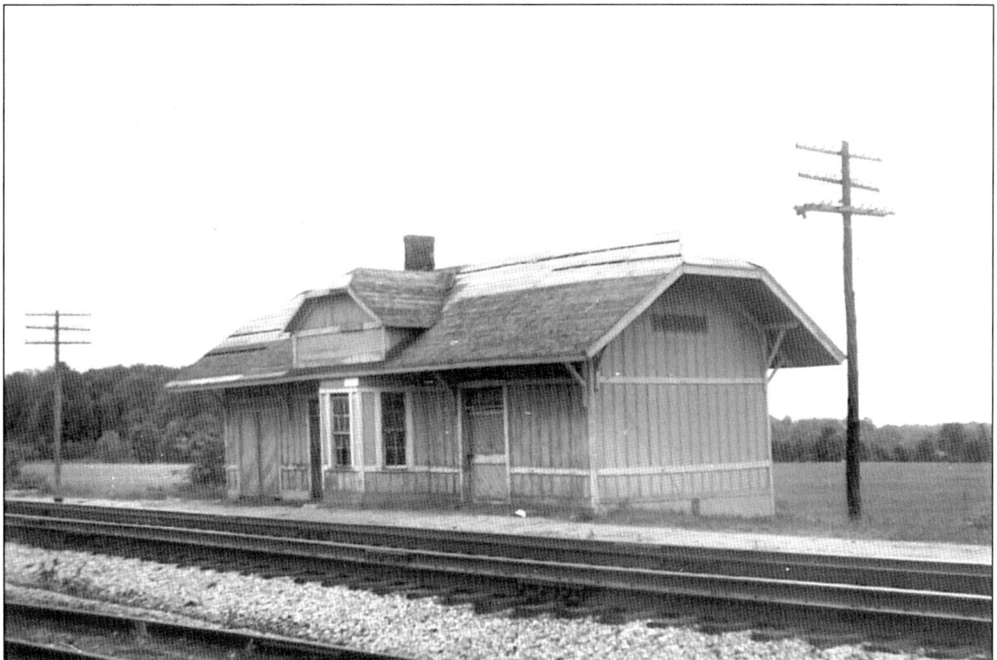

The most prevalent Hocking Valley depot plan is displayed in the Alvada depot. The agency was closed down by the 1960s, and the building was torn down in 1964. (Charles Garvin photograph; Mark J. Camp collection.)

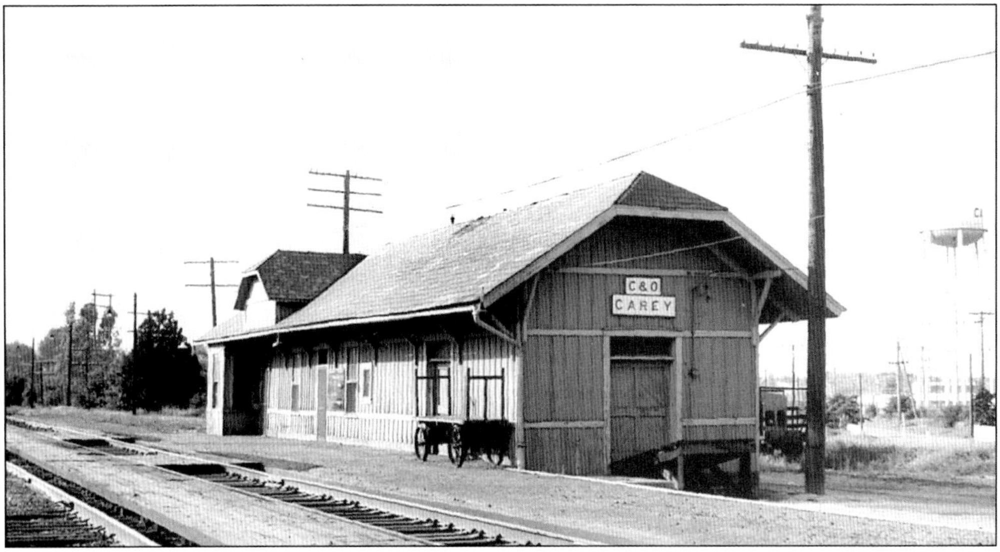

The Carey depot was an extended version of Alvada. Carey's Hocking Valley and later C&O agents were kept busy with stone shipments from the several local quarries. The last passenger train left at the end of April 1971. The depot was demolished in the 1980s; however, C&O's C cabin remains nearby. The concrete remnants of a coaling station at Crawford, just south of town, also still stand. (Charles Garvin photograph; Mark J. Camp collection.)

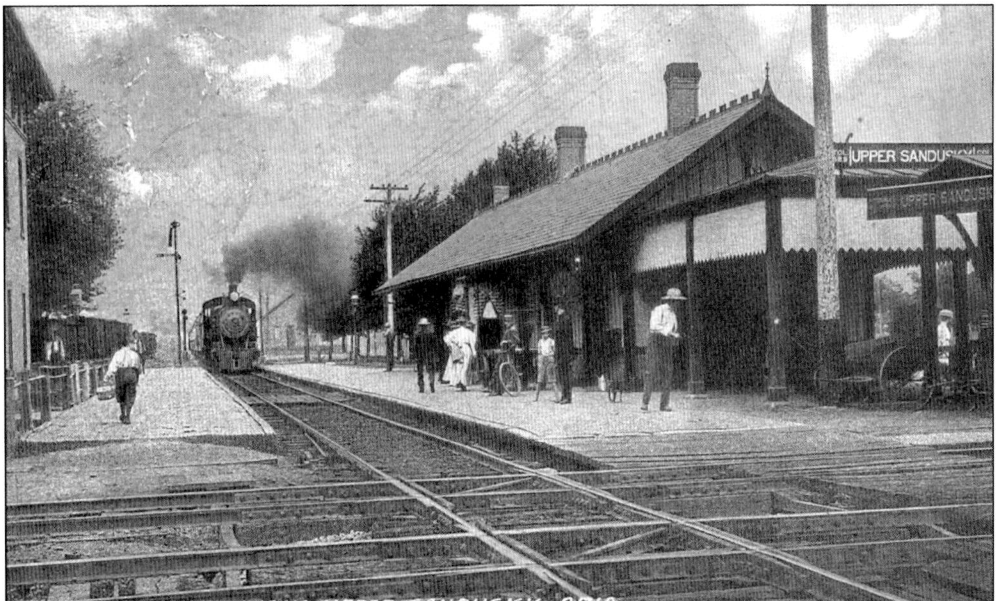

The Hocking Valley crosses the PRR on the west side of Upper Sandusky. This depot, looking north, became a joint depot in October 1901, as the PRR passenger facility was moved to the junction. Note the new platform shelter extending along the double-tracked PRR to the right, or east. The Hocking Valley earlier had added a covered outside waiting area on the south end of the building. Across the track, from the 1870s to around 1930, stood the Utah House, a railroad hotel and lunchroom. North of the passenger depot was the freight house. The junction is a lonely spot today; the buildings were gone by the late 1970s. (Mark J. Camp collection.)

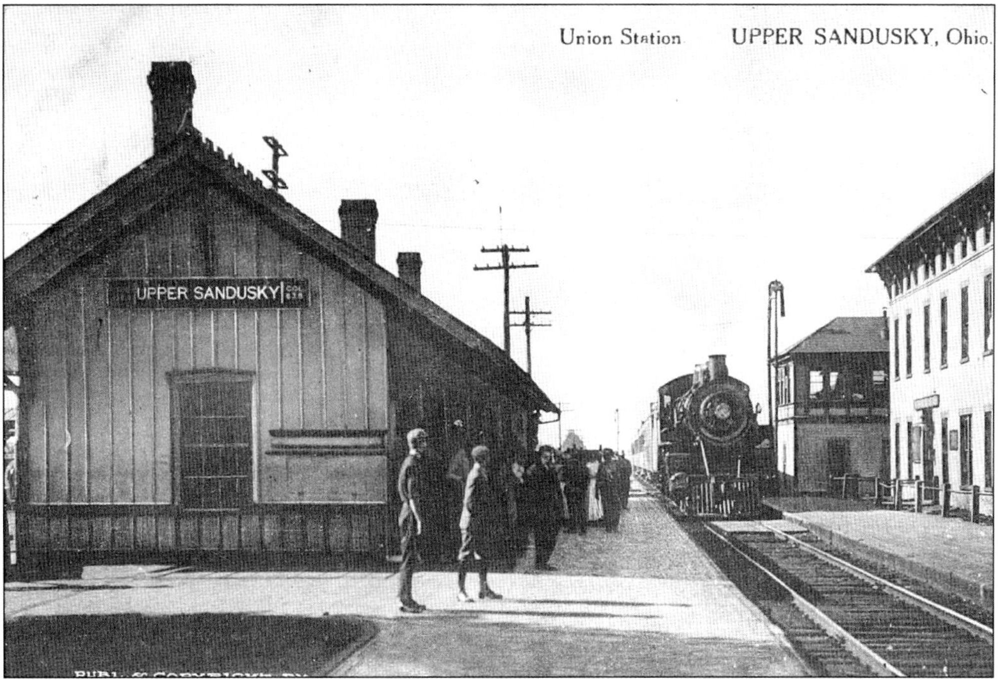

This view looks south down the Hocking Valley at Upper Sandusky. Diagonally across the diamond is Pennsy's interlocking tower; across the tracks is the Utah House. (Mark J. Camp collection.)

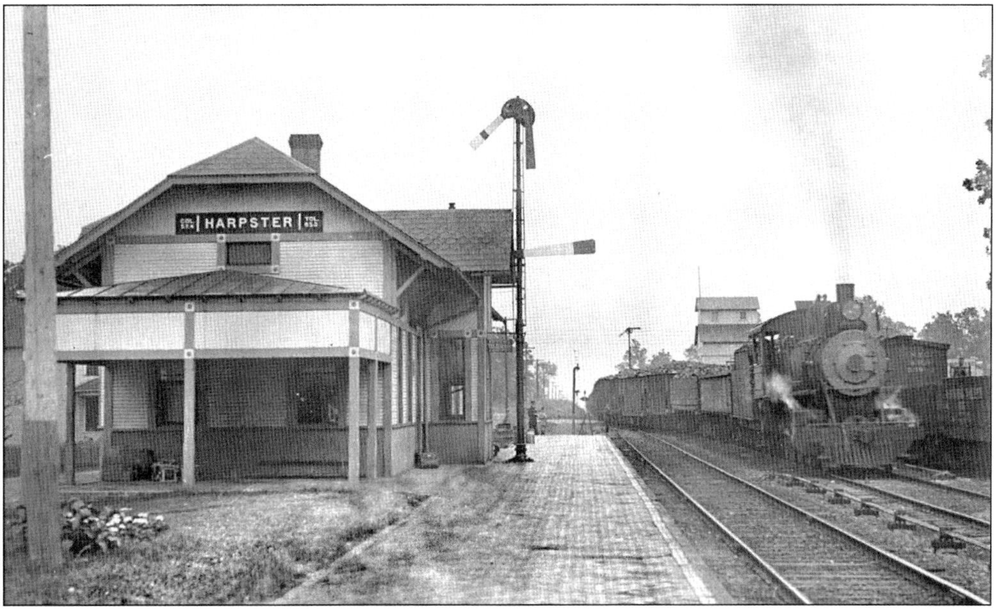

Harpster has had two depots. The first depot probably dates to the early 1880s, and is of CHV&T origin. On the end of the building is a covered outside waiting or storage area, much like at Upper Sandusky. Reportedly, this depot burned down around 1918. (Mark J. Camp collection)

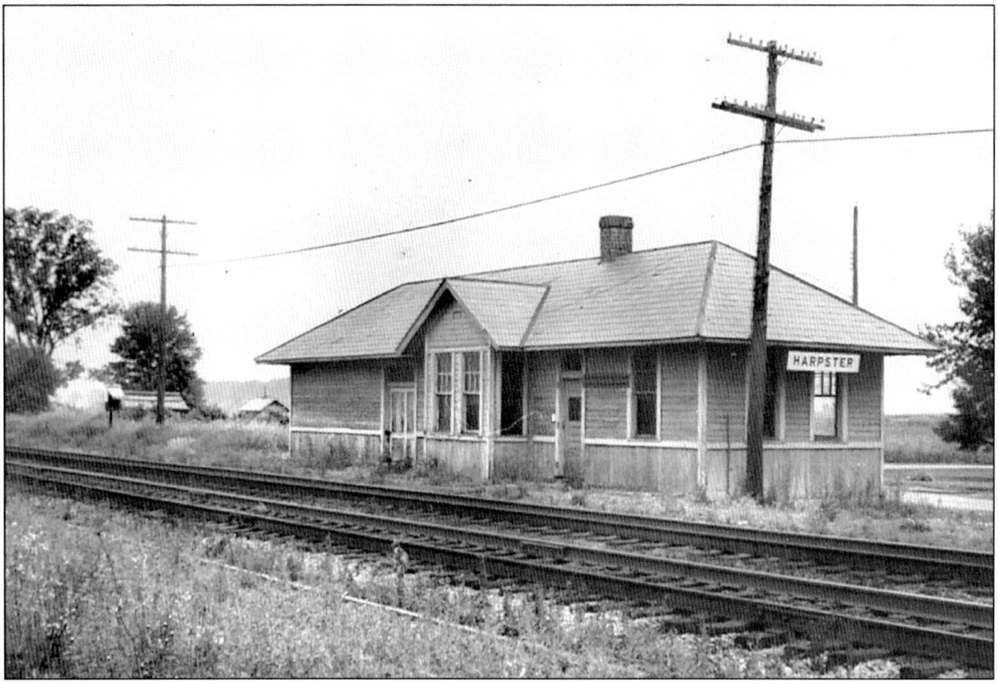

This, the second depot at Harpster, looks like a C&O design, but the C&O did not take over the line until 1920. It was still there in this 1968 view.

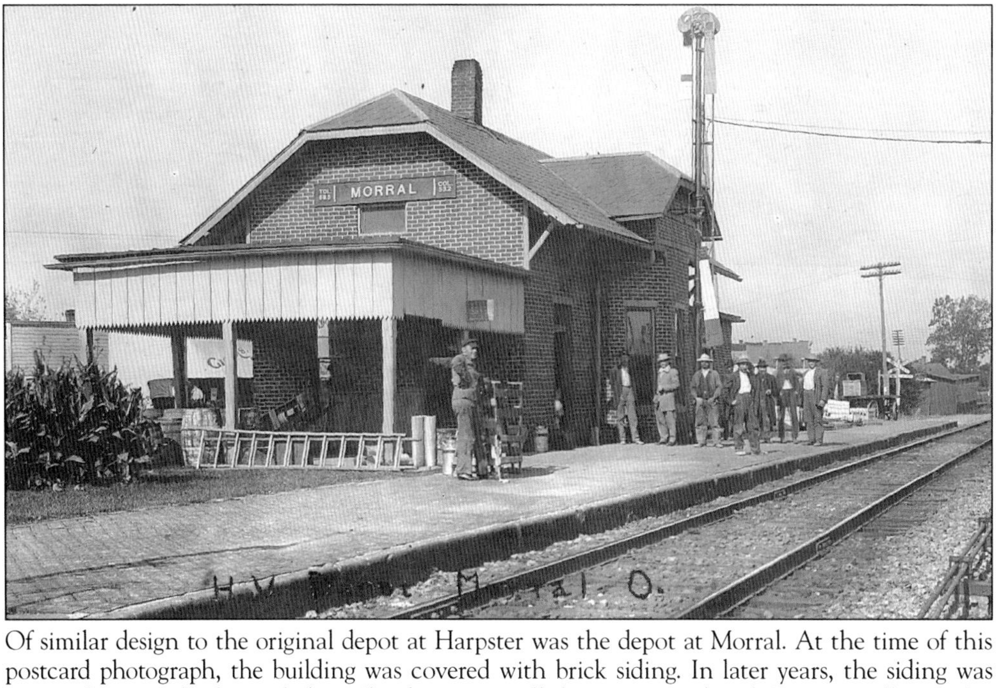

Of similar design to the original depot at Harpster was the depot at Morral. At the time of this postcard photograph, the building was covered with brick siding. In later years, the siding was removed, as was the frame shelter. The depot was still there in 1968. (Mark J. Camp collection.)

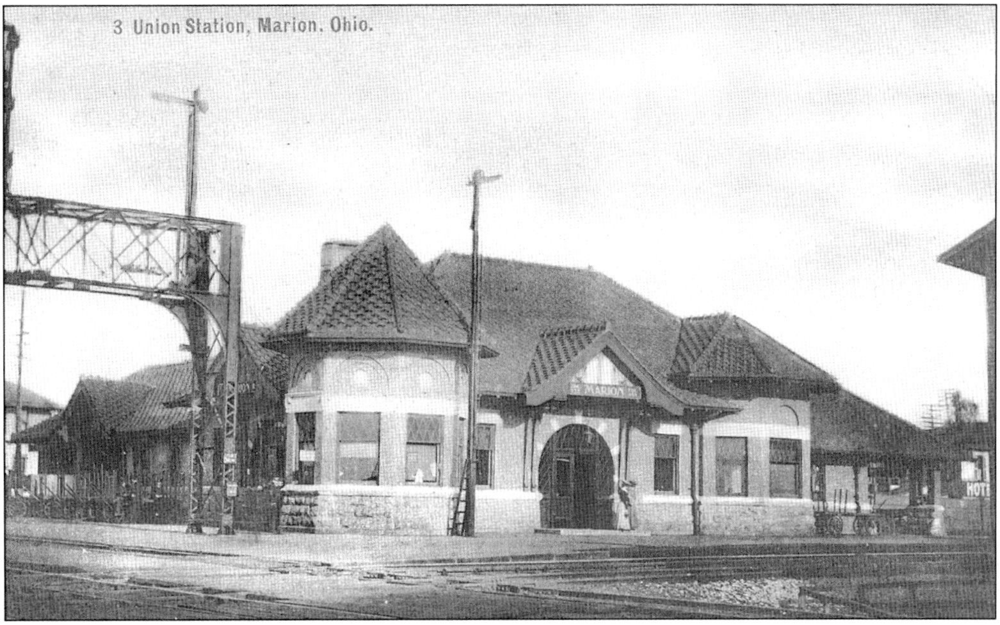

The Hocking Valley used the west side platform of Marion Union Station. The last C&O passenger train stopped at the depot at the end of April 1971. Nearby was a large frame freight house. The view below dates to 1969 and is looking north up the former Hocking Valley tracks. Union Station is now a haven for rail fans and model railroaders. (Mark J. Camp collection.)

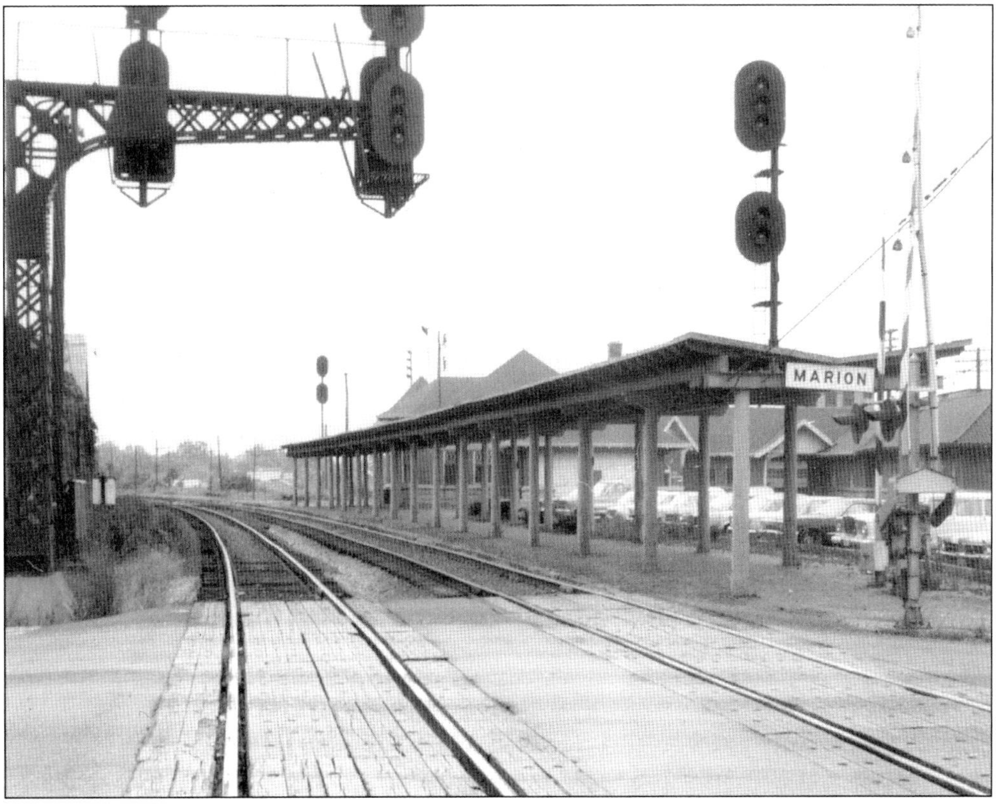

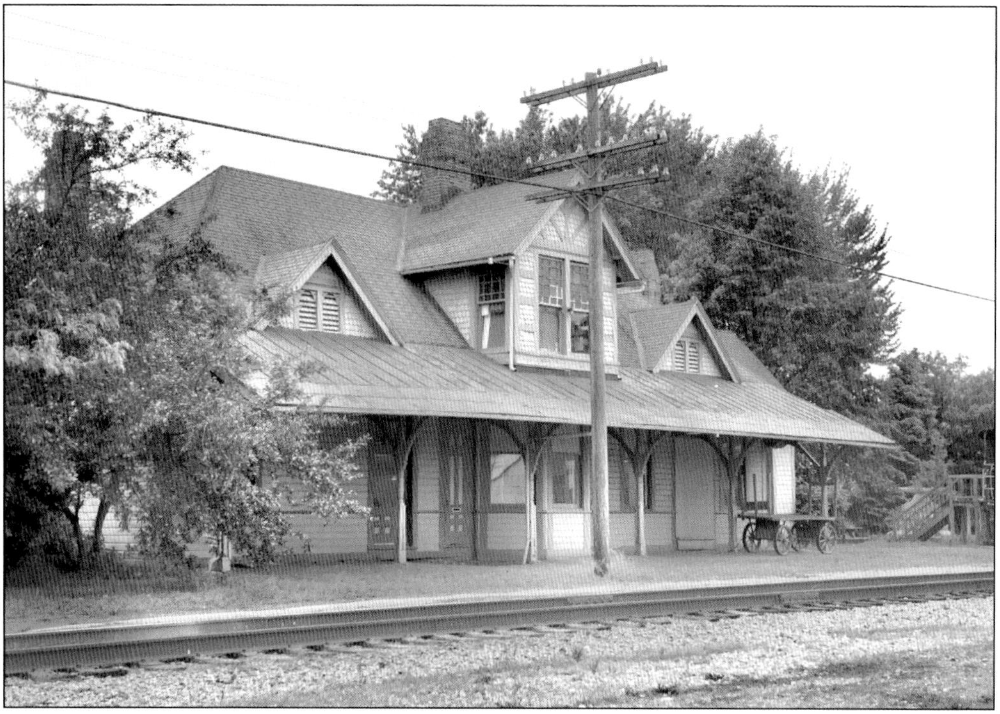

The 1887 Pennsylvania Railroad passenger depot and surrounding park in Ada are on the National Register of Historic Places. Meticulous restoration has turned a run-down property into a pleasant place to visit and experience the historical ambience.

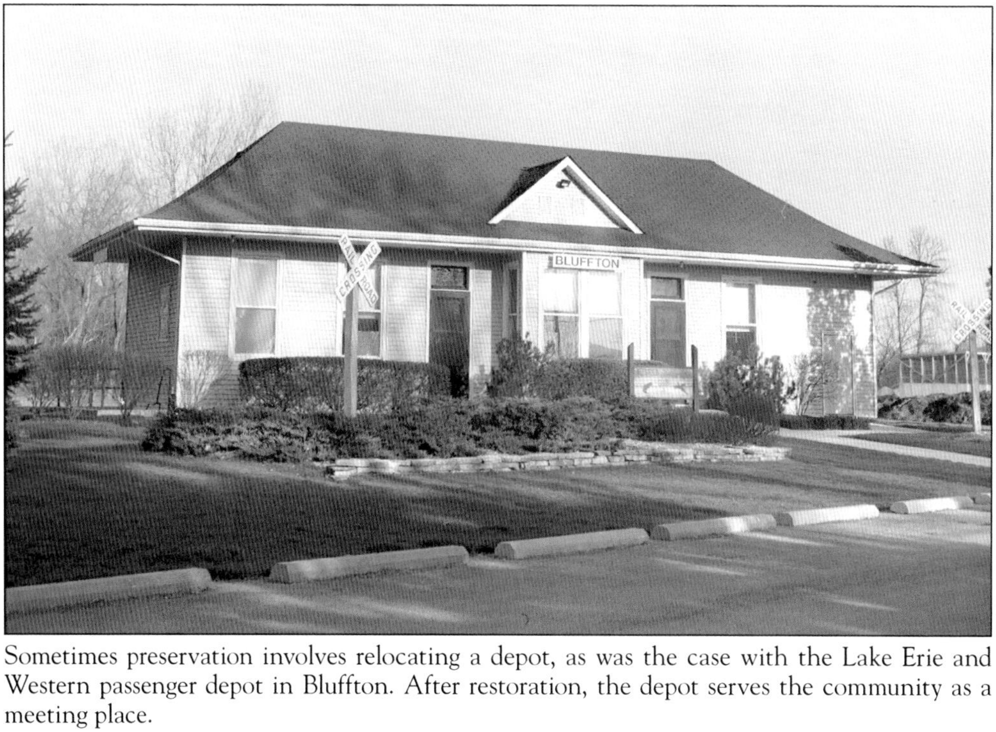

Sometimes preservation involves relocating a depot, as was the case with the Lake Erie and Western passenger depot in Bluffton. After restoration, the depot serves the community as a meeting place.

Seven

Reuse of Depots

Some 50 passenger and combination depots remain in this part of Ohio; obviously many have disappeared. Through the years, around 300 depots served the various communities of west central Ohio. Some of these were depots built to replace outmoded buildings or those destroyed by fire, storm, or train derailment. Economics determined what communities would thrive and require continued passenger service. The smallest communities saw the closing of their depots around World War I. Sometimes these buildings were reused by the railroads at other points along their lines, sometimes continuing as a depot, sometimes converted to other uses. Some were carted off to neighboring farms for use as storage buildings. Some became homes. Many were torn down for their lumber. Brick and stone depots were less likely to be moved and so were either converted to other uses on-site or demolished. By the 1950s, more and more depots were closed or open for only a certain time each week with one agent splitting time between two or three nearby depots. Sometimes the depot would be closed, and business was conducted from a portable prefab building or trailer adjacent to the old depot.

As historical preservation gained emphasis in the 1970s, the railroad depot was viewed as a part of vanishing Americana. Communities and individuals became aware of how few depots remained and took steps to preserve what was left. Some depots in west central Ohio have become museums of local history and railroading, for example, Fort Recovery, Rawson, and Uniopolis, and centers for the arts like Union City. The depots from Jackson Center, New Washington, and Williamstown have also been carefully restored but moved far from their original sites. Depots at Bucyrus, Galion, Marion, and St. Paris are also undergoing restoration. A library with historical displays now operates out of the Forest freight house. The remaining depot in Carey is a senior center. Others including Ada, Bluffton, and Coldwater serve as community centers. Model railroads ran in depots at Ada, Marion, and Sidney. Various businesses have relocated in depots including a frozen custard shop at Bluffton, insurance offices at Kenton, a garden shop at Ludlow Falls, a computer shop at Urbana, a grain company office at Versailles, a candy shop in West Liberty, and automobile repair shops at Versailles and Wharton. Restaurants once operated in depots at Forest and Lima. Depots from Anna, Kemp, McCutchenville, New Winchester, Raymonds, Richwood, and Spore became residences. New Bremen is now a private guesthouse. Depots at Ansonia, St. Marys, Troy, and Wapakoneta remain in railroad use. A number including Belle Center, East Liberty, Fort Jennings, and Spencerville sit vacant or relatively unused, awaiting an unknown future.

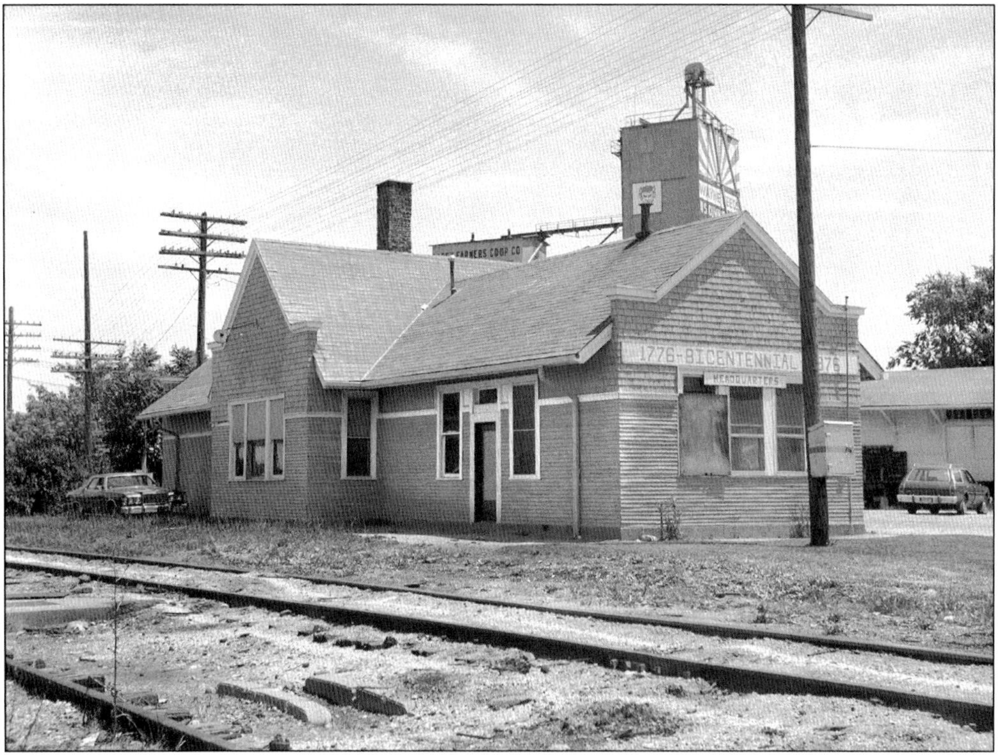

Carey's Big Four depot now serves as a senior center. It is on the original site. The liability of a nearby active track no longer exists since the rail line was pulled up.

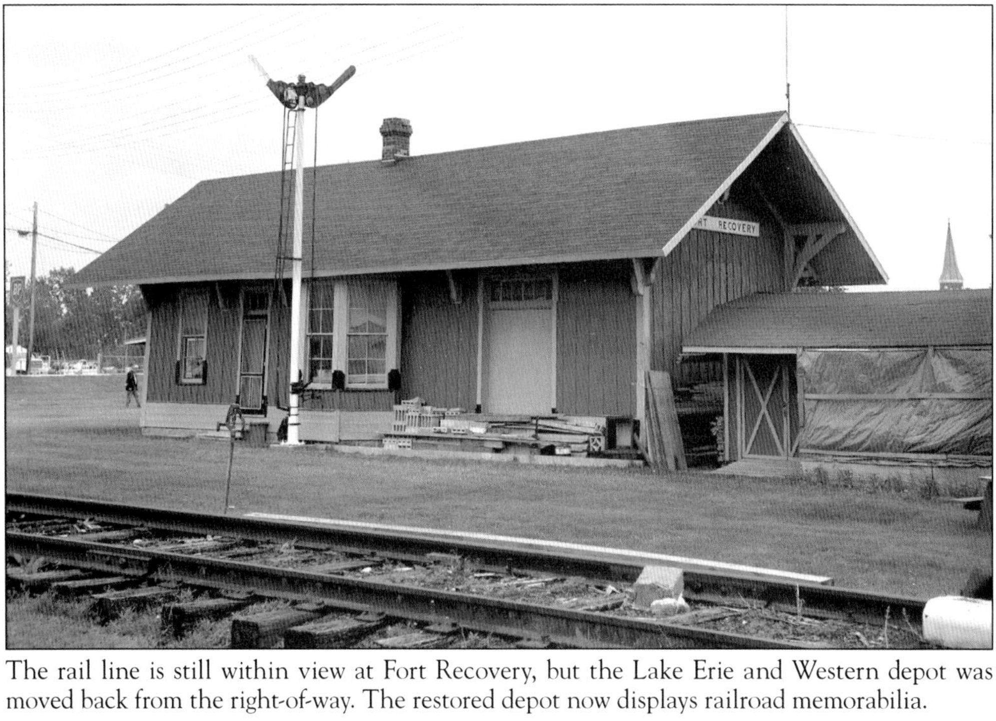

The rail line is still within view at Fort Recovery, but the Lake Erie and Western depot was moved back from the right-of-way. The restored depot now displays railroad memorabilia.

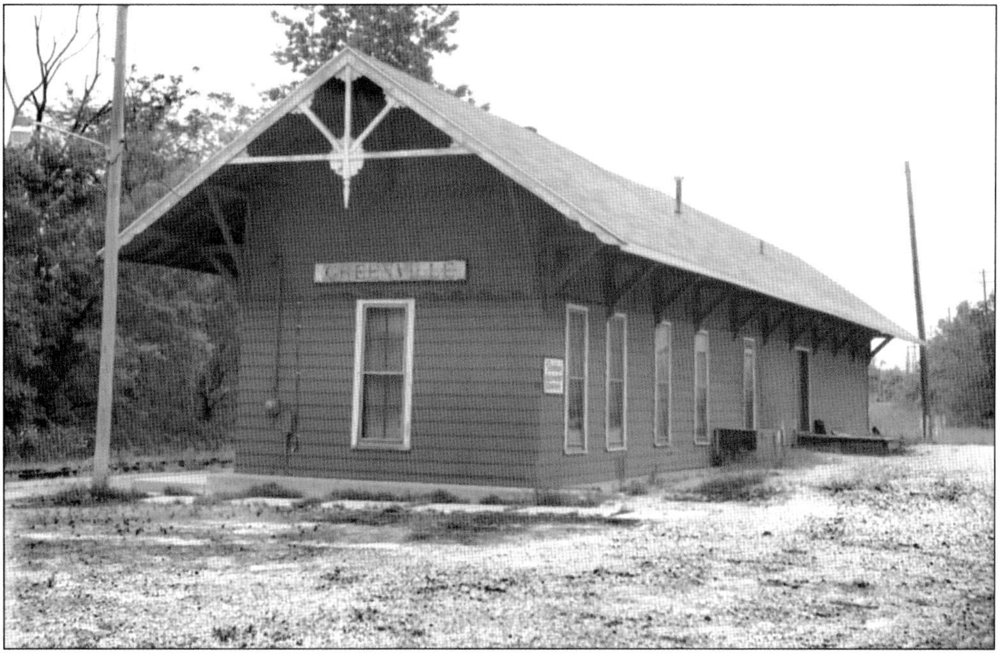

The Cincinnati Northern depot in Greenville is now serving the office and storage needs of a local business.

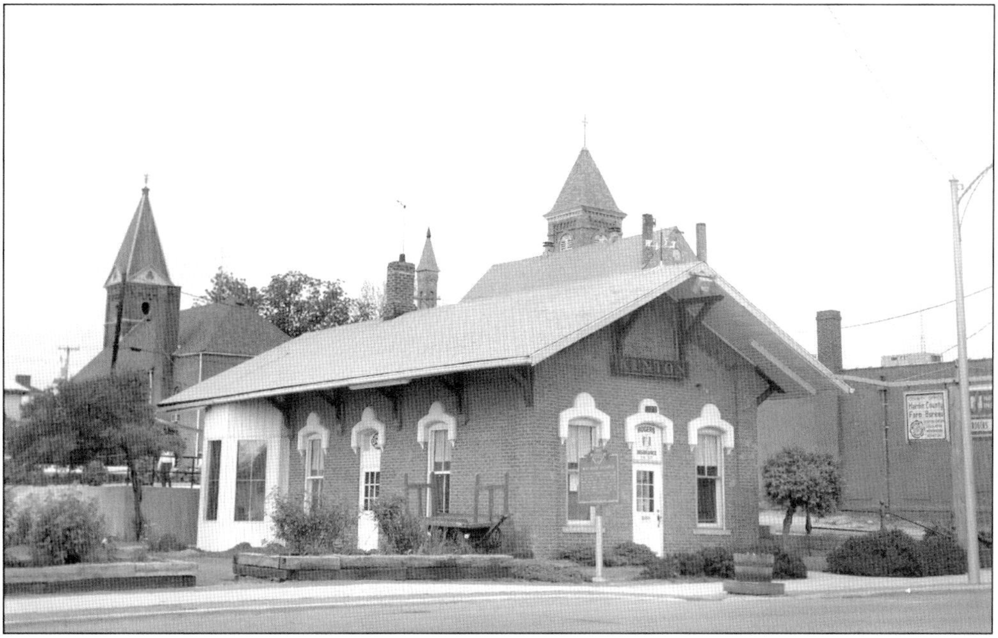

An insurance office now uses the Big Four depot in Kenton still along the abandoned right-of-way. A historical marker tells its history.

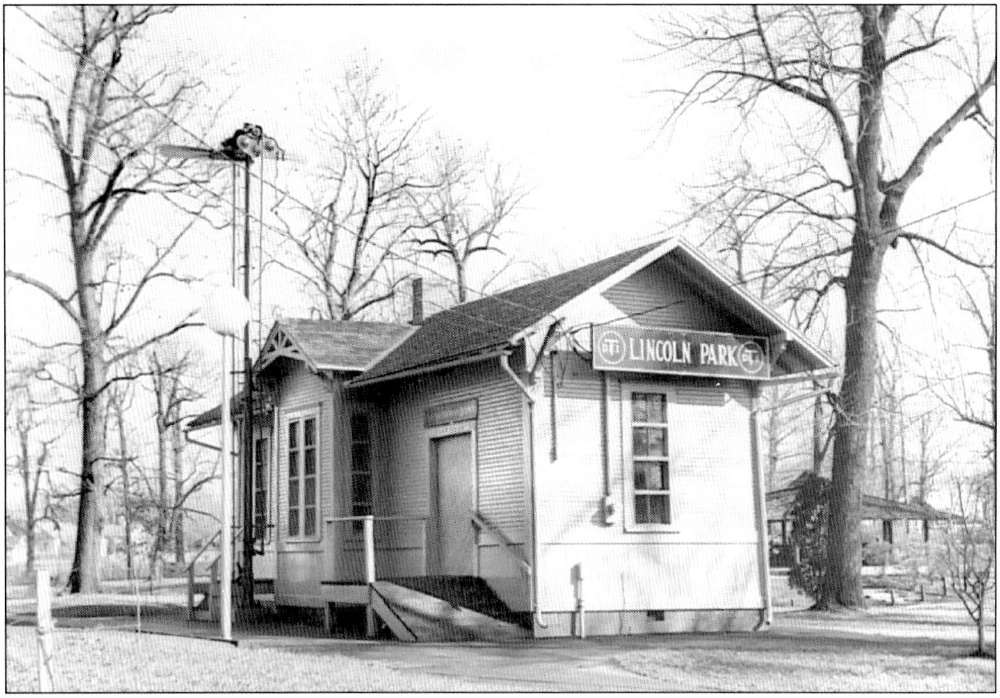

Sometimes depots are moved from one town to another. Preserved in Lincoln Park in Lima is the Detroit, Toledo and Ironton depot from Uniopolis. The Allen County Historical Society maintains the depot as a depot museum but elected to not outwardly designate its original location.

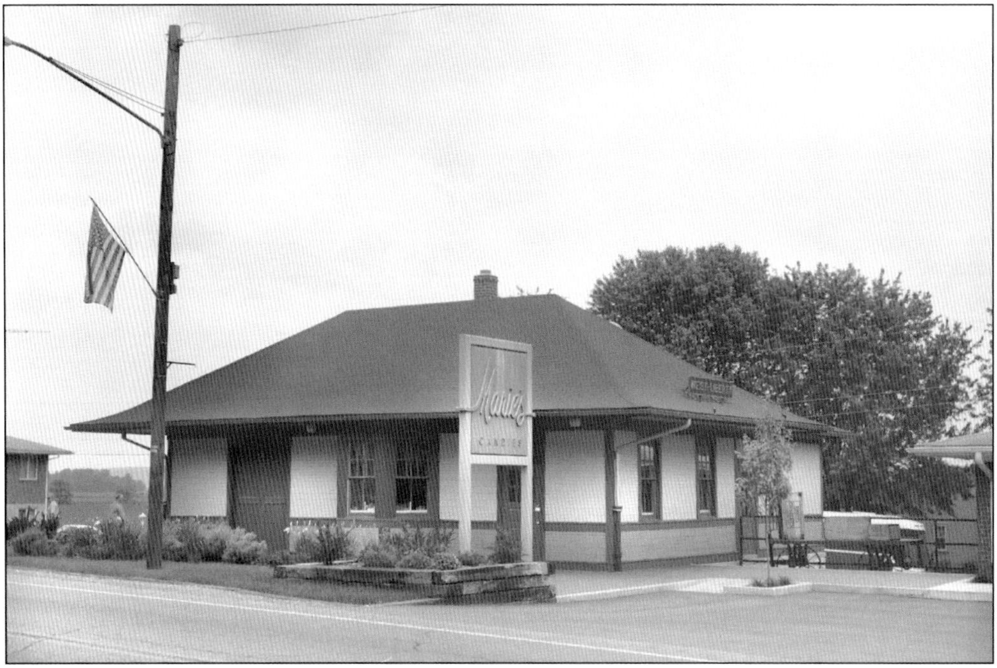

The 1926 Big Four depot in West Liberty was moved to a prominent location on the main highway through town. It was modified as the new salesroom of a local candy company.

Index of Photographs